THE
CRUISING
GUIDE
TO THE
VIRGIN ISLANDS

9th Edition

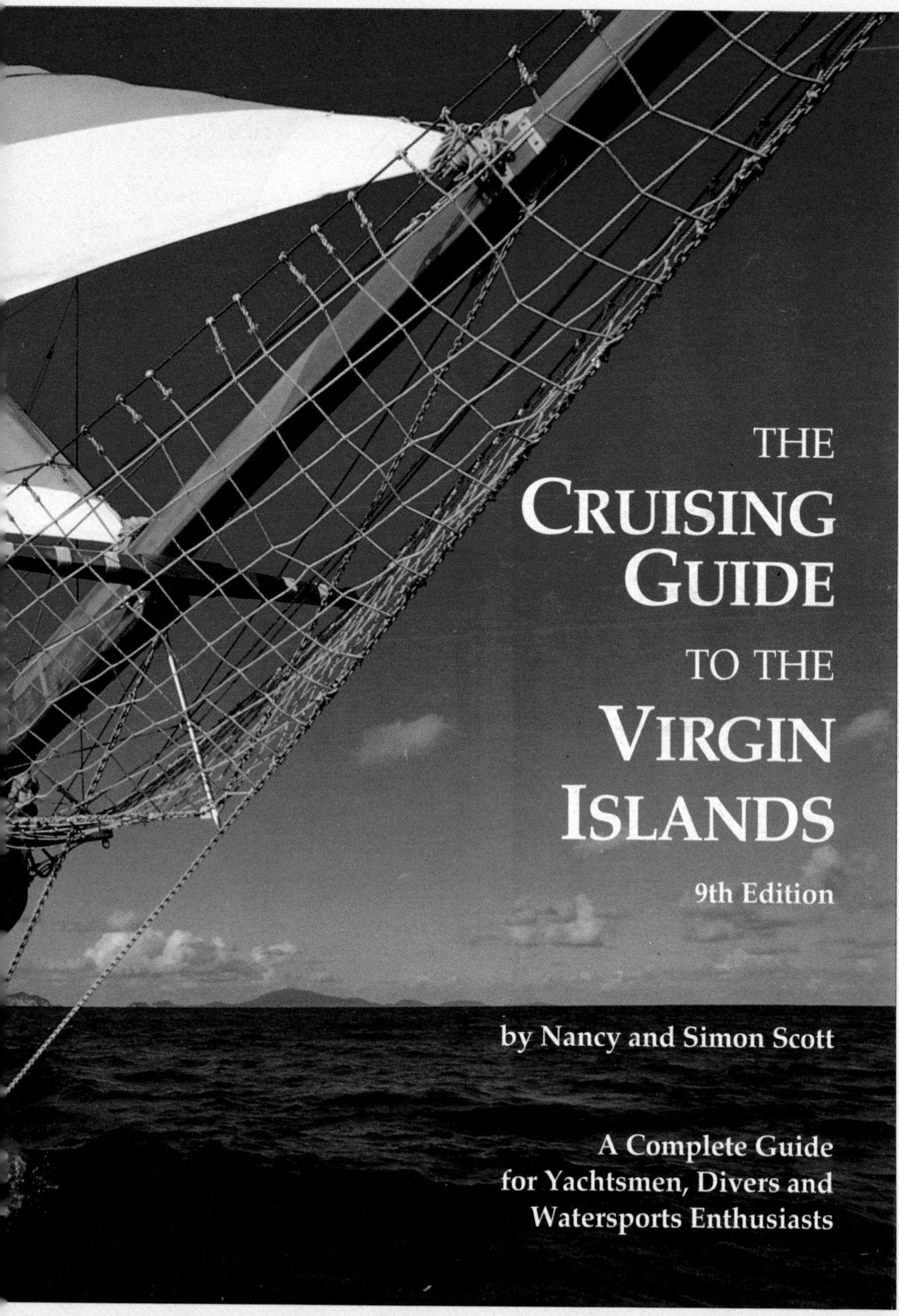

THE
CRUISING
GUIDE
TO THE
VIRGIN
ISLANDS

9th Edition

by Nancy and Simon Scott

A Complete Guide
for Yachtsmen, Divers and
Watersports Enthusiasts

Cruising Guide Publications, Inc. is a special interest publisher of sailing guides to cruising in various areas around the world and other publications of nautical interest. CGP endeavors to provide comprehensive and invaluable materials to both inveterate sailors and less experienced seafarers seeking vital vacationing tips and navigational information relative to the journey to and the enjoyment of their destinations.

The Cruising Guide to the Virgin Islands is intended for use in conjunction with either U.S. National Ocean Survey charts, U.S. Hydrographic Office charts, or British Admiralty charts. Every effort has been made to describe conditions accurately. However, the publisher makes no warranty, express or implied, for any errors or omissions in this publication. Skippers should use this guide only in conjunction with the above charts and/or other navigational aids and not place undue credence in the accuracy of this guide. *The Cruising Guide to the Virgin Islands* is not intended for use for navigational purposes.

Contributing Photographers:
Front cover:
Jim Scheiner, Anthony Blake
Back cover:
top: Dougal Thornton
center: Simon Scott
bottom: Simon Scott

Published by
Cruising Guide Publications, Inc.
P.O. Box 1017
Dunedin, Florida 34697-1017
Phone: (800) 330-9542 • (727) 733-9542
Fax: (727) 734-8179
E-Mail: cgp@earthlink.net

By NANCY AND SIMON SCOTT

Spanish Virgin Island Supplement by:
Bruce Van Sant

Art Direction
Noble Enterprises
Janet Bechtle - Ideas to Images, Inc.

Editor
Nancy Scott

Research Assistants
Thor Downing
Scarlett Steer
Lucie Jefferies
Ashley Scott
Sharon Green

Advertising/Marketing Director
Maureen Larroux

Photography
Jim Scheiner
A.J. Blake
Simon Scott
Dougal Thornton
Carol Lee
Steve Simonsen

Illustrations
Roger Bansemer
Roger Burnett

Cartography
Roger Burnett

Art Production
Traci Blair

Administration
Janet Joyce & Mark Granger

Copyright © Maritime Ventures, Ltd.

Ninth Edition

Printed in Italy by
STUDIO DEER Paris — Medigraf (BS)

ISBN 0-944428-47-9

TABLE OF CONTENTS

Face it,
you showed signs even then.

Just because you're all grown up, you don't have to give up your warm water,

large bath toys and being gently rocked to sleep. Sunsail offers you the

Caribbean, Mediterranean or the Indian Ocean where you can play with your

own 30 to 50-foot yacht or catamaran. Start at one of Sunsail's 39 bases (6 in

the Caribbean), all located in the best sailing and vacation locations on earth.

You can sail yourself or take a captain, or a whole crew. And for a week or two,

breeze from island to island by day and, by night, be gently rocked to sleep

tucked snugly in a moonlit cove. It's comforting to know nothing's really

changed except, of course, the size of your tub, toys and cradle.

1-800-327-2276

You'll love the experience.

SAILING VACATIONS

Sunsail • 410-280-2553 • Fax: 410-280-2406 • Website: http//www.sunsail.com • E-mail: sunsailusa@sunsail.com

INTRODUCTION

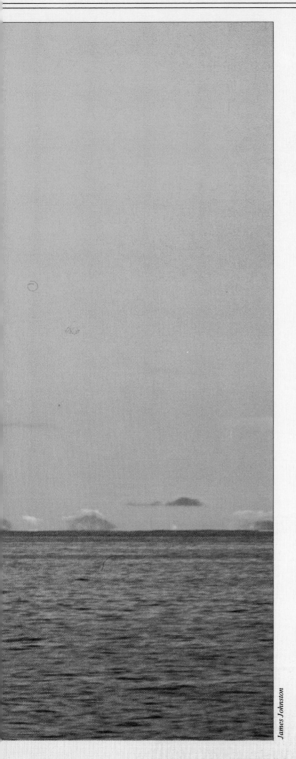

James Johnston

*T*he Virgin Islands are a magical Caribbean archipelago that seem to have been created expressly for the pleasures of yachting and watersports. Whether you are cruising this island paradise aboard your own boat, chartering, or staying ashore, this Guide is designed to help you maximize your visit.

The Guide will assist you in navigation, selection of anchorages, marinas and resorts, as well as steering you towards exciting attractions, shops and dining at restaurants accessible by dinghy or by land.

This year we have added a supplement on cruising in the Spanish Virgin Islands (Eastern Puerto Rico, Culebra and Vieques). These islands share the constant tradewinds, sunshine and balmy weather of the American and British Virgin Islands, and add the spice of Spanish influence. Only a short sail west from St. Thomas, the Spanish Virgins are a great place to extend your Virgin Islands cruising.

Welcome to the Virgin Islands!

Nancy Scott
Publisher

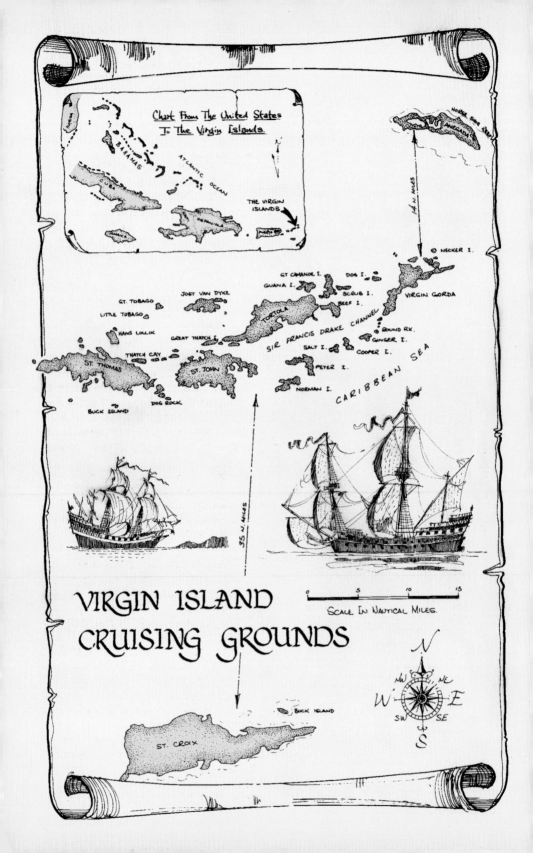

Chart From The United States
To The Virgin Islands.

BAHAMAS

ATLANTIC OCEAN

CUBA

HISPANIOLA

JAMAICA

THE VIRGIN
ISLANDS

PUERTO RICO

HORSE SHOE REEF

ANEGADA

14 N. MILES

NECKER I.

GT. CAMANOE I.   DOG I.

GUANA I.

SCRUB I.   VIRGIN GORDA

GT. TOBAGO   JOST VAN DYKE

BEEF I.

LITTLE TOBAGO

TORTOLA

HANS LOLLIK   SIR FRANCIS DRAKE CHANNEL

GREAT THATCH I.   ROUND RK.

THATCH CAY   GINGER I.

ST. THOMAS   ST. JOHN   SALT I.   COOPER I.

PETER I.

CARIBBEAN SEA

NORMAN I.

BUCK ISLAND   DOG ROCK

35 N. MILES

VIRGIN ISLAND
CRUISING GROUNDS

0   5   10   15

SCALE IN NAUTICAL MILES.

BUCK ISLAND

ST. CROIX

N
NW NE
W   E
SW SE
S

THE VIRGIN ISLANDS

Nothing has influenced the history of the Virgin Islands more profoundly than their geography and physical makeup. Situated at the high point of the curving archipelago that swings from Trinidad to Florida, they survey strategically all of the Americas, and, with their steady trade winds and numerous sheltered harbors, it is not surprising that they rapidly became a center for sea routes to every point of the compass, providing a welcome pause in the lengthy trade lines between Europe and the riches of South and Central America. Having been described as "the place on the way to everywhere," they have long been desirable for both trading and military advantage, from the days when Spaniards sailed through carrying Aztec loot to Spain until this century when the United States paid $25 million to buy the U.S.V.I. from Denmark in order to forestall any unfriendly foreign power from parking on her doorstep.

Sailors and sailing have therefore been at the core of Virgin Islands history from the moment the first Ciboney Indians brought their Stone Age canoes from the Americas to drift nomadically through the Antilles, living off the land and the sea.

The Ciboneys were followed from South America a hundred years or so B.C. by the more down-to-earth Arawaks, who settled throughout the Virgin Islands, cultivated the land, made attractive pottery and ornaments (which can still be found) and maintained a strictly hereditary society. The Arawaks believed that their souls were not only in their bodies but also in trees, rocks and other natural phenomena, and constructed idols called "zemis," carving three-cornered stones in the shape of grotesque human beings, birds or natural forms, which they believed could influence crops and weather. They painted their bodies for ceremonies, grew their hair long and flattened the

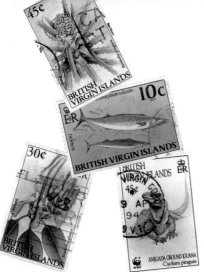

3

fronts of their childrens' heads to make them more beautiful.

The Arawaks dominated the islands for many years and, even now, we still use some of their words: tobacco, barbecue, potato, hurricane and cannibal.

This last referred to the warlike Carib Indians who, about 100 years before Columbus arrived, pillaged their way up from South America like New World Vikings in enormous dug-out canoes. The Caribs were much like the Arawaks and Ciboneys in appearance — medium height, high cheek bones, flat noses and straight, black hair. Unlike the Arawaks they plucked their beards, considering them a deformity. They flattened the fronts and backs of their children's heads to make them beautiful, and scarred and painted their own bodies, presumably toward a similar goal.

The Caribs, quite unlike the Arawaks in temperament, were fierce and aggressive, terrorizing the entire Caribbean with their warlike behavior. A spartan bunch, they kept on the move, raiding the Arawak settlements, stealing their women and capturing the young boys to be emasculated, fattened and eaten. They thought nothing of piling 100 men into an 80-foot dug-out canoe to traverse 1,000 miles in search of battle and plunder. Their social hierarchy was loose, their leaders chosen according to fighting ability rather than ancestry.

Caribs believed that good spirits were invisible except at night, when they took the form of bats; so each Carib had a bat for his personal deity, to whom he would make offerings of cassava bread and fruit to ensure healthy crops and continued well-being. Like the Arawaks, the Caribs practiced euthanasia to rid themselves of the old and infirm, and blamed most unpleasant occurrences — hurricanes, earthquakes or sickness — on evil spirits.

Columbus discovered the Virgin Islands in 1493 on his second voyage to the New World. He anchored off Salt River Bay in St. Croix for fresh water and then was driven by unfavorable winds

to Virgin Gorda. Seeing the numerous islands, he named them "the Virgins" in honor of St. Ursula and the 11,000 virgins who, threatened by the marauding Huns in 4th-century Cologne, sacrificed their lives rather than submit to a fate worse than death. Virgin Gorda got its name (fat virgin) because Columbus, viewing it from seaward, thought that it resembled a reclining woman with a protruding belly.

The Spaniards, whose nation was the most powerful in Europe at this time, had laid claim to the West Indies as they had in their discovery of the Americas. They began to settle in various places throughout the islands to provide stop-over points for their ships carrying spoils from Central and South America to the mother country.

By this time the Caribs had more or less absorbed and digested the Arawaks, either physically or socially, and were thrilled to have new prey to harass, different colored women to steal and a different flavor of enemy to fight. The

5

Always Wanted To Have A Place In The Islands?

Welcome Home.

When you buy a beautiful new yacht with SUN, you're not just buying a boat.

You're buying a home in the islands — your private corner of paradise with a spectacular 360° water view.

You're joining a family — a tight-knit group of sailors who know you and your boat by name, and who take excellent care of both of you.

You're becoming part of one of the industry's most respected ownership programs, the result of over two decades of experience in sensible, worry-free yacht ownership.

And it literally pays for itself.

All your expenses — boat payment, management costs, advertising, dockage, maintenance, insurance — are fully covered by monthly charter revenue. *Guaranteed*.

You're investing in a lifestyle you thought you could only dream of.

Welcome home.

staunchly Catholic Spaniards, right-wing products of the Inquisition's rule, were more than a little horrified at the Caribs' dietary preferences and, by the mid-1500s, had given up any hopes of missionary conversion.

Emperor Charles V ordered that the Indians "should be treated as enemies and given no quarter." Nevertheless, as late as 1620 the Caribs were still raiding mercilessly up and down the Caribbean.

Nor did this fierce tribe confine themselves to settlements. They can truly be described as the first pirates of the Caribbean — the first of many to prey upon the Spanish galleons. They were soon followed in this practice by several European nations who, afraid to challenge Spain directly, gave unofficial backing, in the form of letters of marque, to private enterprise to indulge in smuggling, piracy and the harassment of Spanish settlements.

This combination of privateering and piracy (the distinction between the two wearing very thin at times) was to continue for several hundred years. A vast array of colorful and bizarre characters paused in the Virgin Islands, among them the well-known pirate Henry Morgan and the legendary Sir John Hawkins, who visited the area four times. On his last voyage in 1595 Hawkins sailed with Sir Francis Drake to attack Puerto Rico, the two fleets apparently reconnoitering for a few days in the North Sound of Virgin Gorda to muster their men and prepare for battle.

It was a fateful trip for both of them: Hawkins sickened and died of the fever that was the scourge of the tropics; Drake, himself, after a failed assault on the heavy fortifications of San Juan, soon followed suit.

As the power of Spain waned, other countries began to colonize the West Indies more seriously, although piracy continued for a while, the struggling settlers being happy to trade their agricultural produce and materials for a share of the Spanish gold. The Virgin Islands went through a lengthy period of

Following the example of the original Spanish settlers, early plantation owners brought slaves from Africa. When the introduction of sugar cane production in the 1640s required a large, cheap and stable labor force, the number of slaves began to increase. For some time the colonies thrived. Sugar and cotton were valuable commodities and the plantations diversified into the production of indigo, spices, rum, maize, pineapples, yams and coconuts. In 1717 the first census taken in Virgin Gorda showed a population of 625, about half of whom were black. By the mid-1700s this population had grown to nearly 2,000 and the proportion of slaves throughout the Virgin Islands had increased dramatically.

Life on the plantations was extremely hard for the slaves and, as their majority on the islands increased, so did the restrictions on them and the severity of the punishments meted out to them for the breaking of these. Conflict over the slave trade was increasing; it had been outlawed in England in 1772 and the impetus for its abolition was growing.

"musical colonies" with the English, French, Dutch, Spanish and Danish moving from one island to another, shoving previous settlers on to the next, squabbling amongst themselves in Europe and, as a result, warring in the West Indies.

Eventually, however, the treasures from America dried up and the process of colonization gradually steadied. The Danes formally took possession of St. Thomas and, later, St. John; the English ousted the Dutch and gained a firm foothold in Tortola and Virgin Gorda; and the French settled in St. Croix but later sold it to the Danish West India Company.

The Spaniards continued to raid occasionally from their strongholds in Puerto Rico and Hispaniola through the late 1600s and piracy flared up intermittently in the early 1700s.

Considerable cleaning up and law enforcement took place as the casual farming that had begun, merely in order to colonize the islands and break the Spanish monopoly, gave way to serious plantations which, unsubsidized by stolen Spanish gold, needed to trade at a steady profit.

The obstacles to plantation life increased, several hurricanes and droughts ravaged the islands, and the American Revolution and Napoleonic wars created a revival of enemy raids, piracy and fighting within the islands. The slaves suffered as a result and, as news of abolition elsewhere began to filter through to the West Indies, they began to make use of their by now considerable majority to rebel.

The slave rebellions coincided, more or less, with the introduction of the sugar beet in Europe, which dealt a fatal blow to the once great "trade-triangle" based on West Indian cane. By the mid-1800s the slaves were free and the white population had deserted the colonies.

For almost 100 years the Virgin Islands dozed peacefully, the freed slaves living quietly off the land and sea, though with some difficulty in years of drought and famine. Government was minimal: In 1893, for example, there were only two white men in the B.V.I. — the Deputy Governor and the doctor.

The islands struggled on with tottering economies. Virgin Gorda was visited briefly by Cornish miners who reopened the old Spanish mine in search of copper. An earthquake leveled all the churches in Tortola and the *H.M.S. Rhone* was wrecked off Salt Island. As late as 1869 the steamship *Telegrafo* was detained in Tortola and charged with piracy. Labor riots and rebellions occasionally protested the hardships. The United States began to show an interest in buying the Danish islands, afraid that they would be sold to a hostile nation such as Germany.

The islands moved into the 20th century without much change. An agricultural station was established in Tortola in 1900 in hopes of boosting the faltering economy, various homestead projects were begun throughout the island with little effect and the parent governments of each colony were forced to accept financial responsibility for the islands, which were fast becoming a liability.

The first world was tightening the purse strings further, and by 1917 the Danes were happy to sell their Virgin Islands to the United States, which was eager to have a military outpost in the Caribbean. St. Thomas had long been a useful coaling station and harbor for steamships and was well positioned to defend the approaches to the Panama Canal.

Over the first half of the 20th century there was gradual social reform and progress towards local government. This process began to speed up as the tourist trade, boosted by the increasing ease of casual travel, began to grow.

Finally the geography and physical advantages of the islands began once more to have a major influence on their fortunes. Situated conveniently close to the United States and blessed with a warm climate and a beautiful, unspoiled environment, the Virgin Islands rapidly became popular with tourists. At last, here was an industry which needed only the natural resources of the islands to sustain their economies.

Now stable, friendly places, the Virgin Islands are once more visited by colorful characters from all over the world. Some just sail through nomadically, like the long-departed Ciboneys; others, like the Arawaks, stay to build homes and businesses.

There is still the occasional pirate, although they are more usually found on land these days, and privateering has yet to be revived — unless one applies this label to the tax department.

With the charter industry becoming the backbone of the islands, particularly in the B.V.I., sailors continue to make use of one of the finest sailing areas in the world. The quiet coves where Drake, Columbus and Blackbeard used to anchor are once more havens for fleets of sailing vessels and the modern adventurers who come to explore the Virgin Islands.

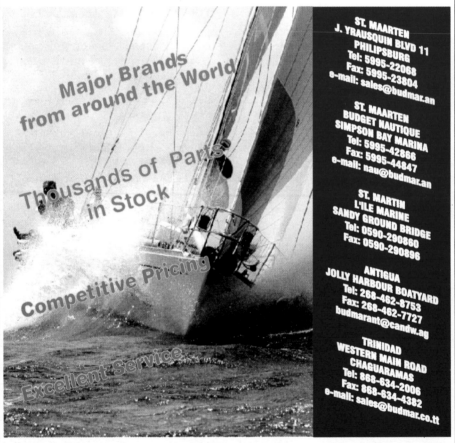

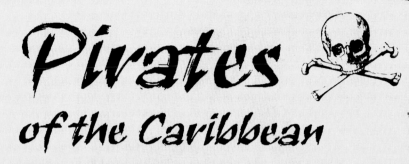

Pirates
of the Caribbean

*I*t is just as well that there are no longer any pirates in the Virgin Islands. Imagine yourself reclining in the cockpit of the yacht after a difficult hour trying to make the anchor stay put. The pina colada is nice and cold. The kids' yelling has receded into the distance as they explore the shoreline, collecting sea urchin spines in their feet. Your wife is perfecting her suntan on the foredeck and the other couple, who used to be your oldest friends until you decided to charter a yacht together, are arguing through clenched teeth in the galley. A perfect vacation in the Caribbean.

Then, as the sun begins to sink towards the horizon, a small sloop veers into the cove you thought you had to yourselves. An anchor splashes overboard and, before you have finished spraying your ankles with insect repellent, a horde of noisy, unshaven thugs row across to your boat and, without so much as a by-your-leave, swarm on deck, empty your wallet, your liquor cabinet and your fridge, and steal your camera and your wife.

It wouldn't do much for the charter business.

Although piracy is no longer a popular pastime in the VI, it is really not that long since it was all the rage throughout the Caribbean. In the early 1700s, a sympathetic governor in St. Thomas was still fencing goods for pirates like Charles Vane and Edward Teach (the legendary Blackbeard), and as late as 1869 the steamship *Telegrafo* was detained in Tortola and charged with piracy.

Nor is there anything new about sailors dabbling in "the sweet trade."

As long as men have transported anything of value across the ocean, there have been others willing to relieve them of it. Even the Bible speaks of "princes of the sea." Julius Caesar had first-hand experience of these — he was kidnapped and held for ransom by them, and his invasion of Britain was partly in order to subdue the Veneti *pirata* and their British crews.

For several hundred years the Vikings made annual raids along the coasts of Western Europe, and in the Middle Ages, as trade and travel by sea expanded, piracy got underway with a vengeance.

"Privateering" also came into vogue at this time. A pirate called Eustace The Monk, who was believed to have black magic powers, did well plundering French ships on behalf of England's King John. Privateering was basically government-sponsored piracy — tacit approval given to raids on the ships of potential enemies. Privately owned vessels manned by civilians were commissioned with "letters of marque" as auxiliaries to the Royal Navy. They were used mainly against merchant shipping and were actively encouraged by monarchs in times of war or hostility. (As the 16th and early 17th centuries saw Europe in a fairly constant state of turmoil, this meant that they were encouraged most of the time.) Since a healthy percentage of the "purchase" went to the Crown, there was an added incentive for Royalty to turn a blind eye to the often extreme actions of the privateers and a deaf ear to the whining and complaining of the Ambassadors from semi-hostile nations.

A prime example of this sanctioning of successful piracy was, of course, the way in which Queen Elizabeth I dealt with Sir Francis Drake. His famous round-the-world voyage actually evolved from a plan to raid the Spanish-American towns along the Pacific coast during an interval when England was theoretically at peace with Spain.

However, when he returned with a treasure worth at least $5 million, the Virgin Queen boarded his ship, the *Golden Hind*, ignoring the Spanish demands that "El Draque"be hanged, and knighted him instead. This led Sir Walter Raleigh to make the (still pertinent) comment, "Did you ever know of any that were pirates for millions? They only that work for small things are pirates."

Having laid claim to all of the Americas and the West Indies, Spain was the most powerful nation in the world at this time. Other nations, though afraid to challenge the monopoly directly, were happy to see pirates siphoning off funds intended for the Spanish Reformation by intercepting the treasure ships loaded with Aztec gold. The increasing number of privateers also provided a handy pool of trained sailors who could be called upon in times of outright conflict.

Numerous ex-pirates played an important role in the eventual defeat of the Spanish Armada. In times of covert hostility they could go back to being privateers (the "legality" made visiting ports for supplies easier), and in the infrequent and uneasy intervals of peace they resorted to plain piracy — their status was largely dependent upon the diplomatic label given to it at the time.

In reality their lives changed very little. If pressganged into the Navy they could expect long voyages, harsh discipline, vile food and a good chance of an early demise — all for a pathetic pittance which would be cut off abruptly in peacetime. As pirates, their conditions at sea were little better but were offset by a freer democratic lifestyle, a similar chance of survival and the possibility of vast financial reward. As Bartholomew Roberts, one of the most successful pirates of the early 18th century, commented, "In an honest service there is thin rations, low wages and hard labor; in this, plenty and satiety, pleasure and ease, liberty and power; and who would not balance creditor on this side, when all the hazard that is run for it, at worst, is only a sour look or two at choking. No, 'a merry life and a short one' shall be my motto."

The defeat of the Armada intensified the harassment of Spanish merchant ships and allowed English, French and Dutch colonies to germinate in the now undefended West Indies.

Some of the first colonists were the itinerant French *boucaniers* who settled on Hispaniola.

They made a meager living barbecuing beef in smokehouses called *boucans* and selling it to passing vessels. Foolishly the Spaniards drove them off the island; in revenge they took to the sea where, instead of hunting wild cattle, they went after Spanish ships instead.

"Buccaneer" became a new and fearful term for "pirate," and their ranks

swelled as out of work naval crews drifted to the new world. New colonies struggling desperately to gain a foothold were a willing market for plundered goods. The governors of these new settlements gained a 10% commission for issuing letters of marque to privateers and, as a result, Jamaica's Port Royal became one of the richest towns in the hemisphere because of pirate gold. It also became known as "the wickedest city in the world," but it was largely due to the transient population of fighting sailors that the British were able to keep Jamaica. As late as 1774, historian Edward Long wrote, "It is to the buccaneers that we owe possession of Jamaica to this hour."

So the pirates were a vital part of the colonization of the West Indies. Henry Morgan, for example, dealt terrible blows to Spanish dominance when he attacked Spanish shipping, ransomed Puerto de Principe in Cuba, assaulted Porto Bello and burned Panama City to the ground. Despite a new treaty with Spain, neither Morgan nor the governor who issued the commission was ever punished, possibly because of the shares received by the King and his brother, the Duke of York.

The Spanish meted out their own punishment if they caught pirates or privateers. They made no distinction between the two except that privateers were sent to the gallows with their commissions tied around their necks. Hanging was the usual end for captured pirates, although, if they were unlucky enough to fall into the hands of the Inquisition, they might receive a more drawn-out demise on the rack.

Some of the evil vermin who gravitated to a life of piracy were very capable of perpetrating their own unique atrocities. Most pirates had a weakness for "rumbul-lion" and in their cups would often torment their prisoners for entertainment. Blackbeard was said to have made one victim eat his own nose and lips; another Englishman named Thomas Cobham sewed 20 Spaniards up in a mainsail and threw the whole squirming package overboard.

"Going on the account" was the term used when a man signed up for a career in piracy; this basically meant "no prey, no pay," but all the crew were shareholders in the "company" and part owners of the ship. The company typically began with a very modest vessel — some of the early buccaneers used dug-out canoes —but after a few killings on the market, they would generally acquire more suitable headquarters.

The ideal pirate vessel was small and fast. Bermudan sloops were felt to be ideal because of their speed (over 11 knots) and maneuverability, and could carry up to 75 men. A bigger company might go for a brigantine, a two-masted vessel that could carry either a square or fore-and-aft rig or a versatile combination of the two.

This was often how pirates made their assaults, sneaking out from the coast in poor light to spring upon a sluggish merchantman. The Virgin Islands made an excellent hunting ground with their myriad coves and passages. Situated right on the treasure route from South America to Europe, the area was visited by many notorious Caribbean pirates such as Edward England, whose kind treatment of prisoners so disgusted his crew that he was deposed; Charles Vane, who Defoe reported, "died in Agonies equal to his Villainies but showed not the least Remorse for the Crimes of his past life"; Calico Jack, well known for his romance with lady pirate Anne Bonny; Bartholomew Roberts, who became one of the greatest pirates of all "for the love of novelty and change alone"; and the formidable Blackbeard, who would go into battle with slow-burning matches alight in his beard and behind his ears to enhance his devilish resemblance.

By the early 18th century, competition for prizes in the Caribbean was strong. A treaty in 1713 allowed the Navy time to begin protecting merchant shipping (for a price that was almost robbery in itself).

As the colonies in the island began to stabilize, law and order made the pirates less welcome as members of the community. Many of them set off for the North American mainland, where the newer colonists, already muttering about Independence, were quite pleased to help the newcomers harass British shipping magnates. Others headed for the Orient, the Red Sea, the Indian Ocean and Madagascar.

Since then piracy has continued to flourish in the Far East, but has been quelled fairly effectively in the West.

Smuggling, however, is another matter — recent years have seen a resurgence in the "sweet trade."

The traditions haven't changed much; seaport bars still abound with tales of sailors sneaking around dark shores in small, fast boats, dodging the authorities, sending coded messages at dead of night and risking life and liberty for high stakes.

Anthony Blake

AIR SERVICE

Traveling to and from the Virgins is very straightforward. Most of the larger bareboat companies have travel agents who work closely with them and are in touch with special air fares and hotel accommodations. San Juan, Puerto Rico is the main routing for passengers destined to the B.V.I., St. Thomas and St. Croix. There are numerous non-stop flights from major U.S. Gateways with ample local connections. St. Thomas and St. Croix have direct service from the U.S. mainland. There are plenty of good hotels throughout the islands and it is advisable to plan a one night stay before checking in

at the appropriate marina. This will enable you to "acclimatize" slowly, watching the sun set and sipping a rum punch while the frustrations of the day's travel diminish to insignificance.

The Virgins are an extremely popular tourist destination not only for sailors, but for all sorts of tourists and water sports enthusiasts; consequently, air travel and hotel accommodations should be reserved well in advance.

If you are planning to travel between the islands, there are numerous methods available to you.

ISLAND AIR TRAVEL

Air Anguilla
776-5789 • St. Thomas
Air St. Thomas
495-5935 • Virgin Gorda
American Airlines
1-800-474-4884 • St. Thomas
American Eagle
495-2559 or
494-2449 • Tortola
For info or to reconfirm 1-800-751-1747
British Airways
494-2215 • Tortola
Caribbean Wings
284-495-2309 • Tortola
919-956-8990 • For Information
Caribair
777-1944 • St. Thomas
Clint Aero Inc
776-3958 • St. Thomas
Coastal Air Transport
773-6862 • St. Thomas

Delta Airlines Inc
1-800-221-1212 • St. Thomas
Fly BVI Ltd
495-1747 • Tortola
Four Star Aviation
495-2256 • Tortola
776-8847 • St. Thomas
Gorda Aero Service Inc
495-2271 or
495-2261 after hours • Tortola
Liat Ltd
495-1187/8/9
Flight info/check in 495-2577 • Tortola
Seaborne Seaplanes
777-4491 • St. Croix
US Airways
1-800-622-1015 • St. Thomas
Vieques Air Link Inc
778-9858 • St. Thomas
Winward Island Airways
775-0183 • St. Thomas

FERRIES

The following ferries operate between the U.S. and British Virgin Islands, and between Tortola and Virgin Gorda:

Smith's Ferry...	775-7292	St. Thomas
	494-4430	Tortola
The Native Sun...	774-8685	St. Thomas
	495-4617	Tortola
Speedy's Fantasy...	774-8685	St. Thomas
	495-5240	Tortola

The North Sound Express (495-2271) operates between Beef Island, and North Sound, Virgin Gorda. The Peter Island Ferry (494-2561) runs between the Peter Island dock at Baugher's Bay, Road Town and the Peter Island Yacht Club.

There is ferry service from Underwater Safaris at the Moorings dock to Cooper Island most days. Call them by telephone or radio to confirm times.

The Jost Van Dyke Ferry (495-2997) shuttles passengers between West End and Jost Van Dyke.

For service between West End and Cruz Bay, call Inter-Island Boat Services at 495-4166 in Tortola or at 776-6597 in the U.S.V.I.

From Redhook, St. Thomas to Cruz Bay, St. John, ferries leave at 6:30a.m. and 7:30a.m. on weekdays and on the hour from 8a.m. through noon. From Cruz Bay, ferries leave from 7a.m. through 10p.m. on the hour, and at 11:15p.m.

Ferries are available between the National Park Dock, St. Thomas, and Charlotte Amalie to Caneel Bay Plantation, St. John. Call 776-6111 for schedules.

Ferries are available directly from Charlotte Amalie to Virgin Gorda — check with the Native Sun, Smith's Ferry and Speedy's Fantasy — as well as between St. Thomas and Jost Van Dyke.

See the directory at the back of this guide for a complete listing of ferry services.

CAR RENTAL

Both the British and the U.S. Virgin Islands have developed adequate car rental agencies to cope with the needs of the growing tourist industry.

Prices are slightly higher than on the U.S. mainland, but considering the high cost of freight and the limited life expectancy that vehicles enjoy in the island environment, the differential is not excessive. Most of the major car rental companies have local branches throughout the Virgins and advance reservations can be made through your travel agent.

In addition, many locally owned and operated companies are also represented. If you are chartering during the peak months (December-April), try to reserve well in advance to avoid delays.

In both the U.S. and British Virgins, remember to drive on the left.

TAXI SERVICE

All points of debarkation are more than adequately serviced by taxis. The airports and ferry docks are often lined three deep, with the drivers pushing hard to capture their share of the market.

It is common in the islands to see open safari buses, which can carry up to 20 passengers in natural "air-conditioned" comfort. Taxi fares tend to be expensive throughout the islands and taxis are not metered! However, there are official taxi rates in both the British and U.S. Virgin Islands, and the prudent traveller should inquire of the rate beforehand so that there are no misunderstandings.

The major charterboat companies will arrange transportation to pick you up upon arrival at the airport, but such service should be arranged at the time of booking the charter.

A SAMPLING OF TAXI FARES

The fares listed below are "per person". Many fares will be "charter fares" and therefore should be lower. This is just to give you an idea of the maximum you should be expected to pay. Always inquire before accepting a taxi and if you have a question ask to see the government passenger fares regulations.

TORTOLA

From Beef Island Airport to:
East End, Long Look - $2.00
Maya Cove - $3.00
Wickhams Cay II (Moorings, Tortola Yacht Services), Road Town, $5.00
Nanny Cay - $7.00
West End, Long Bay, Cane Garden Bay - $8.00

From Road Town to:
Prospect Reef, Treasure Isle, Wickhams Cay II - $2.00
Prospect Reef Hotel - $5.00
Baughers Bay - $3.00
Maya Cove, Brandywine, Skyworld, Nanny Cay - $4.00

Cane Garden Bay, West End, Beef Island Airport - $5.00

From West End Jetty To:
Frenchman's Cay - $2.00
Sugar Mill, Long Bay Hotel - $3.00
Cane Garden Bay, Nanny Cay - $4.00
Prospect Reef, Road Town, Treasure Isle, Wickham's Cay II - $5.00
Beef Island - $8.00
Note: Tours of a maximum of 2 1/2 hours and 3 persons $45.00 Fixed
Tours over 3 persons - $12.00 PP

ST. THOMAS

From downtown Charlotte Amalie to:
Airport Terminal - $4.50
Compass Point - $6.00
Crown Bay Dock - $3.00
Frenchman's Reef - $6.00
Frenchtown - $2.00
National Park Dock - $9.00
Ramada Yacht Haven - $2.50
Red Hook - $9.00
St. Thomas Yacht Club - $11.00
Sapphire Resort - $8.50
Vessup Bay - $11.00

PACKING FOR THE CRUISE

Almost without exception, most sailors coming to the Virgin Islands for a week's sailing bring far too much gear. Try not to carry hard suitcases as they do not stow easily on a boat. If possible, use duffel bags or sea bags that can be folded up when not in use.

If you are traveling from the northern climates during the winter months, try to shed your heavy overcoats and boots prior to boarding the airplane. You will only have to carry them around for the duration of your stay in the islands.

Lay out everything you intend to bring and ask yourself if you really need each item. During the days aboard the boat, you will need only bathing suits and perhaps a cover-up, shorts and a few casual shirts or blouses. If you intend to eat ashore at resorts like Caneel Bay, Little Dix and Peter Island, include a jacket and tie for the men and a light cocktail dress for the ladies. Otherwise, in most island restaurants, casual slacks and shirts are acceptable.

You will need some reef shoes for wading in shallow water and T-shirts.

You may wish to include an inexpensive snorkel for each crew member...using a second hand snorkel can be like borrowing someone else's toothbrush.

If you are sailing in the Caribbean, call us and we'll put you in touch with the rest of the world. Whether you'll be on or near land, connect to the

 **IT'S YOUR CHOICE** most extensive cellular communications network in the region with your own AMPS capable (North American analogue) cellular phone. Or allow us to install a high quality 3 watt cellular phone with low loss cable, and fiberglass cellular marine antenna on your yacht. For as low as $495!* Our rates are competitive, and our service extraordinary.

For voice, fax, or to check your e-mail.

To discover how easy it is, call us right

now at: 1-800-BOATFON.

CABLE & WIRELESS
CARIBBEAN CELLULAR

Say hello to the call of the Caribbean, On Land or Sea.

Anguilla • Antigua • Barbados • British Virgin Islands • Cayman Islands • Grenada
Guadeloupe • Jamaica • Martinique • Montserrat • St. Kitts & Nevis • St. Lucia • St. Maarten/St. Martin
St. Vincent & The Grenadines • Turks & Caicos

In Canada 1-800-567-8366. In the Caribbean and elsewhere 1-268-480-2628. © Cable & Wireless 1998
*This low price may not be available in all locations. Please call.

CUSTOMS AND IMMIGRATION

For visitors entering the U.S. Virgin Islands from the United States, there is no customs or immigration clearance, as you are still in U.S. territory. However, you will have to clear back in on your return from this free port area. U.S. citizens are allowed to bring in $1200 duty-free every 30 days from the U.S.V.I.

Those U.S. visitors sailing from British Virgin Island waters and those entering the British Virgin Islands through the airport or West End should be advised that proof of citizenship will be required for all members of your party. A birth certificate, passport or voter registration card and photo I.D. is the normal I.D. expected. For all other visitors, a valid passport is required.

B.V.I. customs must be cleared upon entry and little problem will be encountered for bona fide sailors. All items carried for commercial use are subject to local duties at the going tariff.

CURRENCY

The U.S. dollar is the local currency in both the U.S. and British Virgin Islands. Since you will be spending a lot of time on small islands, it is a good idea to keep traveller's checks in smaller denominations. Major credit cards are honored at most U.S.V.I. stores and hotels and the larger B.V.I. establishments, but do not expect to use them at small restaurants during your cruise. Personal checks are not accepted anywhere.

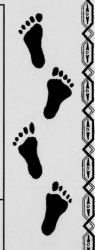

PROTECTION FROM THE SUN

Although it may seem difficult to comprehend as you dig your car out of the snow to get to the airport, the tropical sun is *hot*, especially on pale bodies that have been kept undercover throughout a northern winter.

The constant trade breezes keep the temperature pretty much ideal, but be careful not to spend too long out in the sun, as the combined effect of overhead tropical sun and reflection from both sails and water can cause severe sunburns.

Most charter yachts are equipped with bimini tops; however, it is still a good idea to bring along a pair of light-weight or surgical pants and tops if you have access to them. These will enable you to cover up.

If you are fair, then perhaps you should think about a wide-brimmed hat.

Suntan lotions are available throughout the islands. Heed the warnings of dermatologists regarding excessive sun exposure and do not go out into the sun without using an appropriate sun block or coverup. Start with at least SPF-15. If you are careful, you will gradually develop a rich, golden tan without suffering a painful and potentially dangerous sunburn.

WHAT NOT TO BRING

Apart from an abundance of clothing, there are a few items that don't make any sense to lug back and forth:

A) Scuba gear — If you have your own regulator, face mask, etc., fine, but don't bring down weight belts and tanks. They are available for rent from many outlets and dive shops throughout the islands and will save you the hassle of lugging them around.

B) Food items — Once again, unless you have special dietary needs, these items are readily available throughout the islands and the marginal savings on some frozen steaks could be offset if the box thaws or goes astray.

C) Surfboards and windsurfers — These items represent a problem for the major airlines and a nightmare for the smaller commuter airlines. They are available for rent and anyone interested should make prior arrangements with the appropriate charter company or agent.

Remember that you will probably purchase a few items while in the islands and some allowance should be made for such purchases when packing.

The ideal amount of luggage to bring on a sailing holiday should fit in a duffel bag underneath your airline seat. This will save your worrying about checking bags and waiting with baited breath to see if they show up on the other end.

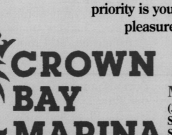

Jim Scheiner

PROVISIONS FOR THE CRUISE

Most charter companies in and around the Virgin Islands offer the charter party a choice of provisioning programs or options.

The original concept was designed to cope with the lack of supermarkets. But in recent years, both in the U.S. and British Virgin Islands, the selection of goods has increased tremendously. Therefore, your provisioning options are as follows:

A) Allow the charter company to provision for you from a pre-selected plan, to save on sailing time. The main plans are *full provisioning*, which includes 3 meals a day, or the popular *split program*, which eliminates some evening meals so you can eat ashore. If you are considering this, ask the charter company for a sample menu.

B) Provision yourself from one of the local markets or delicatessens. This is a good idea if you have specific dietary needs, but it is time-consuming, and when analyzing costs, taxi fares and sailing time should be considered. However, many of the local markets have a surprisingly sophisticated array of products.

C) Have an independent provisioner prepare your provisions in advance and have them delivered to the boat or swing by and pick them up. Provisioning lists are available in advance, allowing you the luxury of choosing your provisioning from home.

Restocking Along the Way

However you provision your vessel, you will probably wish to augment your supply at some point along the cruise. Major items are normally available only in Road Town, Virgin Gorda Yacht Harbour, Cruz Bay, Charlotte Amalie, Redhook and Christiansted, St. Croix. Many smaller shops have a surprising selection of provisioning items, including those in Maya Cove, Nanny Cay, Cane Garden Bay, at the Bitter End Hotel in North Sound, at Harris's Place and Rudy's Superette in Jost Van Dyke, and at Sapphire Beach Marina and Compass Point in St. Thomas.

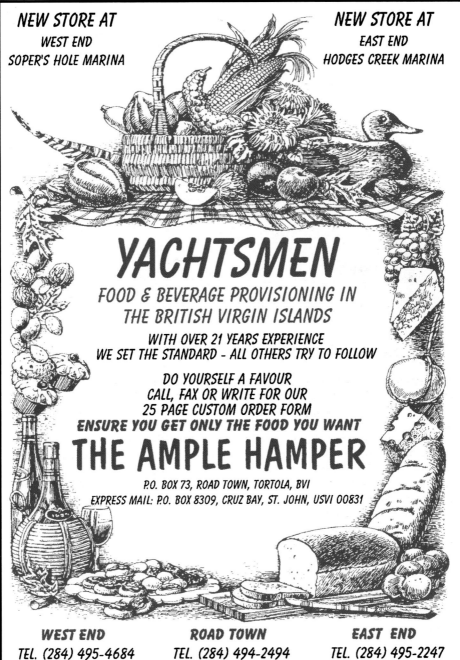

PHOTOGRAPHY IN THE ISLANDS

Jim Scheiner

The verdant green hillside tumbles down to a deserted golden beach, fringed with majestic coconut palms. Tall ships and sleek yachts glide by on an azure sea. You and your companions spend joyful days sailing, snorkeling and exploring. As the water laps against the side of your yacht, you wonder how you'll ever be able to recapture this carefree feeling after you return to the hustle and bustle of the "real world." How will you convey the unspoiled beauty of the Virgin Islands to your friends back home? Well, while memories and tans fade fast, photos last and last.

Camera

It's hard to go wrong with today's cameras; top of the line models now offer auto-everything, simplicity and the basic point and shoot cameras deliver control, sophistication and zoom lens capability previously reserved for high-end machines. Serious shooters will probably want to bring a 35 mm single lens reflex (SLR) with a full complement of lenses. A wide-range zoom lens (35mm to 135mm or longer) will cover most situations. For capturing onboard action, a wider angle lens (24mm) will be good. A long telephoto lens (longer than

210mm) is difficult to use on a moving boat, but can deliver some dramatic shots. Today's automatic "fill flash" is ideal for filling in the deep shadows caused by the tropical sun and for shooting sunset portraits. A polarizing filter can intensify some colors and make the water appear clearer, but it adds a lot of contrast and eats up light. Remember, if you bring every gizmo and accessory you own, you'll spend your entire holiday lugging it around and worrying about its safety. If you're a snap-shooter thinking about upgrading, consider one of the new, water resistant automatic cameras. While not waterproof by any means, they are a little more durable in a marine environment. Even if you're a serious shooter, you might also want to bring a simple camera rather than risk your expensive SLR.

Video

These days, legions of holiday makers are leaving their SLRs and "snap shot" cameras behind and going forth armed with video camcorders. The latest generation of video cameras are small enough to be taken anywhere and deliver an incredible "broadcast quality" picture with point and shoot ease. But they're equally capable of recording endless hours of meaningless, boring video. With a little planning, practice, and discipline, your vacation movies can be quite entertaining.

Here are a few basics: Hold the camera steady (use a tripod or brace yourself),
set the zoom at widest angle setting and get close. Don't over do panning and zooming. Film selectively, you don't need to record every activity every time it happens. When you do decide to record an activity, shoot it in a logical order — establishing big view shots to set the scene, medium shots to show the action and close up shots to show details — you should try to tell a story. Keep it short unless something *very* special is happening. Limit each scene to 10 to 20 seconds of meaningful video. Try in-camera editing, where you shoot your scenes in the order and length that you want to view them. Don't forget live "voice over" narration to explain what and where, but don't over do it. And while you don't want to have the date superimposed over

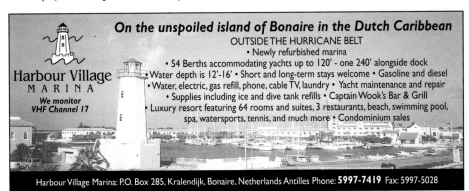
31

all your video, it's not a bad idea to do it for the first shot of each day, sort of like the entry line in a diary. Remember, keep it short, interesting and steady, and think before you push the record button.

Bring plenty of batteries and tape they're not readily available on the islands. A wide angle adapter lens for use in the narrow confines on the boat helps capture all the action. Video cameras are especially sensitive to water/spray damage, including condensation formed when coming from a cold, air conditioned

new "Underwater" film has confused a few people. Basically, it's a slide film with increased sensitivity to red in order to compensate for the predominantly blue light at depths below 20 feet. We've found it to be useful for wide-angle shots in shallow water. For bright colorful shots of divers or marine life, the best technique is to get close, use a strobe and "normal" film. Film processing (both E6 slide and print) is available on the island. As always, keep your film out of the sun and avoid having it repeatedly X-rayed

room to warm, humid air. A good case is essential. Charging batteries on board can be complicated so find out in advance how much 110 AC power there is. If there's only 12 volt, then invest in a 12 volt charger, but double check the polarity before plugging it it.

Film

Bring the type of film (print or slide) you normally use. There is plenty of light in the tropics, so make sure you bring some fine-grained, slower speed film (ISO 100 and lower) for crisp and clear shots. Four hundred speed film is great for sunsets and twilight scenes. ISO 200 is great, an all around compromise. For slide film photographers, Fujichrome's new Velvia (ISO 50) is very color saturated and makes the images come alive. Kodak's

at airport security stations. If you transport your film in a ziplock or mesh bag, it's easy to have it hand checked.

Protecting Your Equipment

Even though you've come all this way for the sun, sea and sand, it doesn't mean that your cameras should partake as well. Salt water and sand kills cameras! While an outright dunking in the sea is certainly catastrophic, it's the cumulative damage caused by spray and carelessness that needs to be prevented. Today's state-of-the-art electronic still and video marvels are especially sensitive to salt water damage. Specialized cameras, protective cases, and preventative measures all help, but a little bit of common sense and awareness go a long way.

Salt water is *very* corrosive and it does most of its damage invisibly, destroying the hidden inner-workings of your camera. Even if you quickly wipe off the occasional splash, the few drops of saltwater that seeped inside your camera will continue to absorb moisture out of the air, damaging your camera long after it appears to be dry.

On board the boat, keep your camera protected from waves and spray. A gallon size, heavy-duty ziplock or even a small (5 gallon) garbage bag will work wonders. Keeping your camera hidden under a lightweight *waterproof* jacket until you're ready to shoot also is a possibility. But if it's really blowing, simply leave your camera below decks, out of harm's way. A UV, or skylight filter, will help protect your lens from salt spray. Don't forget that the salt water "contamination" you collect on your hands and face just from being on a yacht is passed to your camera every time you pick it up. Freshwater face washes and "camera only" towels and paper towels help to minimize this. I always have a dry, clean paper towel in my pocket. Never change film or lenses when there is any chance of spray or splashes.

Getting your camera ashore is another matter. Dinghies are a lot wetter than you think. On a professional shoot, I place my camera bag inside a heavy duty garbage bag (tied closed) and then place that in a canvas bag. Sometimes I use a waterproof, hard "pelican" case, but they're heavy and bulky and difficult to work out of. Be wary of placing an unprotected camera bag on the floor of the dinghy, there's likely to be a lot of water sloshing around. If you want to take pictures from the dinghy *and* keep your camera dry, slow the dinghy down (stop it if necessary) and avoid shooting while motoring into the wind. A lot of cameras get soaked climbing out of the dinghy to go ashore. Seal everything back up before you splash your way through the surf. If you're at all unsure of your balance, pass your camera bag to someone already ashore and hold it high against big waves.

Ashore, the biggest problem is sand. Even waterproof cameras are not sandproof; sand gets into the o-ring seals and destroys them. Practice the same care on the beach as you did on you yacht and you'll do fine. A "camera only" ziplock and beach bag will prevent others from inadvertently throwing wet, sandy towels and clothes on top of your camera. After a swim, dry (and rinse) your hands, face and hair before shooting. As discussed below, disposable cameras are perfect for dinghy and beach trips.

Underwater Photography Equipment

The easiest and cheapest way to get started in underwater photography is to purchase a couple of waterproof, disposable "snorkel" cameras (i.e., the Kodak Weekender or Fuji Waterproof). Not only are they waterproof, but they're also

dinghy- and beach-proof. Take one everywhere and enjoy worry-free vacation photography. While we don't sanction "one time use" cameras, in this situation it's far better to trash a $10 to $20 disposable camera than your $600 Nikon.

The Weekender is rated to about a dozen feet and ideal for swimming and snorkeling. But if scuba diving is in your plans, you'll need to move up a notch. Ikelite, a manufacturer of professional underwater camera housings and strobes, also makes the Aquashot housing (around $80) for use with Fuji or Kodak disposable cameras-with-flash. The advantage over the snorkeling cameras described above is twofold. First, the cameras have a built-in flash which will bring out the brilliant colors of the fish and corals. Without flash, everything deeper than 20 to 30 feet underwater is blah blue. Second, the Aquashot housing is rated to 125 feet, as deep as you are likely to go. This combination of housing and disposable camera-with-flash is a great trouble-free way to get started in underwater photography with minimal risk or investment. The pictures rival those taken by expensive underwater cameras.

An Underwater Photography Primer

Regardless of what kind of camera you use to take underwater pictures, there is one maxim that holds true — *get close.* The less water you shoot through, the clearer, brighter and more color-saturated your pictures will be. There are exceptions of course, but most good underwater photographs are shot within four feet

of the subject, which is quite close, within conversational distance. If you can reach out and touch your subject, you're too close, much further away and you're too far. The perfect distance is a handshake distance — reach out and shake hands with your buddy and fire away. If your subject (a fish, say) isn't interested in shaking hands, then just imagine a double arm length. However you measure it, it's pretty close, but that's what it takes to get *good* underwater photos.

With most cameras, at three to four feet from your subject the dimensions of the area photographed will be roughly two by three feet. Angelfish, parrotfish and coral and sponge formations are appropriate subjects. Tiny fish and huge vistas requires specialized lenses. Remember, that while pictures of coral and fish are fun and challenging to take, make sure that you take plenty of your companions. Try to avoid shooting down on your subject. If at all possible, aim across or even up slightly, this helps separate your subject from the background and even adds a little drama to the image.

Most published underwater photographs boast brilliant colors. However, due to the natural absorption of sunlight by water, your pictures will suffer from the underwater "blues," unless you use a flash to bring out the reds and yellows. Smaller cameras with built-in flashes do a fine job of balancing the flash with the available light. Even the most powerful underwater strobe won't reach past five or six feet. Try to avoid stirring up the bottom, the resultant strobe lit "back scatter" will look as if you were diving in a blizzard.

The coral reef and its inhabitants are very fragile, so please, no standing on or grabbing delicate coral structures or removing anything from the sea. Take only pictures, leave only bubbles.

Jim and Odile Scheiner are the owners of Rainbow Visions Photography in Tortola, specializing in underwater photography and video.

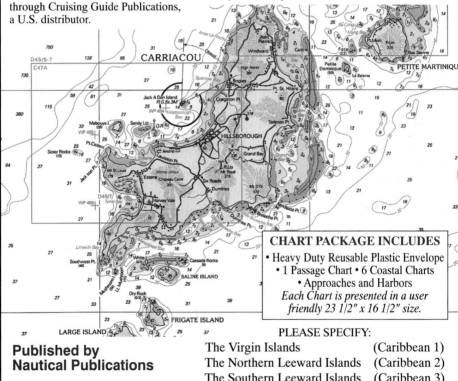

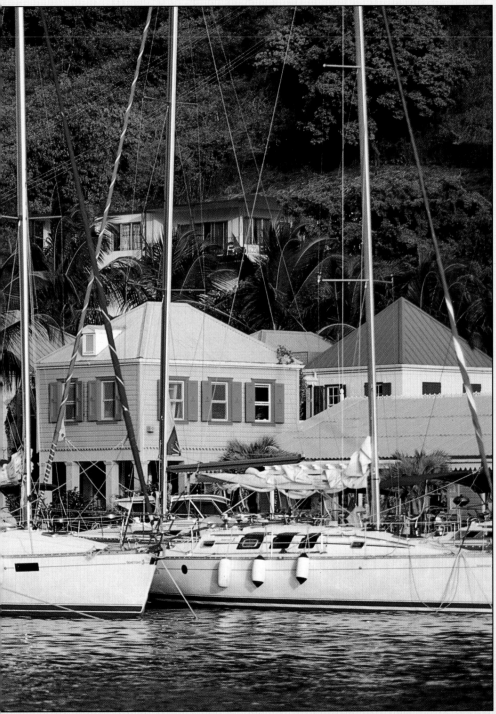

Dougal D. Thornton

CHARTS

Paper Charts

It is possible to navigate through the U.S. and British Virgin Islands with a single paper chart, NOS 2564. Many of the charter companies have duplicated this chart in one form or another as a handout for each charter group. If you're chartering, be sure to ask your charter company in advance which charts they'll provide you, when you'll receive them, and whether the charts are yours to keep. Then take a careful look at the areas you intend to cruise and order any additional chart coverage you may want.

Your own charts will allow you to plan your trip in advance and will also serve as a nice memento of your trip. Complete paper chart coverage of the Virgin Islands will range from about $50.00 to several hundred dollars, especially if you include electronic charts which are now very popular. Charts can be hard to obtain in the Virgin Islands, so taking your own charts is the best way to be sure you have the coverage you're comfortable with.

The following paper charts cover the Virgin Islands and surrounding areas, and they are available from larger chart agents in the U.S., Canada and Europe:

Caribbean Yachting Charts
(These charts are cross referenced in our anchorage sections).

CYC-Series 1 - Puerto Rico and the
    Virgin Islands, Fajardo to Anegada
C-11 - St. Thomas to Anguilla
C-12 - Anegada to Virgin Gorda
C-12A - Virgin Gorda - North Sound
C-13 - Tortola to Virgin Gorda
C-13A - Tortola-Road Harbour
C-14 - St. John to Tortola
C-14A - St. John-Coral Bay
C-15 - St. Thomas - St. John - Pillsbury
    Sound
C-16 - St. Thomas

C-16A - St. Thomas - Charlotte Amalie
C-17 - St. Croix
C-17A - Christiansted Harbour

Imray
A13 - SE Coast of Puerto Rico
A131 - Isla de Culebra and Isla de Culabea
A23 - The Virgin Islands, St. Croix
A231 - St. Thomas to Virgin Gorda
A232 - Tortola to Anegada
A233 - A231 & A232 (two sides)
A234 - St. Croix NE Coast

Chart Kit
Reg. 10 - U.S. and British Virgin Islands

U.S. National Ocean Service (NOAA)
25640 - Puerto Rico and the Virgin Islands
25641 - Virgin Gorda to St. Thomas;
    St. Croix
25644 - St. Croix, Frederiksted Road
    and Pier
25645 - St. Croix, Christiansted Harbour
25647 - St. Thomas, Pillsbury Sound
    and St. John
25650 - Virgin Passage and Vieques Sound
25653 - Island of Culebra and approaches

U.S National Imagery and Mapping Agency (former DMA)
25600 - Anegada Passage
25609 - Tortola to Anegada
25610 - Approaches to Gorda Sound
25611 - Road Harbour and approaches

British Admiralty
130 - Anguilla to Puerto Rico
485 - St. Croix
2005 - Road harbour to Capella Islands
2008 - NE Virgin Gorda to Anegada
2019 - Tortola to Virgin Gorda
2183 - St. Thomas Harbor
2452 - Tortola to Culebra, including
    St. Thomas

Electronic Charts

Used in combination with GPS and paper charts, electronic charts have become extremely popular in the Caribbean, though they remain hard to purchase in the islands. The following electronic charts cover the Virgin Islands (and beyond) and are available from selected chart agents and electronic dealers in the U.S., Canada and Europe.

C-Map Standard (CF - 85)
J150 - Puerto Rico and the U.S. Virgin Islands
J151 - British Virgin Islands to Monterrat

C-Map NT (CF 95)
NAB-604 - Hispaniola to U.S. Virgin Islands, including BVI

Navionics
CX005 - Dominican Republic to Virgin Islands
CX010 - Puerto Rico to Grenada

Garmin
GCX005 - Dominican Republic to Virgin Islands
GCX010 - Puerto Rico to Grenada

BSB/NOAA
Reg. 10 - Puerto Rico and U.S. and British Virgin Islands

Maptech
Chartpack 9 - Imray-Iolaire: Puerto Rico to Venezuela
Chartpack 10 - NOAA/DMA Puerto Rico to Grenada

Courtesy of Bluewater Books & Charts

Caribbean Yachting Charts —
The References at the Bottom of the Pages

We have cross-referenced all of our sketch charts for the U.S. and British Virgin Islands this year with the Caribbean Yachting Charts — Series 1 — St. Thomas to Anguilla. You will note at the bottom of the anchorage pages a number such as "C 14" which denotes the Caribbean Yachting Chart that the anchorage discussed appears on. The charts have been recently resurveyed and use WGS 84 map datum for the GPS waypoints. We think you will find these charts very accurate and easy to read. The charts are available from our order form at the back of the book or by calling 800-330-9542.

NAVIGATION

Pilotage through unknown waters is one of the major concerns of the cruising yachtsman. However, in the Virgins, where there is very little tide rise and fall and only minimal current to worry about, pilotage is extremely simple.

Since the weather is so warm, we don't experience any fog and you can always see the island for which you are heading.

Reefs and shoals are not a major problem as they are well marked and, provided time is taken to study the pertinent charts on a daily basis, your cruise around the island will be most enjoyable.

The islands themselves are high and volcanic, rising steeply from the crystal clear water. In many cases, it is possible to position your bow almost on the beach, providing you have a stern anchor set.

Since the island chain is close together, you will have no difficulty in distinguishing them. Using the contour marks on the charts you will usually be able to pinpoint your location without the use of navigation tools.

Equipment

Every cruising yacht should be equipped with the basic tools of navigation — parallel rules, triangles, dividers, plotters, etc. However, it should be noted that in order to navigate throughout the islands, the only equipment needed is a compass, chart, pencil and leadline or fathometer. Those wishing to brush up on navigational skills will find ample opportunity, although celestial observations are often difficult because of the proximity of the islands.

Reef Reading

There is no dark secret attached to the ability to read the reef. It is merely the ability to distinguish water color. Experience is, of course, the best teacher; however, with a few practical hints, even the novice will be able to feel his way to an anchorage within a few days.

It is important to have the sun overhead in order to distinguish reef areas. That is why most charter companies insist that the boats be at anchor by 1600 hours. Do not attempt to negotiate a reef-fringed entrance with the sun in your eyes, and always have someone on the

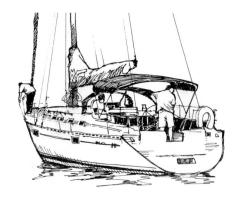

bow keeping an eye on the water in front of the boat.

Deep water of 50 feet and over will be "inky" blue. This can be lighter if the bottom is white sand.

A light green or turquoise would indicate a depth of 15-25 feet. If the bottom has rocks or coral, these will change the color to a brownish shade.

Water of 10 feet and under will show as a very pale shade of green if there is a sandy bottom, or a light brown if rocks and coral are present.

Right of Way and Night Sailing

A general rule of thumb is to stay out of everyone's way. There are times, however, when this is impossible and, in such instances, power boats should give way to boats under sail. This being the case, it is important in close quarters to hold your course so that the other skipper can take appropriate action to avoid you, without having to double-guess your actions.

If you are crossing ferry traffic, it is prudent to keep a weather eye on approaching vessels and make every effort to stay well clear.

Many schooners trading between the islands are underway at night, and very few use running lights.

Don't sail at night!

Cruising Etiquette

During your cruise through the Virgins, please remember that there are a limited number of places on the smaller islands capable of dealing with garbage.

Check first before carrying it ashore — *don't throw it over the side,* even if it means keeping it a couple of days in a plastic bag. Always carry any refuse back to your boat, rather than leaving it on the beach.

Many of the beaches throughout the Virgins are private property and the cruising yachtsman must exercise care to respect any notice indicating such restrictions.

GPS — Global Positioning Satellite

Although the Virgin Islands are mostly line of sight navigation it is still quite helpful to have a GPS system aboard your vessel for occasional reference. It is certainly valuable when making passages to destinations outside of the Virgin Islands or for those very occasional days when the weather may somewhat obstruct your view of prominent landmarks.

GPS is a fantastic aid to navigation, but it should be used in conjunction with visual sightings and depth readings. It can be quite helpful for getting you near a harbor entrance, but it is not accurate enough to take you into the harbor. There

have been reports of navigators finding themselves a couple of miles away from where they expected in places where our GPS showed good correspondence. Occasional errors are a possibility.

The latitudes and longitudes we give in our guide are courtesy of Nautical Publications, publishers of the Caribbean Yachting Charts that we cross reference in our guides. They are taken from the series 1 — Virgin Islands — St. Thomas to Sombrero and use WGS 84 map datum. To order a set of charts please refer to the order form in the back of the book.

GPS Waypoint	Location	Latitude (north)	Longitude (west)
149	Great Harbour Jost Van Dyke	18°26.0 north	64°45.0 west
139	Road Harbour Tortola	18°24.8 north	64°36.2 west
138	Brandywine Bay Tortola	18°24.5 north	64°35.0 west
133	Beef Island Bluff	18°25.3 north	64°30.9 west
144	Water Point Norman Island	18°19.3 north	64°37.5 west
142	Rock Hole Peter Island	18°21.4 north	64°37.0 west
136	Cooper Island	18°23.5 north	64°31.0 west
134	Round Rock (north)	18°24.1 north	64°28.2 west
135	Round Rock (south)	18°23.3 north	64°27.1 west
132	The Baths Virgin Gorda	18°26.0 north	64°27.0 west

GPS Waypoint	Location	Latitude (north)	Longitude (west)
125	Mountain Point Virgin Gorda	18°30.4 north	64°25.2 west
131	St. Thomas Bay Virgin Gorda	18°27.2 north	64°26.9 west
124	Mosquito Rock Virgin Gorda	18°31.3 north	64°23.1 west
121	Setting Point Anegada	18°42.4 north	64°24.5 west
162	Charlotte Amalie St. Thomas	18°18.6 north	64°55.6 west
161	Packet Rock	18°17.6 north	64°53.4 west
165	Middle Passage Western St. Thomas	18°21.5 north	64°50.7 west
153	Jersey Bay St. Thomas	18°18.2 north	64°51.3 west
154	Maria Bluff St. John	18°18.5 north	64°47.7 west
151	Durloe Cays St. John	18°18.5 north	64°47.8 west
146	Ram Head St. John	18°17.8 north	64°42.2 west
145	Red Point St. John	18°19.4 north	64°40.3 west
171	Christiansted St. Croix	17°46.0 north	64°41.9 west
172	Green Cay St. Croix	17°46.6 north	64°40.1 west
173	Salt River St. Croix	17°47.8 north	64°45.0 west

THE BUOYAGE SYSTEM OF THE VIRGIN ISLANDS

In an international effort to standardize buoyage systems, the International Association of Lighthouse Authorities (IALA) has agreed that, in order to meet conflicting requirements, there will be two systems in use throughout the world. These are to be called systems A and B, respectively. The rules for the two systems were so similar that the "IALA" Executive Committee felt able to combine the two sets of rules into one, known as the "IALA Maritime Buoyage System."

This single set of rules allows lighthouse authorities the choice of using red to port or red to starboard on a regional basis, the two regions being known as region A and region B.

The latter system, system B, is used in North and South America and throughout the waters of the Caribbean. In system B the color red is used to mark the starboard side of the channel when approaching from seaward.

In this respect, it should be noted that the respective buoyage systems for both U.S. and British Virgins are the same.

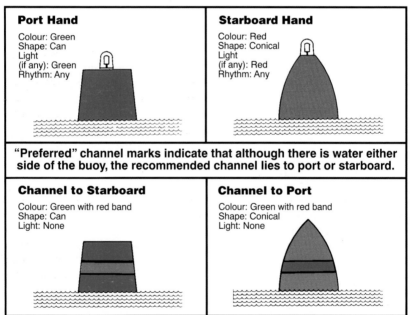

RED RIGHT RETURNING!

The lateral 'system B' as seen entering from seaward.

Port Hand
Colour: Green
Shape: Can
Light
(if any): Green
Rhythm: Any

Starboard Hand
Colour: Red
Shape: Conical
Light
(if any): Red
Rhythm: Any

"Preferred" channel marks indicate that although there is water either side of the buoy, the recommended channel lies to port or starboard.

Channel to Starboard
Colour: Green with red band
Shape: Can
Light: None

Channel to Port
Colour: Green with red band
Shape: Conical
Light: None

VIRGIN WEATHER

Located in the northeast trade wind belt, the Virgin Islands are blessed with almost perfect weather the year round. The seas from the north are broken by the island chain, providing the seafarer with ideal weather conditions.

Weather Forecasts

Unlike that of most other parts of the world, the weather in the Virgin Islands is extremely stable. Forecasts are broadcast daily on most of the local stations:

St. Thomas: WIVI 99.5 FM; (Forecasts at 0730, 0830, 1530, 1630 with hourly updates WVWI — 1000 AM (Forecasts hourly); WSTA — 1340 AM; Radio Antilles — 830 AM

St. Croix: WSTX 970 AM

Tortola: ZBVI — 780 AM

Puerto Rico: WOJO — 1030 AM (English speaking all day at 6 minutes past the hour)

The following weather reports will be found on your VHF radio:

Virgin Island Radio WAH gives detailed weather. It is announced on VHF Channel 16 switching to VHF Channel 28 and Channel 85.

NOAA Weather is broadcasted throughout the day on WX 3 or 4 on your VHF radio.

Tides

The tidal range throughout the Virgin Islands is about 12 inches, depending upon the time of year. You will probably be unaware of any fluctuation. However, you cannot rely upon the rising tide to float you off the odd sandbar. Currents in certain areas can reach 1-2 knots, namely through Pillsbury Sound between St. Thomas and St. John, the Durloe Cays in St. John, and in the narrows between St. John and Tortola.

Ground Swells

During the winter months of November through April, any significant weather in the North Atlantic will produce heavy swells along the entire north coast of the Virgins several days later. These ground seas have little effect on vessels under sail, but can turn a normally tranquil anchorage into pounding surf. Most anchorages exposed to the north are prone to this phenomenon—choose your anchorage accordingly.

Winds

Owing to the northeast trade winds, the wind direction throughout the Virgins is dominated by the movements of the Bermuda High. During the winter months of November to January, the prevailing wind is from the northeast at 15-20 knots. The fabled Christmas Winds can produce 25-30 knots for several days at a time. By February, the winds start to move around to the east, and by June, they are blowing out of the southeast at 10-15 knots.

During September to October, the trade winds are weakest, and the weather can be less settled. Although these months are considered hurricane season, Hurricane Hugo was the first to hit in 50-odd years. By November, the high pressure system around Bermuda starts to stabilize and 15-20 knot breezes become the norm.

Rain

While late summer to fall is considered rainy season, rain squalls can come at any time of year. Be aware of approaching squalls by watching the sky and clouds to windward. If a dark squall is approaching, it probably has considerable wind velocity on the squall line, and the prudent skipper should shorten sail beforehand.

It also will give the crew a chance to arm themselves with soap and enjoy a shower.

Winter Storms and Hurricanes

Despite hurricanes Marilyn and Bertha, the Virgin Islands have fewer storms than does the Long Island Sound in New York. When the islands do experience a tropical storm or depression, it is usually in the early development of the storm center, and the storms usually do not reach full intensity until they are north of the area. Should a storm approach the islands, remember that they travel very slowly; consequently, with the communication systems used today, sailors can be assured of at least 48 hours' warning.

COMMUNICATIONS

Telephone Service

The U.S. Virgin Islands (area code 340) and Puerto Rico (area code 787) are on the same system as the U.S. Calls can be made at pay phones, as on the mainland, either collect, or with a telephone credit card.

The British Virgin Islands, serviced by Cable and Wireless, have a different area code 284, and can be accessed from the U.S. by using the prefix of 1 plus area code plus seven digit number. You can also use your credit card, or call collect. Several USA Direct Dial telephones are available throughout the islands as well as coin and telephone card phones. Fax and email service are also available.

The Customer Care office of Cable and Wireless is located on Wickham's Cay near the banks, or by calling 221 or the main office at 284-494-4444.

> **AREA CODES:**
>
> *British Virgin Islands 284*
>
> *U.S. Virgin Islands 340*
>
> *Puerto Rico 787*

How Can I Be Reached In An Emergency?

If you are expecting urgent business calls or if you should be needed for a medical emergency, it would be wise to leave the phone number of both Virgin Island Radio and Tortola Radio, and the marina from where you are sailing. The party will not be able to contact you directly unless you happen to be monitoring the radio, but they can leave a message and the list of yachts for which they are holding traffic would be read during traffic hours.

Virgin Island Radio broadcasts traffic every hour on the hour between 0500 and 1200 daily. They will place collect calls, credit card calls, third party calls, and take Master Card and Visa. Their telephone number is (340) 776-8282.

Tortola Radio (British Virgin Islands) broadcasts traffic at 0700, 1100, 1900 and 2300 daily. Weather is broadcast from VHF channel 16 at 0900 and 1200 daily. To call Tortola Radio by land phone call 284-494-4116.

VHF

Almost every boat sailing the Virgins will be equipped with a VHF radio. Apart from single side band for offshore communications, VHF is used for all local traffic.

The channels vary from boat to boat, but the most commonly used frequencies are listed below.

Channel 16: Standby and international distress frequency

Channel 12: Portside operations (Charter company to yacht)

Channel 6: Ship-to-ship, safety

Channel 27, 84: Radio Tortola

Channel 25, 85, 87: W.A.H. Virgin Islands Radio

Channel 68: Ship-to-ship communications

Channel 22A: Coast Guard

Channel 3: Weather

Channel 16 is used as a calling frequency, but the operator must switch to a second channel once contact has been established in order to keep 16 open.

And Now For The Good News
No Surcharge On Credit Card Calls

CABLE & WIRELESS
BRITISH VIRGIN ISLANDS

DIAL 111

To make a credit card telephone call from the British Virgin Islands simply dial 111 from any phone - public or private - and follow the recorded instructions to complete your call. You'll be connected in seconds. No complicated access codes. No Fuss. No credit card surcharges. You pay only normal operator rates.

Phone Cards

Or, you can purchase a prepaid Phone Card from a wide network of card agencies located throughout the islands. Simply insert the card into any of our specially marked payphones and dial the required number. It's that simple!

Dial 1 + AREA CODE + NUMBER for North America and the Caribbean, 011 + COUNTRY CODE + NUMBER for Europe and the rest of the world. Nothing could be easier than calling home from the BVI.

Can I Call Home From the Boat?

It is possible for VHF calls made from your vessel via Virgin Island Radio or Tortola Radio to be patched into the phone system.

As stated above, calls may be made through Virgin Island Radio with payment by several methods. Also, Tortola Radio will place collect calls for you. If you are a bareboat charterer, make arrangements with the marina prior to leaving. If you are aboard a crewed charter yacht, the skipper will assist you with radio calls.

Private yachts must make arrangements to open an account with either Tortola Radio or Virgin Island Radio if not using one of the above methods of payment.

EMERGENCY
U.S. COAST GUARD
787-729-6770
VISAR
999 OR 911

Cellular Telephones

For Virgin Island yachtsmen who need to keep in touch, cellular telephone service is now available. Cellular phones can be used for everything from checking in with the office, the family, or for local applications like ordering more provisions and making dinner reservations. Installed on many bareboat charter fleets as well as crewed yachts, this offers the yachtsman the choice of using a telephone for more privacy, or the radio.

You can rent cellular phones in the Virgins or bring your own from home. There is service by two cellular phone companies, Boatphone in the BVI and Vitel Cellular in the USVI. Information is available from your charter company regarding the availability and operation of cellular phones. All that is required is a major credit card.

How About Dinner Reservations?

Where telephone service is nonexistent, many restaurants stand by the VHF on Channel 16 or 68, which is reserved for ship-to-ship operation.

It is frowned upon by the local licensing authority to use the VHF Channel 12 for reservations if the restaurant can be reached via Tortola Radio on a phone patch.

Radio Procedure

Before attempting to make a VHF radio call, think it through. Understand the procedure and the limitations of the equipment you are using.

The call should begin with two repetitions of the station or vessel being called, followed by the name of your yacht, followed by the word "over." It is important to terminate with the "over" as the other party will then key his mike and reply.

Example: "...Moorings, Moorings, this is the vessel *Bodacious* ZJL 172, over..."

If you get no response, repeat the call. If there is still no response, try again in 5 minutes. When contact is to be terminated, the party will sign off: "...This is *Bodacious*, ZJL 172 clear with Moorings..."

Distress Calls

In case of a real emergency, you should come up on Channel 16, "...Mayday, Mayday, Mayday. This is the vessel *Bodacious*, over..."

Repeat three times until contact is made. Then give your location and the nature of your problem. It is important to state only the pertinent information and not to cloud the situation with emotion.

• Stay calm; *don't panic.*
• Don't allow anyone to use the radio unless they are familiar with the procedure and the problem.

The U.S. Coast Guard in San Juan monitors 24 hours per day.

Virgin Island Radio in St. Thomas monitors 24 hours per day.

Tortola Radio monitors from 0700 to 1900, but in a Mayday situation an operator will respond.

Unbeatable Convenience

Marine and Land Mobile Cellular Service

Caribbean Cellular Telephone gives users the quality service they deserve with the features they need.

Buy, rent, or bring your own cellular telephone. Your own personal incoming telephone number awaits you, so you're never out of touch with the rest of the world. With CCT's voice mail and fax service, your cellular phone works for you IF you choose not to receive calls. Never search for a payphone again! Call one of our friendly customer service representatives today for personal attention, or activation is as easy as dialing "0" and SND from your cellular phone. Reliability, privacy, and mobility you can't afford to live without.

CARIBBEAN CELLULAR TELEPHONE
MILL MALL, BOX 267, ROAD TOWN, TORTOLA, B.V.I.
PHONE: (284) 494-3825 FAX: (284) 494-4933

BOATPHONE
Put The World in YOUR Pocket!

CUSTOMS AND IMMIGRATION

Since the Virgin Islands are divided between the U.S. and Britain, you will be crossing international boundaries during your cruise. Therefore, it is necessary to clear customs when entering and leaving each respective territory. Failure to observe this formality could result in substantial fines or even loss of your vessel. Should you pick up your charter boat in the U.S.V.I. and wish to cruise the waters of the B.V.I., it would be necessary to "clear" the vessel with U.S. Customs and Immigration. Then proceed to the nearest British port of entry for clearance "inbound." You are required to clear the vessel out again before departing for U.S. territory. Often, if your stay is short and of a known duration, you will be permitted to clear in and out at the same time.

At the time of clearance, it is necessary to have in your possession the ship's papers and passports or identification for all crew members, in addition to your clearance from the last port. All crew members must be present for clearance. It is also recommended that you wear proper attire when making your clearance.

B.V.I. Cruising Permits

For yachts cruising in B.V.I. waters, there is a daily tax payable at the time of clearance or at the commencement of charter. Dive boats, day charter, and sport fishing boats should contact customs for the required fees at 284-494-3701.

The rates are as follows:

A. Charter boats based outside of the BVI: $4/person per day all year.

B. Charter boats recorded in the BVI: Dec. 1-Apr. 30: $2/person per day; May 1-Nov. 30: $0.75/person per day.

Fishing Permits in the B.V.I.

It is illegal for a non-resident to remove *any* marine organism from the waters of the British Virgin Islands without first obtaining a recreational fishing permit. Call the Fisheries Department at 494-3429.

Locations of Customs

St. Thomas:	Wharfside at the ferry dock.
St. John:	Waterfront at Cruz Bay.
St. Croix:	Gallows Bay at Christiansted.
Tortola:	Roadtown at the Government Dock. West End ferry dock.
Virgin Gorda:	Airport or Yacht Harbour.
Jost Van Dyke:	Great Harbour.

Office Hours

U.S. Customs are open from 8a.m. to noon and 1-5p.m. Monday through Sunday, but vessels clearing in on Sunday will incur overtime charges. Vessels arriving after hours must raise their quarantine flag, remain on board and clear the next morning. Customs and immigration are located next to each other for ease in clearing.

British Customs are open: Monday through Friday, 8:30-3:30 for normal business, with extended hours to 6p.m. (with overtime fees); Saturday, 9-12:30, with extended hours until 6 p.m.; Sunday carries overtime charges all day. Customs officers can be found clearing in the ferries on Sundays for yacht clearance. Outside these hours, raise your quarantine flag and clear at the first available opportunity. Do not leave your vessel except to go straight to customs and immigration.

Schedule of Charges

Clearance into and from U.S. waters is free during normal working hours except for a token charge for the forms involved.

Typical charges for a 10 ton yacht clearing into the B.V.I. are as follows:

Harbor Dues $2.00
Ship's Dues $3.00
Forms .... $ .40
Overtime fees .... additional $4.00

Please note that there is a 10-cent stamp duty payable throughout the B.V.I. on all travelers checks.

B.V.I. Immigration

One of the following types of identification is required by U.S. and Canadian citizens entering the B.V.I.:

    A. Passport
    *B. Birth Certificate
    *C. Voter's Registration Card
    *Plus a photo I.D.

All other countries must have a current passport. If you have questions regarding the need for visas contact your nearest British Embassy or telephone the B.V.I. Immigration Department at 284-494-3701.

- All crew members are to present themselves for clearance.
- Yachts dropping passengers off must first clear both customs and immigration.
- All private yachts will be given no more than 30 days' entry. Extensions will incur a fee.
- Late fees, in addition to customs charges, are as much as $8 per vessel and higher on Sundays and public holidays.

Jet Skis

It is against B.V.I. law to import jet skis. If you have a jet ski aboard you must declare it at customs when entering the B.V.I. Jet skis can be rented from local rental shops in certain locations.

WATER SAFETY

The waters of the Virgin Islands are essentially a benign area. When people think of tropical waters, man-eating sharks, barracuda and giant moray eels come to mind. The truth of the matter is that more injuries are sustained by cuts from coral or by stepping on sea urchin spines, than by encounters with underwater predators.

Sharks

There are many large sharks around the waters of the Virgins, but they remain largely in deep water. It is highly unlikely that you will ever see a shark during your cruise.

Barracuda

You will, without doubt, see numerous barracuda of various sizes while snorkeling the reefs. They are curious fish and are likely to stay almost motionless in the water watching your movements. They will not bother you, and it is best to show them the same courtesy.

Moray Eels

These creatures are shy by nature and make their homes in rocks and crevices in the reef. They will protect themselves from perceived danger, so do not reach into caves or crevices unless you can see inside.

Coral

Exercise extreme caution around all coral as cuts and scratches can become infected quickly. Familiarize yourself with the various types of coral and remember to stay well clear of the fire coral.

Wear good foot protection when wading on shallow reefs.

Sea Urchins

These black, spiny creatures are found in abundance throughout the islands. They can be seen on sandy bottoms and on reefs and rocks. If you stand on one or inadvertently place your hand on one, it is likely that one or more of the spines will pierce your skin and break off. Do not try to dig the spines out. (See Medical Information on page 215.)

Don'ts

If you observe the following basic rules on water safety, you will add to your enjoyment of the cruise:

1. Don't swim at night.
2. Don't swim alone.
3. Don't swim in heavy surf.
4. Don't dump refuse in the water — it is illegal and attracts sharks.
5. Don't wear jewelry when swimming or diving.
6. Don't reach into crevices or caves.
7. Don't spear a fish and leave it bleeding in the water or in a bag at your waist.
8. Take *no* marine life without a permit!

While the moray eel is a fearsome looking crature, they are actually shy by nature.

VISAR (VIRGIN ISLANDS SEARCH & RESCUE, LTD.)

VISAR (Virgin Islands Search and Rescue Ltd.) is a nonprofit organization that provides an invaluable and often lifesaving service to sailors voyaging in the British Virgin Islands.

Based in Road Town, Tortola, VISAR generally responds to medical emergencies or other cases where life or limb are endangered. The organization will also assist in communications to calls for help of a commercial nature and will put anyone in need of assistance with commercial towing operations, salvors or mechanics.

VISAR can be reached in the following ways:

- Through Tortola Radio — ask for Fire and Rescue and relate to them that you need Search and Rescue.
- By telephone (either cellular or regular phone) you can dial either 999 or 911 and ask for Search and Rescue.

In either case you will be put in touch with a VISAR coordinator who will be able to assist you. Once this initial contact has been established, make every effort possible to ensure that lines of communication (either VHF radio or phone) are kept open.

In emergency situations requiring assistance, VISAR recommends that you have the following information available:

- Location is most important. (Be accurate — e.g.: there is a Great Harbour on both Peter Island and Jost Van Dyke and several Long Bays throughout the islands. You must be specific.)
- State the exact nature of your distress, such as fire, suspected heart attack, or other similar emergency.
- State the name of your vessel.
- Speak slowly and clearly.
- Remain as calm as possible. Panic can only make the situation worse.
- Listen carefully to what is said. In an international community like the islands, you are as likely to speak to responder that may be other than American. An accent can make it very difficult to translate, and consequently listening carefully as you talk is extremely important.

VISAR is largely supported by membership dues. These range from $25 for an individual to $1,000 for a life member. For further information, contact: VISAR, P.O. Box 3042, Road Town, Tortola, B.V.I.; phone: (284) 494-4357.

Jim Scheiner

ANCHORING

Many sailors visiting the Virgin Islands have all sorts of sailing experience, both inshore and offshore; however, it is interesting to note that many have little experience anchoring.

Since you will be subjected to the constant trade breezes on a heavy displacement-type vessel, follow these suggestions for safe, hassle-free anchoring:

1. Pick your anchorage and arrive there early enough in the afternoon to assure both good light and a choice of spots. Bear in mind that during the peak season, December to April, some of the more popular spots become crowded.

2. Before doing anything else, work out a system of communication between the person on the helm and the crew member dropping the anchor. Remember that your engine will be running and therefore you will be unable to communicate verbally. Hand signals are needed and should be worked out beforehand.

3. Furl the sails and generally make the boat shipshape before entering the anchorage. Also shorten the dinghy painter to prevent its being sucked into the prop.

4. Pick your spot. Make sure you will have enough room to fall back on the anchor without lying too close to the yacht anchored behind, once you have laid out 5-to-1 scope. Sand makes the best holding ground. Do not anchor on coral.

5. Motor up to the desired spot slowly, ensuring that you are head to the wind. Stop the boat exactly where you wish the anchor to lay. Take note of the depth.

6. Once the vessel has lost all forward way, lower the anchor to the bottom.

7. Let the wind slowly push the vessel back. Don't try to reverse. Pay out adequate scope as the vessel moves aft. Don't worry about being broadside to the wind.

8. When the desired amount of scope has been paid out, snub the rope and allow the wind to straighten out the vessel.

9. Put the engine into reverse and increase throttle to 1500 rpm. This should set the anchor and the anchor rope should start to tighten. If you notice it "skipping," pay out more scope. Once you are satisfied that the anchor is set, take the engine out of gear. The vessel should spring forward.

moor seacure limited

THE OTHER ALTERNATIVE

Tired of straining the old back? Tired of waking up all night worrying about your anchor dragging, thinking that THIS is supposed to be a vacation? WELL, now there is an alternative... Located throughout the British Virgin Islands at most popular anchorages there are professionally maintained moorings available for overnight use. The small fee for the mooring use is well worth the good night's sleep it affords.

Here are a few tips on picking and leaving a mooring...

1. As in anchoring, approach the mooring area slowly with your dinghy pulled on a short line.
2. Have a crew member ready with a boat hook at the bow to direct you and to pick up the mooring pennant.
3. Approach the mooring buoy slowly from the direction that keeps the bow of your boat into the wind.
4. You may find that at idle speed by shifting alternately from forward to neutral you can coast to the buoy, then shift into reverse for a second to stop the boat as the crew member lifts the pennant on board and attaches it to the bow cleat.
5. Please do not be embarrassed if you miss picking up the pennant for the first time. It happens to all of us at sometime. Just circle around and make another approach.
6. To leave the mooring with your dinghy once again on a short line simply let go the pennant and set off for your next destination. Take care not to run over the mooring buoy and pennant as you leave.

These helpful hints are brought to you by Moor-Seacure Ltd.-the premier mooring company in the BVI. And remember, "If it doesn't say MOOR-SEACURE, it probably ISN'T!"

Moor-Seacure moorings are available at these and other fine locations...

• LAST RESORT AT TRELLIS BAY
• COOPER ISLAND • MARINA CAY • ANEGADA REEF HOTEL
• RHYMERS AT CANE GARDEN BAY
• SOPERS HOLE MARINA AT WEST END • VIXEN POINT
• DRAKES ANCHORAGE • LEVERICK BAY
• PENN'S LANDING AT FAT HOGS BAY
• NEPTUNE'S TREASURE, ANEGADA
ABE'S BY THE SEA AND HARRIS' AT JOST VAN DYKE IN LITTLE HARBOUR

DON'T BE A DRAG

P.O. Box 139, Road Town, Tortola, B.V.I. • 284-494-4488 • Fax: 284-494-2513

10. Put on your snorkel gear and visually check your work. This is the best way to ensure a good night's sleep. If the anchor is lying on its side or caught in coral, or if the rope is caught around a coral head, reset it. Better now than later.

11. Check your position relative to other vessels and/or landmarks. Is there enough room between you and the boats around you? If swinging room is tight or if you are expecting squalls during the night, you might think about laying out a second anchor at 45 degrees to the first. This can be accomplished best with the dinghy.

If the hook doesn't set the first time, don't feel embarrassed! There is not a skipper afloat who hasn't encountered this problem. It is due not to your technique, but to the nature of the seabed. Discuss the situation with your crew, pick it up and try again.

PUBLIC HOLIDAYS

Although the observance of public holidays will make little difference to you when sailing, it is prudent to plan your cruise so that you are not needing shore based facilities during the following holidays:

MONTH	U.S. VIRGIN ISLANDS	BRITISH VIRGIN ISLANDS
January	New Year's Day Three Kings' Day (Observed) Martin Luther King's Birthday	New Year's Day
February	Presidents' Day	
March	Transfer Day	Commonwealth Day
April	Holy Thursday Good Friday Easter Monday Children's Carnival Parade Adults' Carnival Parade	Good Friday Easter Monday
May	Memorial Day	Whit Monday
June	Organic Act Day	Sovereigns Birthday
July	Emancipation Day (West Indies) Independence Day Supplication Day	Territory Day
August		Festival Monday Festival Tuesday Festival Wednesday
September	Labor Day	
October	Columbus Day Local Thanksgiving Day	St. Ursula's Day
November	Liberty Day Thanksgiving Day	Birthday of Heir to the Throne
December	Christmas Day Christmas Second Day	Christmas Day Boxing Day

Should any holiday fall upon a Sunday, the Monday following shall be a legal holiday.

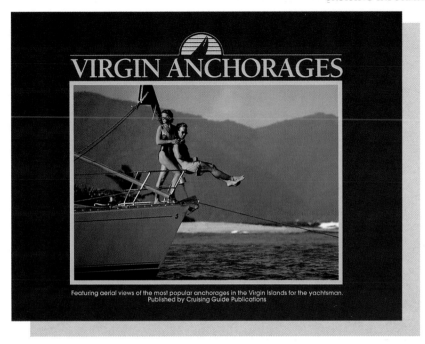

VIRGIN ANCHORAGES

Featuring aerial views of the most popular anchorages in the Virgin Islands for the yachtsman.
Published by Cruising Guide Publications

A WORLD OF ISLANDS AWAITS...

The Virgin Islands are a magical world that awaits your exploration. The new edition of *Virgin Anchorages* graphically, and through spectacular aerial photography, depicts dozens of favorite anchorages throughout the U.S. and British Virgin Islands.

Each anchorage is featured in a two-page full-color spread. One page provides an aerial photograph of the anchorage. The adjoining page offers advice on approaching the anchorage with navigational instructions.

The book, to be used in conjunction with navigational charts and Cruising Guide Publication's *Cruising Guide to the Virgin Islands*, is indispensable for the yachtsman or charterer visiting these legendary Caribbean islands.

TROPICAL FISH POISONING

Ciguatera, also known as tropical fish poisoning, is a disease which can affect people who have eaten certain varieties of tropical fish.

The results of such poisoning can be very serious and, although seldom resulting in death, can cause severe discomfort. Victims of ciguatera poisoning are often ill for weeks and some symptoms may persist for months.

Ciguatera occurs only in tropical waters and in the Atlantic area, predominantly in the waters of south Florida and the islands of the Caribbean.

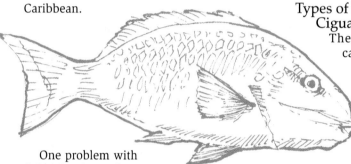

One problem with fish poisoning is that it is impossible to differentiate between toxic and nontoxic fish. The fish itself is not affected by the toxins and therefore appears quite normal and edible. The toxins cannot be tasted and washing, cooking or freezing will not render them harmless.

Many tales exist throughout the Caribbean on how to tell toxic from nontoxic fish, including cooking silver coins with the fish and if the coin turns black, it is toxic. Another is that flies will not land on a piece of toxic fish. While such homespun ideas are interesting bits of Caribbean folklore, they do not work and should not be relied upon.

Symptoms of Ciguatera

In most cases, the symptoms will appear within three to ten hours after eating the toxic fish. The first signs are nausea, vomiting, diarrhea and stomach cramps.

Later, the patient may also start to suffer from a wide variety of neurological ailments, including pains in the joints and muscles, weakness in the arms and legs, and/or a tingling sensation in the feet and hands. A tingling sensation around the lips, nose and tongue is also common.

At the onset of any of the above symptoms, the patient should ask him- or herself, "Have I eaten any fish today?" If the answer is "yes," seek medical attention.

Types of Fish Carrying Ciguatera

The fish most likely to carry the toxins are the larger predatory fish associated with coral reefs. These include barracudas, grouper, snapper, jacks and parrot fish. It should be noted that only certain species in each family are associated with the toxins. Therefore, it is a good idea to check with a local fisherman before eating your catch.

The fish that are considered safe are offshore fish such as tuna, wahoo, swordfish, marlin, and dolphin. Others include sailfish, Spanish mackerel, small king mackerel and yellowtail snapper.

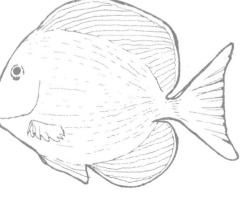

FISH TRAPS

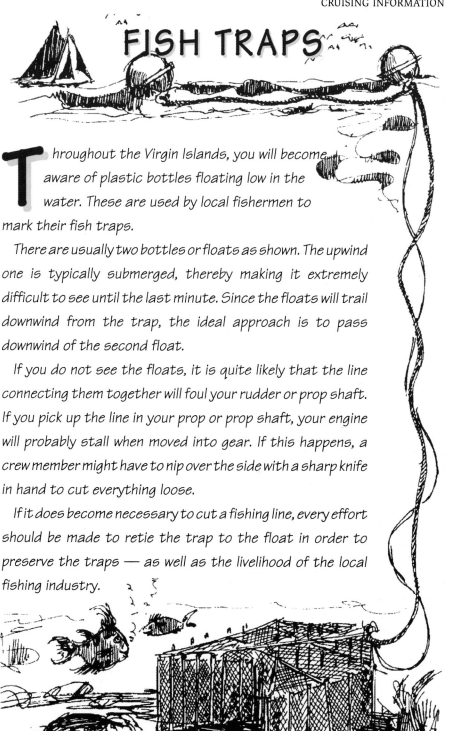

Throughout the Virgin Islands, you will become aware of plastic bottles floating low in the water. These are used by local fishermen to mark their fish traps.

There are usually two bottles or floats as shown. The upwind one is typically submerged, thereby making it extremely difficult to see until the last minute. Since the floats will trail downwind from the trap, the ideal approach is to pass downwind of the second float.

If you do not see the floats, it is quite likely that the line connecting them together will foul your rudder or prop shaft. If you pick up the line in your prop or prop shaft, your engine will probably stall when moved into gear. If this happens, a crew member might have to nip over the side with a sharp knife in hand to cut everything loose.

If it does become necessary to cut a fishing line, every effort should be made to retie the trap to the float in order to preserve the traps — as well as the livelihood of the local fishing industry.

DIVING AND SNORKELING

Jim Scheiner

NATIONAL MARINE PARKS

British Virgin Islands

Visitors come to the Virgin Islands to savor the magnificence of the area's natural resources — the steady, gentle trade winds, glorious sunshine, crystalline waters, the splendor of the coral reefs and abundant sea life. This is a fragile area, however, which must be protected if it is to be enjoyed for many years to come.

The anchors of the charter boats have taken their toll in broken coral, destroying the incredible beauty below the sea that once housed many different forms of sea life. In an effort to defend the reefs against the carelessness of yachtsmen, the National Parks Trust has taken a firm stand and has installed mooring buoys developed by Dr. John Halas of the Key Largo National Marine Sanctuary. This mooring system is being used worldwide to protect reefs and prevent damage from anchors. It calls for a stainless steel pin cemented into the bedrock and a polypropylene line attached to a surface buoy. The system is very strong and extremely effective in eliminating damage when used properly.

Marine Park Regulations:

- Do not damage, alter or remove any marine plant, animal or historic artifact.
- All fishing — including spearfishing — is strictly prohibited. Lobstering and collecting live shells are also illegal.
- Use correct garbage disposal points; do not litter the area. Water balloons are prohibited.
- Water skiing and jet skiing are prohibited in all park areas.
- No anchoring in the restricted area in and around the wreck of the *Rhone*. When the mooring system is full, vessels should utilize the Salt Island Settlement anchorage and arrive by tender, using the dinghy mooring system provided.

Mooring Usage Regulations:

- Vessels must legally have met BVI Customs and Immigration requirements, and have in their possession valid clearance forms and cruising permits.
- The buoys of the reef protection system are color-coded:
  Red: Non-diving, day use only.
  Yellow: Commercial dive vessels only.
  White: Non-commercial vessels for dive use only on first-come, first-served basis (90-minute time limit).
  Blue: Dinghies only.
- **Large Yellow:** Commercial vessels, or daysailing boats or vessels over 55' in length.
- Vessels must attach to the buoy pennant, making sure to avoid chafing of the pennant against the vessel. If the configuration provided is not compatible with your vessel, an extension line must be attached to the pennant eye.
- All buoys are used at user's risk. While the moorings are the property of the B.V.I. Government and are managed by the B.V.I. National Parks Trust, neither bears the responsibility for any loss or injury resulting from the use of the system. Charterers may purchase permits through their charter companies, and visiting private yachts may purchase permits through customs. The fees are nominal and go directly to the Parks Trust for the installation and maintenance of the buoys.

The British Virgin Islands National Parks Trust Maintains Moorings On The Following Islands

- Norman
- Pelican
- The Indians
- Peter Island
- Dead Chest
- Salt
- Cooper
- Ginger
- Guana
- West Dog
- Great Dog
- Cockroach
- Virgin Gorda

United States Virgin Islands

For years the National Park areas have been a favored cruising area for many yachtsmen. As a result of increased numbers of pleasure boaters enjoying the park, the damage to the underwater reefs and corals has dramatically escalated. Anchors and, even worse, the sweep of the anchor chains have swept the undersea life away leaving only broken pieces of what were once beautiful living corals. The National Park Service, with the support of the community, has installed moorings and established protected zones around the more susceptible grass and reef areas.

National Park Regulations:

- Do not damage or take any dead or live marine creatures such as sea fans, coral and shells.
- Anchors must not cause damage to underwater features of the Park.
- All sea turtles are endangered or threatened species. Do not harass or harm them.
- Do not disturb or remove shipwrecks or their contents.
- Tying to shore vegetation is prohibited.
- Feeding of any wildlife in the park, either on land or in the water, is prohibited.
- Fishing is permitted except in Jumbie and Trunk Bays, with hand-held rod and handline.
- Possession or use of any type of spearfishing equipment within park boundaries is prohibited.
- Florida spiny lobsters may be taken by hand or by hand-held snare. *Do not* take female lobsters with eggs. *Limit*: Two per day. *Legal size limit*: 3½ inches carapace. Do not take rock lobster or the lobster species variously called slipper lobster, buccaneer or locust lobster.

- Queen conch may be taken from Oct. 1-June 30. Conch must be 9 inches long and landed in shell. Two per person, per day.
- Overnight stays in park waters are limited to 14 nights per year.
- Maintain quiet aboard boats from 10pm. to 6am.
- Water skiing and jet skiing are prohibited in the park.
- National Park rangers may board any vessel in park waters at any time in order to conduct official business.

Trash may be placed in receptacles located at Cruz Bay, Francis Bay, Annaberg, and Little Lameshur.

Mooring Usage Regulations:

- Moorings located within the park boundaries may not be used by vessels greater than 55 feet in length.
- Moorings are maintained by Park Service personnel. The National Park Service accepts no liability for damage, loss or injury resulting from the use of defective moorings.
- Help keep moorings safe by reporting defects or damage to Park personnel.
- National Park Service moorings are not intended for use in heavy weather conditions when it is recommended that boats anchor in a protected bay.
- No anchoring in Reef Bay, or Little or Great Lameshur Bay, or Salt Pond Bay. Moorings are available in these locations.

The U.S. Virgin Islands National Parks Trust Maintains Moorings At The Following Locations

- Lind Point
- Jumbie Bay
- Hawksnext
- Maho Bay
- Francis Bay
- Whistling Cay
- Leinster
- Ginger
- Salt Pond
- Bay Reef
- Greater Lameshur
- Little Lameshur
- Rams Head

DIVING THE VIRGIN ISLANDS

The Virgin Islands are one of the best sailing and cruising areas in the world. They are also recognized as one of the top dive destinations.

The wreck of the *R.M.S. Rhone* has become synonymous with the B.V.I. in dive circles, regarded by many as the best wreck dive of the Western Hemisphere.

Superb reefs for both snorkeling and diving are found in and around most of the anchorages. The U.S. Virgin Islands have a series of underwater parks: Trunk Bay, St. John, Buck Island, St. Croix, Coki Beach, St. Thomas. In the British Virgin Islands, the island of Anegada has over 300 documented shipwrecks.

Servicing the needs of the visiting yachtsmen, many professional dive shops and dive tour operators have set up businesses, providing complete services from equipment rental and air tank refills, to tours and instruction.

For the non-diver, a resort course will enable you to explore the underwater world with the aid of an instructor. Full certification courses are available from the individual dive shop operators conveniently located throughout the islands.

The rules and regulations of the marine parks of both the U.S. and British Virgins are similar.

DIVING IN THE BRITISH VIRGIN ISLANDS

Dive operators of the Virgin Islands, through a cooperative effort, have pooled information to give you these brief but picturesque descriptions of 20 of their favorite locations:

Painted Walls — Long canyons, a cave, a sponge-encrusted tunnel, barracudas, rock beauties, angelfish and a variety of pelagic fish make the Painted Walls an exciting and picturesque dive with 28- to 50-foot depths.

The *Rhone* — Just about everyone in diving has heard of the classical wreck, the *RMS Rhone*. Even those who have not visited the B.V.I. have seen the *Rhone* in Columbia Pictures' treasure diving epic, *The Deep*. An ocean steamer, 310 feet in length, this magnificent vessel sank off Salt Island during an extremely violent hurricane in 1867. After 117 years of silent slumber in 20-80 feet of water, this great ship remains remarkably intact with much of her decking, rigging, steam engine and propeller still visible. Gilded with colorful sponges and flourishing corals, the *Rhone* is perhaps the most impressive shipwreck in the entire Caribbean.

Rhone Reef — Two coral-encrusted caves are located in less than 25 feet of water at Rhone Reef, Salt Island. A variety of hard and soft corals, fish, turtles and the occasional shark can be found here. Due to its proximity to the *Rhone,* it is a protected area.

Great Harbour — Directly across the channel from Road Town Harbour lies a large, protected bay on the north side of Peter Island. At the center of this bay is a shallow coral reef less than 20 yards offshore, beginning in 8 feet of water. Loaded with colorful sponges and a marvelous array of small marine life, the reef slopes gently to approximately 18 feet, then drops vertically to a depth of 40 feet.

Indians — The Indians are four large rock formations that rise from the ocean floor to a height of about 90 feet. Deepest depth is 50 feet on the westward side. The Indians have just about everything for the snorkeler as well as the scuba diver; brain, finger, star and elkhorn corals are abundant, as are gorgonians and sea fans.

Caves — The caves at Norman Island can provide many hours of fun for snorkelers. There is a large variety of subjects for the underwater photographer such as schools of dwarf herring or fry. These fish provide food for the many pelicans in the area. The reef in front of the shallow caves slopes downward to a depth of 40 feet.

Angelfish Reef — One of the best sightseeing dives is a sloping reef located off the western point of Norman Island. Depths here range from 10–90 feet. The high point of your dive will be a visit to the bottom of the channel where a large colony of angelfish resides. There is plenty of fish action at this particular site because of the swiftly flowing currents in the nearby channel and the close proximity to the open sea.

Cooper Island — The southeastern shore of Cooper Island, called Markoe

Medical Emergencies

In the event of diving related emergencies, contact the U.S. Coast Guard Search and Rescue on VHF 16 or telephone (340) 729-6770 for immediate assistance. There is a recompression chamber in St. Thomas at the Hospital Chamber [telephone (340) 776-2686] or Divers Alert Network (919) 684-8111, 24 hours.

Your charter company also can be of great assistance, and should be contacted if you run into a problem.

Point, is a sheer rock wall that plunges some 70 feet to the ocean floor. Nurse sharks are frequently encountered lying on sandy floors at the base of small canyons formed by the rugged walls of the island.

Scrub Island — The south side of Scrub Island is a splendid reef with depths of up to 60 feet.

Little Camanoe — The northeastern tip of Little Camanoe offers a 30-foot reef dive. The coral overhangs in this area are exceptionally good. *Caution*: ground seas.

Seal Dog Rock — Plenty of pelagic fish. Depth of 80 feet. *Caution*: may have a current. This dive is recommended for experienced divers.

George Dog — The rocky point in the anchorage at George Dog is an easy 25-30 foot dive for beginning divers.

Invisibles — (East of Necker Island) Spectacular soaring peaks from 4-70 feet from surface. Flashing schools of every kind of fish, sleeping nurse sharks and all forms of sea life abound.

Visibles — (Southwest under Water Pinnacle off Cockroach Island) Caves, canyons, resident 8-foot green moray and nurse shark. Depths to 70 feet. Spawning area for many species of jacks, snappers, groupers.

Chimney — (West Bay of Great Dog) Winding canyon goes to a colorful un- derwater arch. Many coral heads with an unbelievable variety of small sea creatures.

Joe's Cave — (West Dog Island) Cathedral-effect cave with schooling glassy-eyed sweepers. Clouds of silversides overshadow a variety of eels, pelagic fish and other species, with an occasional school of bulky, splashing tarpon.

Van Ryan's Rock — (Off Collison Point, Virgin Gorda) Huge lobsters, turtles, and plenty of fish among brilliant corals and swaying sea fans.

Ginger Island — Mushroom coral heads 15–20 feet high, great visibility. Graduated shelves ending at 70–90 feet in a huge sand patch. Pet the stingrays and play with huge jewfish.

Southside of Great Dog Island — Reef runs east and west, 100 yards of island coral, butterfly fish. Exciting dive locations, each more unusual than the next. Expect to see just about anything!

Anegada Reef — Graveyard of some 300 documented shipwrecks dating from the 1600s to the present. Spanish galleons and English privateers with uncountable treasure.

The Chikuzen — This 245-foot ship was sunk in 1981 and provides a fantastic home for all varieties of fish, including big rays and horse-eye jacks. The depth here is less than 80 feet. Located about 5 miles north of Camanoe Island.

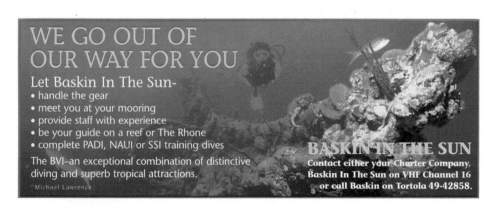

Jim Scheiner

DIVING IN THE U. S. VIRGIN ISLANDS

Cartenser Sr. — (Off St. Thomas, near Buck Island) A spectacular dive on the intact, coral-encrusted hull of a World War I cargo ship in 50-foot depths. Tours easily arranged.

Cow and Calf — Two rocks between Christmas Cove and Jersey Bay, 5 feet below the surface. The lee side of the western rock provides intricate arches, ledges and caves. Many angelfish and beautiful coral.

Christmas Cove — Good beginner's dive on the northwest side of Fish Cay in 40 feet of water. Swim amongst the coral heads. Plenty of fish.

Dog Rock — For advanced divers on the northwestern side of Dog Island in 40-50 foot depths. Rock and coral ledges and caves. *Caution:* This one can be rough.

Coki Beach — A good place to snorkel off the beach. Coral ledges.

Little Saint James — A 40-foot dive on the lee side has some deep ledges to explore, sheltering various schools of fish.

Twin Barges — Located off Limetree Beach lie two wrecks sunk approximately in the 1940s. Although visibility is limited outside the wrecks, the clarity improves inside the ships' chambers.

Carvel Rock — Off of the northern side of this rock, near St. John, in depths to 90 feet, big schools of pelagic fish pass through colorful, sponge-encrusted caves.

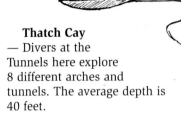

Thatch Cay
— Divers at the Tunnels here explore 8 different arches and tunnels. The average depth is 40 feet.

Scotch Bank — Off St. Croix, this popular dive spot is a favorite for spotting stingrays and manta rays.

Long Reef — A 6-mile-long reef which provides dives at depths from 30–50 feet. A forest of coral, including pillar and elkhorn colonies.

Salt River — This area has 2 distinct walls. The East Wall plunges from depths of 50-100 feet, revealing many caves and caverns. The West Wall peaks at 30 feet and tumbles to 125 feet. The colors of the sponges grasping the crevices and pillars are awesome.

Buck Island
— Off St. Croix, this national monument features abundant tropical fish and a jungle of huge staghorn and elkhorn coral. An absolute must for anyone visiting St. Croix.

Frederiksted Pier — (St. Croix) 30-foot-deep pilings offer splendid diving day or night. The pilings provide a home for bright sponges and algae, as well as sea horses, crabs and octopus.

Cane Bay, Davis Bay and Salt River — All have walls of coral from 20 feet to over 1000 feet. Several anchors have been discovered along the wall. One of the most-photographed anchors is nestled in sand at 60 feet on the Northstar Wall.

Jim Scheiner

The Royal Mail Steamer Rhone

On the morning of October 29, 1867, the *R.M.S. Rhone* was at anchor outside Great Harbour, Peter Island. The *Rhone*, under the command of Captain Robert F. Wooley, had left Southampton on October 2, 1867, and was taking on cargo and stores for the return crossing.

The *R.M.S. Conway*, commanded by Captain Hammock, lay alongside.

The stillness of the tropical day was undisturbed as the sun blazed down from a clear sky upon calm seas. As the morning wore on, the barometer began to fall, hinting the weather might deteriorate. The seas, however, remained untroubled. Although the captains alerted themselves, work was allowed to continue. Captain Wooley hailed Captain Hammock that he did not like the look of the weather and, as the hurricane season was over, it must be a northerly brewing. Wooley felt they should shift to the northern anchorage of Road Harbour, Tortola.

About 11am., the barometer suddenly fell to 27.95 degrees. The sky darkened, and with a mighty roar a fearful hurricane blew from the north/northwest. The howling wind whistled through the shrouds and tore at the rigging. With engines going at full speed, the ships rode the storm.

At noon there came a lull in the storm. The *Conway* weighed anchor and headed toward the northern anchorage of Road Harbour. As she steamed across the Sir Francis Drake Channel, she was hit by the second blast of the hurricane. Her funnel and masts were blown away, and she was driven onto the island of Tortola.

The *Rhone* tried to weigh anchor during the lull, but the shackle of the cable caught in the hawse pipe and parted, dropping the 3,000-pound anchor and some 300 feet of chain. With engines running at full speed, she steamed seaward in order to seek sea room to weather the second onslaught. She had negotiated most of the rocky channel and was rounding the last point when the hurricane, blowing from the south/southeast, struck, forcing her onto the rocks at Salt Island where she heeled over, broke in two, and sank instantly, taking most of her company with her.

— *Courtesy of R.M.S. Rhone by George and Luana Marler*

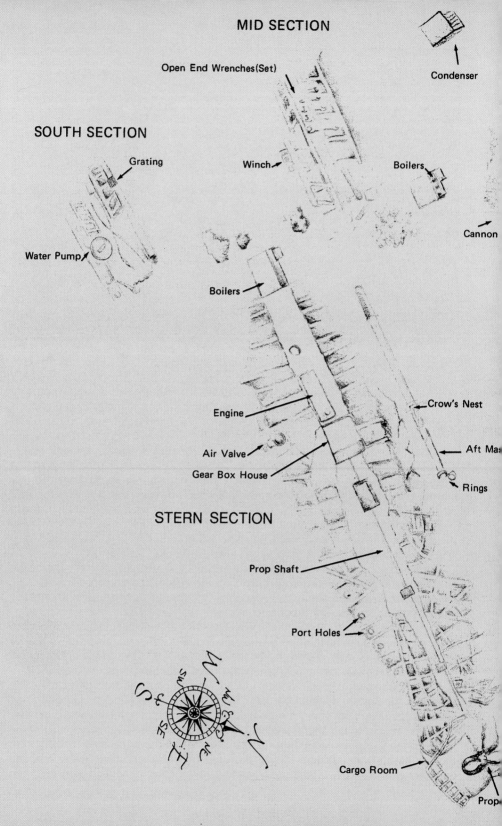

MID SECTION

Open End Wrenches (Set)

Condenser

SOUTH SECTION

Grating

Winch

Boilers

Water Pump

Cannon

Boilers

Engine

Crow's Nest

Air Valve

Aft Mas

Gear Box House

Rings

STERN SECTION

Prop Shaft

Port Holes

Cargo Room

Prop

BLACK ROCK POINT

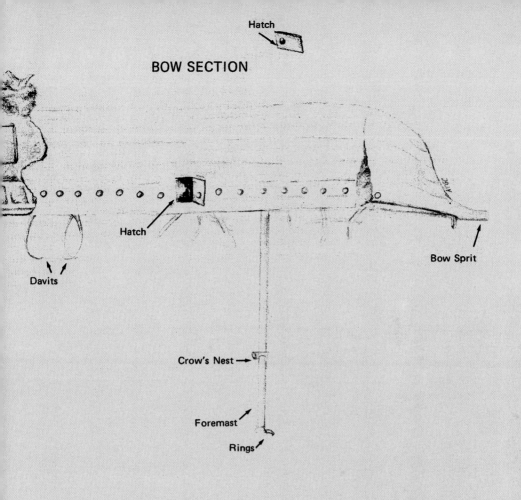

Hatch

BOW SECTION

Hatch

Davits

Bow Sprit

Crow's Nest →

Foremast

Rings

R.M.S. RHONE NATIONAL PARK
No Spearfishing, Linefishing, Taking of
Coral or Shells, or Anchoring in the Wreck.
GOVERNMENT OF THE BRITISH VIRGIN ISLANDS

This is a diagram to the Rhone
as it is positioned underwater.

LEE BAY

SAILING ROUTES of the BRITISH VIRGIN ISLANDS

SCALE IN NAUTICAL MILES

ANEGADA

NECKER I.

MOSQUITO I.

VIRGIN GORDA

DOG ISLANDS

FALLEN JERUSALEM

ROUND ROCK

GINGER I.

GREAT CAMANOE I.

BEEF I.

COOPER I.

DRAKE CHANNEL

GUANO I.

SALT I.

TORTOLA

SIR FRANCIS

PETER I.

NORMAN I.

LITTLE J.V.D.

JOST VAN DYKE

GREAT THATCH I.

UNITED KINGDOM
UNITED STATES

ST. JOHN

Dear Yachtsmen:

Welcome to the Yacht Chartering Capital of the World! The British Virgin Islands are homeport for the largest bareboat fleet in the world.

The B.V.I. is an archipelago of some 40 islands, islets, rocks and cays offering a wide variety of water-based activities. Whether you are a first-time charterer or a seasoned sailor, you will find that the British Virgins are ideal for testing your skills.

If you wish to test your angling skills, the B.V.I. is renowned for sportsfishing, deep and shallow water, e.g., bonefishing on Anegada. Or, if your wish is to get even closer to nature, you may explore our undersea world. We have some of the most varied dive sites in the Caribbean and, perhaps, more wrecks than any other Caribbean destination, several completely unexplored.

Our waters are safe and extremely manageable, surrounded by numerous protected anchorages. Our people are warm and as friendly as the balmy tradewinds constantly blowing over the islands.

I have always been a strong advocate of making sure that the B.V.I. remains a competitive "Yachtsman-Friendly Destination." To this end, the government has recently enacted legislation to make sure that the destination remains on the cutting edge of the chartering industry, and to broaden the mix of yachts based in the British Virgin Islands. This legislation also streamlines the process of clearing customs and immigration at our ports of entry, ensuring that you have more time to enjoy your vacation.

We are glad to have you and we look forward with anticipation to your next visit, with your friends.

Sincerely,
Ralph T. O'Neal
Chief Minister

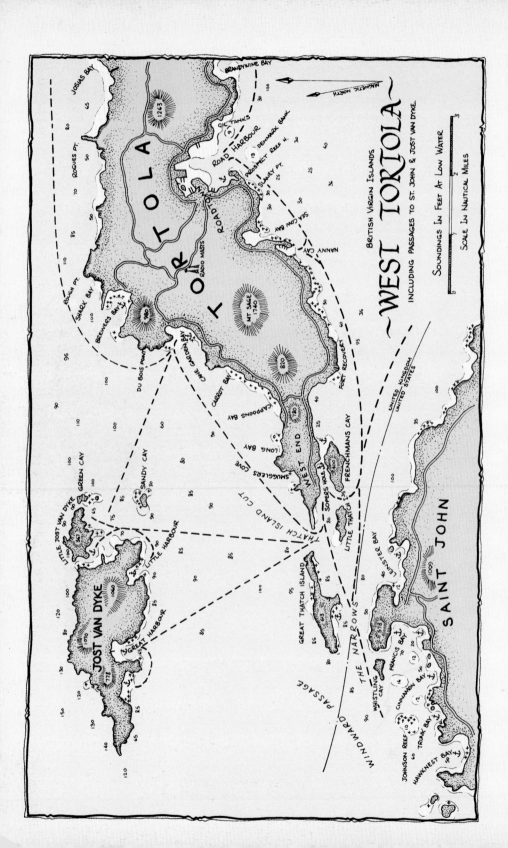

~WEST TORTOLA~

BRITISH VIRGIN ISLANDS

INCLUDING PASSAGES TO ST. JOHN & JOST VAN DYKE.

SOUNDINGS IN FEET AT LOW WATER

SCALE IN NAUTICAL MILES

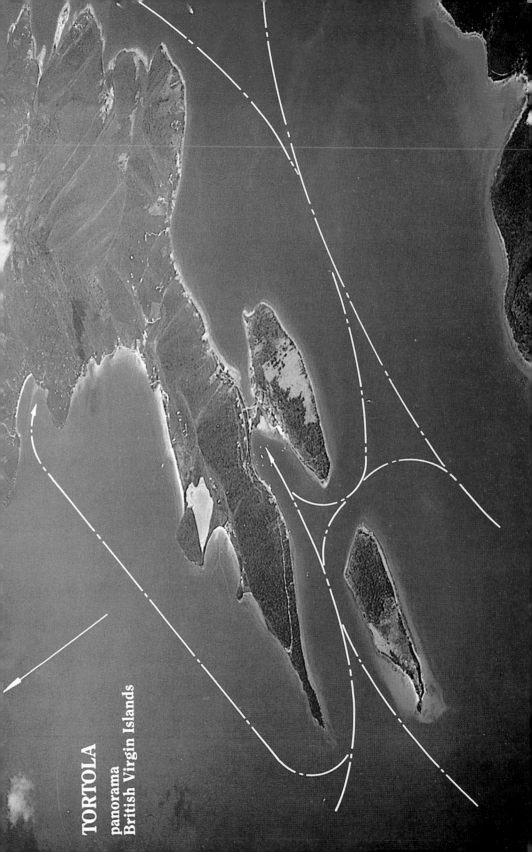

TORTOLA
panorama
British Virgin Islands

DIVERS, SNORKELLERS AND BOATERS

The coral reefs are precious and delicate.
Their future depends on you.

Worldwide coral reefs are suffering degradation from various factors -- pollution, over fishing, excess nutrients.. and tourist activity.

PLEASE TAKE CARE NOT TO INFLICT FURTHER DAMAGE

TOUCH NOTHING — The slightest touch with hands, fins or equipment can irreparably damage coral polyps, the tiny animals that build the coral reefs. Remember most corals only grow a half inch per year.

REMAIN HORIZONTAL in the water and snorkel in water over your depth. Snorkelling on shallow reefs can easily inflict damage to the coral and cause personal injury. In a vertical position, your flapping fins are killers! They break coral and stir up sediment that can smother the coral polyps. For equipment adjustment, swim out and away from the coral into deep water.

UNSURE, UNEASY — Wear a float vest, and practice your skills off a sandy beach.

LOOK, ENJOY AND LEAVE — Take nothing dead or alive from the reef.

DO NOT ANCHOR ON CORAL — Use mooring buoys where available, or anchor on a sandy bottom. Anchors, chain and line should not touch coral (dinghy anchors included). If there is no sandy bottom, don't anchor, but leave an attendant in the dinghy while the rest of the party snorkel or dives.

FEEDING THE FISH — Caution, you may be injured! Feeding can make fish aggressive and dangerous. It also upsets species distribution and may introduce disease.

PHOTOGRAPHERS — Avoid cumbersome rigs. Don't brace yourself on the coral to take a photo. Damaging the reef even inadvertently for the sake of a photo is not worth it.

DIVERS — Adjust buoyancy. Secure all dangling gauges, consoles, and octopus regulators. Know where your fins are. Air bubbles trapped in caves will destroy marine growth. Bubbles rising on a vertical rock face can scour, don't get too close.

THINK, CARE AND ENJOY. HELP THE REEF GIVE CONTINUING ENJOYMENT.
A Message From ARK (Association of Reef Keepers)

JOST VAN DYKE

A large, high island, Jost Van Dyke lies to the north of Tortola and becomes visible to yachtsmen sailing from St. Thomas upon entering Pillsbury Sound. With a population of approximately 200, the island remains relatively unspoiled. The largest settlement is Great Harbour which is also a port of entry into the B.V.I.

Named after a Dutch pirate, the island is known as the birthplace of Dr. John Lettsome, born on Little Jost Van Dyke in 1744. Dr. Lettsome later returned to his native England and founded the London Medical Society and the Royal Humane Society. Known for his good sense of humor, Dr. Lettsome wrote the following:

I, John Lettsome,
Blisters, bleeds and sweats 'em.
If, after that, they please to die
I, John Lettsome.

White Bay

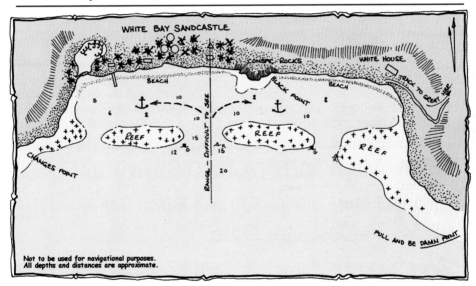

Not to be used for navigational purposes.
All depths and distances are approximate.

White Bay is the western most harbor on the south side of the island. Aptly named for its beautiful stretch of white sandy beach, White Bay is an excellent anchorage under normal sea conditions. During the winter months, however, ground seas can make it an untenable anchorage, suitable for day stops only.

Navigation
White Bay is a relatively small anchorage with very little swinging room once inside the reef; however, there is room for several boats if anchored properly. Although there are three entrances through the reef, it is recommended that you make your approach between the middle of the two reefs, leaving the red buoy to starboard and the green to port.

Anchoring
The channel will carry 10-12 feet. Once inside the reef, anchor to port or starboard in approximately 7-10 feet of water with a sandy bottom. Do not anchor in the channel or block it, and stay well clear of the shoal spot just off the black rocks to starboard of the channel entrance.

The eastern most entrance is also marked with a set of red and green buoys. Once inside the reef anchor to port of the entrance keeping an eye on both the

reef and the shallow area off of the black rocks.

Ashore

White Bay Sandcastle is a small, delightful resort that serves breakfast, lunch and four course gourmet dinners with reservations. The Soggy Dollar Bar is a great spot to swim ashore for a Painkiller and to while away the afternoon under a palm tree. The Painkiller, a delicious, but potent, rum drink was originally invented at the Soggy Dollar Bar. White Bay Sandcastle monitors VHF 16.

To the west down the beach is Gertrude's Beach Bar another good excuse to perfect your skills at doing little else but sunning, swimming and hanging out.

On the eastern end of the beach is Ivan Chinnery's White Bay Campground and Local Flavour Beach Bar. He offers small cabins or prepared camp sites on one of the most exquisite beaches you'll find.

Great Harbour

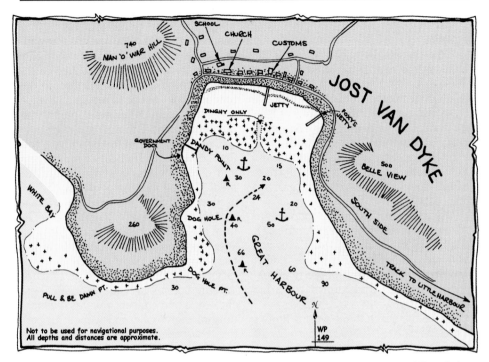

Not to be used for navigational purposes.
All depths and distances are approximate.

WP
149

A normally sheltered harbor at the foot of 1000 foot high peaks, Great Harbour is a port of entry into the BVI and is the largest settlement on the island.

Navigation
On your port side upon entering are three lit red buoys designating a channel to the government landing for official government business only. This channel carries a depth of about 12 feet. Most boats, however, head down the middle of the harbor giving the shorelines on either side a reasonable berth. There is a large reef extending out 300 yards from the inner shoreline, so anchor before you reach it.

Anchoring
Anchor anywhere outside the reef in 15-30 feet of water. It can be difficult to get your anchor to hold, but once well set

you should be okay. This would be a good place to put your snorkel on and check your anchor visually.

Ashore

Take the dinghy ashore through the break in the reef. Head directly for the dock in order to avoid shallow coral heads. The customs officer for Jost Van Dyke will clear vessels in or out of British waters for both customs and immigration. Customs and the police are located just at the base of the dock. Across from the police station at the base of the dock is a dumpster for garbage disposal.

Great Harbour has a worldwide reputation for having great beach parties. It is amazing the countries and places you will see someone with a Foxy's t-shirt walking by! The atmosphere is casual with flip flops and shorts welcome everywhere.

Down the beach to the west is Rudy's Superette for necessities, and Coco Loco's for t-shirts, bathing suits and jewelry. Club Paradise (gaily painted in pink and purple) serves lunch and dinner with live entertainment on Wednesdays and Sundays. Ali Baba's restaurant is next for local food: breakfast, lunch and dinner

with a Monday night pig roast. The customs/police building is at the center of the beach at the base of the dock.

On the road perpendicular to the beach you will find Nature's Basket with locally grown fresh fruits and vegetables and Christine's Bakery with her delectable fresh baked bread. Further up the road is the ice house to replenish the ice on board. Around the corner, next to the fire department is a small gas station.

On eastern end of the beach you will first come to Happy Laury's for burgers and chicken with occasional entertainment. Tucked into the corner on the far eastern end of the beach is Foxy's Tamarind Bar and Grill with a dinghy dock in front of the restaurant. Foxy and his wife, Tessa have hosted the Wooden Boat Regatta for many years, as well as other races. Now almost a legend, Foxy's has become famous over the years amongst charterers and cruisers alike, as the location for many wild and wonderful parties where the music and dancing in the sand go on until the wee hours. Stop in at their gift shop and sport your own Foxy t-shirt. You can still catch Foxy singing calypso and playing his guitar. Foxy's monitors VHF 16 and serves lunch and dinner.

Little Harbour

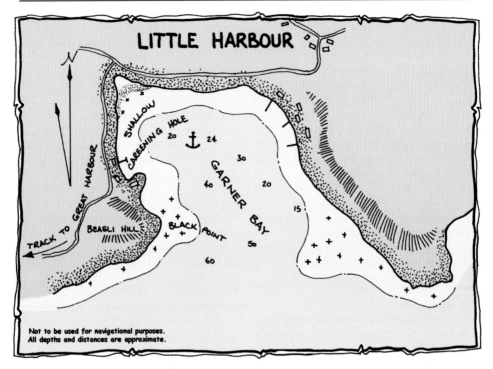

Not to be used for navigational purposes.
All depths and distances are approximate.

Little Harbour, or Garner Bay, as it is sometimes called, lies to the east of Great Harbour. Once used as a careenage for island sloops, the harbor now caters to charter parties, with three restaurants ashore.

Navigation

The entrance to Little Harbour is straightforward and deep. There is a shoal area to port when entering, but the channel is wide and clear.

Anchorages

The traditional anchorage is off the western end of the bay in 12 feet of water, but in recent years boats have been anchoring all over the bay.

The shore is rocky along the east side, but the bottom is clean, hard sand. Insure that your anchor is well set with sufficient scope, as parts of the harbor are very deep. Or pick up one of the moorings and pay for it ashore at the appropriate restaurant.

Ashore

For those who enjoy hiking, there is a small track that takes you about 1000 feet up the mountain. For those ambitious enough to make the climb, the views are spectacular.

There are three restaurants in the bay. On the eastern side is Abe's By the Sea, serving lunch and dinner with reservations. Abe's also has a little grocery store where you can buy ice and provisions for yachtsmen. On the other side of the bay are Sidney's Peace and Love and Harris's Place. Sidney's is open at 9am for breakfast, lunch and dinner with live music on Monday and Saturday nights. Harris's can provide you with ice, groceries, fax and phone facilities, as well as serving breakfast, lunch and dinner. Monday nights they have live entertainment and all you can eat lobster. All of these restaurants monitor VHF 16.

Sandy Cay, Green Cay, Little Jost Van Dyke

The following three anchorages offer spectacular beaches and snorkeling, but should be considered day stops only.

Little Jost Van Dyke

There is a small anchorage on the southeastern end of Little Jost Van Dyke. Entrance from the south presents no hazards. You will find a concrete bulkhead and should anchor off it in 15-25 feet of water. The bottom is sandy and provides excellent holding.

If the wind is out of the south, the anchorage becomes very sloppy and during northerly ground seas the surge is excessive.

There is no passage between Jost Van Dyke and Little Jost Van Dyke, but good snorkeling exists along the south side.

Green Cay

Green Cay offers a superb daytime stop with excellent snorkeling. Anchor due west of the sand bar in 20 feet of water. It is better to stay close to the bar, as the prevailing wind will keep you clear and the water depth increases rapidly once you are off the bar. During the winter months the ground swell manages to work around the island, making the area untenable as an overnight anchorage.

The best snorkeling will be found on the reef that extends south of the cay.

Sandy Cay

To the east of Jost Van Dyke is Sandy Cay. Owned by Laurence Rockefeller, there is a botanical tour on the small path that encircles the island. It also affords some spectacular views of the surrounding islands.

The anchorage is on the southwest side close to shore, in the lee of the island. The holding ground is good, but be careful to avoid the coral heads.

Extreme caution should be exercised during winter ground seas, as the waves make their way around both sides of the island, causing surf to break on the beach, making landing a dinghy difficult, if not disastrous.

To the north of the cay is a ragged breaking reef that provides excellent snorkeling when the seas are flat.

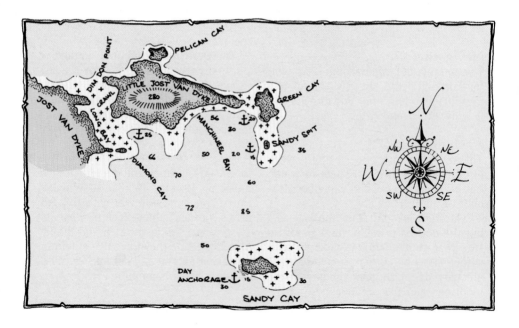

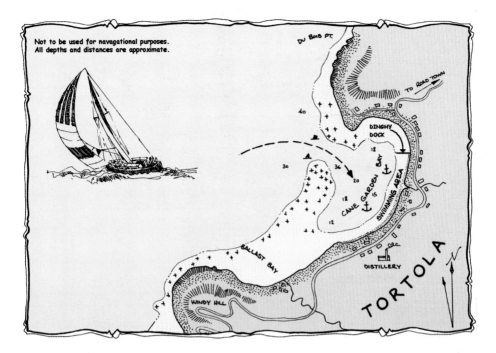

Not to be used for navagational purposes.
All depths and distances are approximate.

TORTOLA
Cane Garden Bay

Regarded by many as one of the more beautiful anchorages in the B.V.I., Cane Garden Bay is picture postcard material, with a white, palm fringed beach stretching the entire length of the bay. When approaching from the west, you will sail past Smugglers Cove, Belmont, Long Bay and Carrot Bay before reaching Cane Garden Bay. If you have any doubt, line up the south side of Jost Van Dyke directly under the peak of Tobago, and this range will bring you to the entrance.

Navigation
There are two reefs at the entrance to Cane Garden Bay. Entering boats should favor the northern end of the bay. The reef is marked by two buoys which simplify the entrance appreciably. Leave the red buoy to starboard when entering. Once clear of the reef, you'll have plenty of room to anchor.

Anchoring
If there is a slight ground swell, the northern portion of the bay will afford more protection. If the swell is considerable, however, it is recommended that you reschedule your cruise to return a few days later when it has subsided.

When anchoring, keep clear of the buoys designating the swimming area. The bottom affords excellent holding in 15-25 feet of water. Mooring buoys are available and can be paid for at Rhymers Beach Bar.

Owing to the mountains, the wind tends to change directions, so check your swinging room in relation to other vessels, particularly if you are anchored and they are on a mooring. You will tend to swing much further on an anchor than a mooring.

James Johnston

Ashore

There is a public dinghy dock which makes going ashore a much easier and drier experience. It is a good idea to drop a stern anchor when motoring in to the dock so that your dinghy will not bang against the dock or any other dinghies. If you are bringing your dinghy ashore, avoid any unpleasant surprises from a rising tide, pull your dinghy well up on the beach and lay out the dinghy anchor.

Cane Garden Bay is lined by several terrific beach bars for the choosing. You can always hear the bands from the anchorage and jump in your dinghy and head for shore to rock the night away. If its a late night ashore, and the wind is right, it can be difficult to get an early night of sleep.

Next to the dinghy dock is Quito's Gazebo serving lunch and dinner. Quito performs alone and with his band on Tuesday, Thursday, Friday and Saturday from 8:30. This is an island favorite amongst both locals and tourists — the place is jamming when the band is going.

The Big Banana Paradise Club is open from 7am serving breakfast, lunch and dinner. It has a delightful setting and is owned by Al Henley who also manages Treasure Isle Hotel in Road Town. The restaurant reflects Al's experience in the restaurant business. The Paradise Club has entertainment on Tuesday, Wednesday, and Friday from 9pm.

Rhymers Beach Bar is the pink building where you pay for your mooring fee. There is garbage disposal, a shop with provisions, ice, telephones and showers for a small fee. Rhymers serves breakfast, lunch and dinner and has live entertainment on Thursday nights.

Stanley's Welcome Bar is open from 10am to 10pm serving lunch and dinner with reservations. Stanley's was one of the original restaurants in Cane Garden Bay and is famous for the tire swing hanging from the palm tree (which has been there for at least 25 years). Stanley has made many friends over the years with charterers who come back year after year for a pina colada and a swing on the tire.

Pleasure Boats handles boat rentals from the beach, with kayaks, pedal boats, motor boats and windsurfers. Cane Garden Bay is an excellent place to hone your kayaking skills.

Nestled in the seagrape trees, Myett's Garden & Grille Restaurant is open for breakfast, lunch and dinner with reservations, daily. A charming renovation offers dining at their new garden grill with lobster, fish, steak, chicken, burgers, amongst the trees while viewing the bay and the sunset. This season they have plans for a breakfast bar with fresh baked goods and specialty coffee and teas. The latest news headlines will be printed off

the internet along with a current daily weather report. Plans for a new boutique are in the works for this next season as well. Myett's has live entertainment on Friday, Sunday and Monday, as well as special occasions.

At the far end of the beach is De Wedding open from 11am serving lunch and dinner with reservations. Their specialty is fresh seafood.

The Elm Bar and Gift Shop are open daily until 7pm, 5pm on Sundays. Sundays feature live music beginning at 2pm.

Supplies can be purchased from Callwood's Grocery Store, Rhymers and a few other local shops. Mr. Callwood's rum distillery affords the visiting yachtsman a glimpse back into history. White and gold rum is still produced from the cane grown on the hillsides. It is recommended that Mr. Callwood be asked permission prior to your wandering through the distillery, and the purchase of a bottle or two is expected.

Brewers Bay

This anchorage is off limits to most charter boats. If you are a bareboat charterer, check to be certain that this anchorage is approved by your charter company.

Without question, Brewers Bay on the north side of Tortola is one of the most beautiful anchorages in the Virgin Islands. Fortunately, however, it is seldom used by visiting yachtsmen, owing to its exposure to the northerly ground seas and the extensive coral formations which make access to the anchorage difficult.

During the winter months, it is not advisable to anchor here overnight, and if there is any indication of a ground sea developing, Brewers Bay should not be considered as even a lunch stop.

When entering the anchorage, do so under power. Make sure you have good light in order to read the bottom, and position a crew member on the bow in order to alert you to the presence of coral heads.

There is a reef that fringes the southwest shoreline and another in the center of the bay. In order to secure a reasonable spot to anchor in, you will have to work yourself up into the southeast corner of the bay, between the reefs, where you can anchor on a sandy bottom in 15-20 feet.

Ashore

While the snorkeling is excellent, time should also be taken to explore ashore. For those interested in a short walk, it would be worthwhile walking up the road to the east, toward Mount Healthy, to see the ruins of Tortola's only remaining windmill. Only the base of the original mill has survived the passing years, along with the broken remains of the old distillery buildings.

Brewers Bay Campground is located on the beach at Brewers Bay. There is also talk of developing Brewers Bay as a destination for tourism with a beach bar ashore.

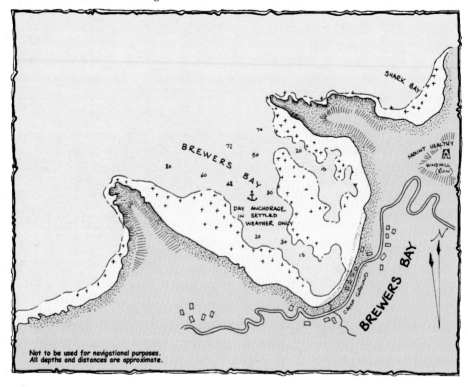

Not to be used for navigational purposes.
All depths and distances are approximate.

Soper's Hole

West End is shown on the charts as Soper's Hole, a protected harbor lying between Frenchman's Cay and Tortola. It is a port of entry for vessels arriving and departing British waters, and a ferry stop between the British and United States Virgin Islands.

Navigation

Whether you enter Soper's Hole between Frenchman's Cay and Little Thatch or Steele Point and Great Thatch, you will be in deep water at all times. A current of up to three knots depending on the tidal flow can be expected. If you are sailing in, then you should cut the points of either Frenchman's Cay or Steele Point as close as is possible.

The government dock is located on the northern shore, but yachtsmen are advised not to tie up while clearing customs because of the movement of the ferries. Rather, it is recommended to pick up a mooring and bring the dinghy in.

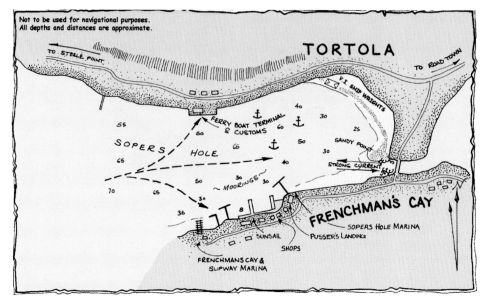

Not to be used for navigational purposes.
All depths and distances are approximate.

Along the front of the ferry dock to the northeast corner of the harbor is a shipping lane for tugboats and sand barges — leave this area clear for their operations.

Anchoring

The harbor is so deep in places that yachts will find themselves in 60-70 feet of water. The best place to anchor is in the northeast corner, where the water depth is 20-35 feet on a sandy bottom.

There are, however, moorings off of the Soper's Hole Wharf & Marina in the southeast section of the bay, which are maintained regularly by Moor Seacure. These moorings may be picked up and paid for at the Soper's Hole Wharf & Marina office ashore.

Moorings are also available in the vicinity of the Frenchman's Cay Shipyard and are marked accordingly. Be advised not to anchor in the way of the slipway as they need ample room to operate the railway and maneuver vessels during adverse wind conditions.

Frenchman's Cay Shipyard has a 200 ton railway for repairs and modifications to just about any vessel. The yard's specialty is repairing, awlgripping, and welding.

Ashore

The West End customs office is located in the building on the ferry dock and is open Monday through Friday from 8:30am to 4:30pm. For clearance outside of those hours overtime fees will apply. Some supplies are available from the grocery and snack bar across from the customs building and from the Ample Hamper. Taxis to Road Town are available in abundance when the ferries arrive.

On the southeast side of the harbor is the Soper's Hole Wharf & Marina with dockage up to 150 feet with a 20 foot depth. Both slips and moorings are available along with 12 air conditioned rooms.

You can fill up on fuel, water, ice and dispose of your garbage. Barclays Bank has an ATM machine located on the premises. This is the home of Sunsail's fleet of 70 bareboat, crewed and flotilla charter yachts as well as the Sunsail Sailing School. The marina monitors VHF 16.

The two story Pusser's Landing, features waterfront dining in two restaurants and bars, an outdoor terrace and the Pusser's Company Store. Downstairs offers a more casual ambiance, with an open air bar, outdoor dining on the terrace and the Company Store, which carries a unique line of Pusser's own nautical and tropical clothing, watches, luggage, nautical accessories and even cigars. Pussers is open seven days a week and monitors VHF 16.

For provisioning needs the Ample Hamper is the place to go. Open Monday through Saturday from 8am to 6pm and Sunday from 8am to 1pm they take credit cards and offer a large variety of provisions, gourmet foods, liquor and wine.

Flamboyance offers perfumes at competitive prices so you may not have to go to the U.S.V.I. Exotic Caribbean herbs and spices, Cuban cigars, soaps, sauces, jams and rums are all available from the Caribbean Corner Spice House.

Culture Classic Boutique and Sea Urchin sell casual clothing and swim wear. BVI Apparel Factory Outlet sells souvenirs and t-shirts. Island Treasures is a gallery of art and sculpture with an emphasis on local and Caribbean art.

Zenaida has some fascinating jewelry, accessories and sarongs. BB's Island Designs sells books, magazines, t-shirts and souvenirs. A popular destination after a long day of sailing and sunning is the Ice Cream Parlor. See Sheppard Boat Rentals for power boat rentals, water taxi services, day charters and island trips.

You will find a dinghy passage behind the sandbar between Frenchman's Cay and Tortola.

The sandspit area in the eastern section of Sopers Hole is the home of V.I. Shipwrights, a yacht repair facility. V.I. Shipwrights have six 70 foot slips with drafts of 12 feet. Water and electricity are available. Plans are underway for haul out capabilities and also possibly mooring buoys as well.

The Frenchman's Cay Marina and Shops are building a new complex currently under construction. The marina and some of the shops should be open by December 1998 and completion is scheduled by December 1999. It will house a full service marina, chandlery, nautical gift shop, arts and craft shop, drug store, laundry service, spa and fitness center and more. The Shipyard and Marina monitors VHF 16.

Near to West End is the Frenchman's Cay Hotel overlooking the Sir Francis Drake Channel. Breakfast, lunch and dinner are served and the pool and tennis courts are available to diners. Jus' Limin' is open Tuesday through Sunday for lunch and dinner and their bar is open from 11am through 10pm daily. The view is spectacular and diners are invited to use the pool.

Located near the ferry dock, the Jolly Roger Inn serves breakfast, lunch and dinner, as well as a late night menu.

The following are some of the restaurants in the West End Area that you may want to visit. See the restaurant section for more details.

In nearby Carrot Bay, Mrs. Scatliffe's restaurant is a wonderful West Indian experience. Mrs. Scatliffe serves chicken family style and sings while you are eating. Sometimes a lively fungi band provides the entertainment.

In Little Apple Bay you will find the Apple restaurant providing complimentary coconut chips and conch fritters at happy hour. Dinner is with reservations only. Sebastians on the Beach in Little Apple Bay serves breakfast, lunch and dinner as well as a daily happy hour. This is a good place to sit on the beach and watch the sunset.

Long Bay Beach Resort is on the northern side of the western end of Tortola. This lovely hotel serves breakfast, lunch and dinner in the Beach Cafe and dinner in the Garden Restaurant with reservations.

Housed in an old sugar mill in Apple Bay, The Sugarmill Restaurant has enjoyed a reputation for excellent cuisine. Dinner is served from 7pm with reservations only.

Nanny Cay

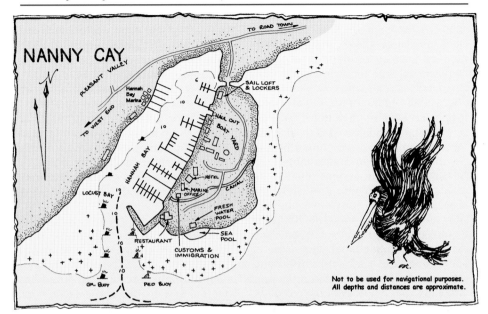

NANNY CAY

Not to be used for navigational purposes.
All depths and distances are approximate.

Approaching Nanny Cay from the West End of Tortola, the first landmark will be the masts of the boats hauled out in the boatyard and slips. Nanny Cay is a peninsula jutting out from the south coast of Tortola, behind which is the Nanny Cay Marine Centre, a full-service marina and boatyard offering a 50 ton lift capable of lifting boats of up to 70 feet.

Navigation

Head for the southern most point of Nanny Cay (the Peg Leg Landing restaurant is an easy landmark), until the red and green channel markers are visible.

The larger reef is to port and marked by a green buoy. Head between the green and red buoys, leaving the red to starboard. The number of buoys may vary, but the marina does keep the channel marked.

The inner harbor has shoal water on the western shore and is marked with a series of green buoys — *do not go west of these buoys*. There is no anchoring, due to the lack of room. Visiting yachts should tie up to docks A & B (the first docks to starboard upon entering) and check with the harbormaster.

Ashore

Amenities available within the marina complex, include showers, water, gift shop, laundromat, ice and fuel. Provisions may be purchased from the Gourmet Chandler and storage lockers may be rented through the marina. Blue Water Divers operates a dive shop and conducts diving tours daily. Nanny Cay is their main base of operations. BVI Marine Management is based at this marina for mechanical repairs, refrigeration, welding and 24 hour chase boat service. Johnny's Maritime Services is also located on the dock. Virgin Textiles and the Seashell Gift and Souvenir Shop sell souvenirs to bring home. Island Marine Chandlery is open from 8am to 5pm daily except on Saturday when they close at noon. Sundays they are closed. BVI Painters and Yacht Restoration Marine Services (shipwrights) complement the boatyard.

Please note: Customs and immigration services are no longer available at Nanny Cay Marine Centre. You must clear through one of the other ports of entry.

Two restaurants complement the marina. The Plaza Cafe is open all day. Peg Leg Landing, a rather whimsical restaurant on the point, serves lunch and dinner and overlooks the Sir Francis Drake Channel. It's a great place to dine, with a view from every table.

Nanny Cay, headquarters for many crewed and some bareboat charterers, offers discounted rates for yachtsmen at the hotel, and use of the pool and tennis court. Windsurfing lessons are also available here at BVI Boardsailing.

Hannah Bay Marina lies to the west of Nanny Cay. Facilities include deep water slips with nine and a half foot draft, condominiums (conspicuous pink structures with teal green roofs) for short or long term accommodation, swimming pool, showers, water, ice, electricity, telephone and cable TV hook-ups. Transient yachts are welcome at the facility for short term dockage and use of facilities. There are plans for a provisioning store and laundry facility at a future date.

Prospect Reef Harbour

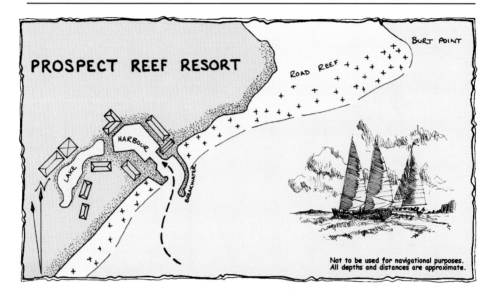

Not to be used for navigational purposes. All depths and distances are approximate.

Just to the west of Road Town is a small harbor that services the Prospect Reef Hotel. It can accommodate vessels up to 40 feet in length and 5-1/2 feet of draft.

Navigation

The harbor entrance has reef on either side. Be sure you know exactly where you are and what to expect, because once in the channel you are committed.

A stone breakwater extends from the shoreline marking the starboard side of the channel. When entering, be prepared to make a "dogleg" to port once you are through the breakwater.

Ashore

The Inner Circle in the harbor provides dockage up to 45 feet with a 5-1/2 foot draft along with fuel, water, electricity, telephones and access to the resort facilities. Prospect Reef offers all the conve-niences of a major hotel complex, including an Olympic size pool and a sea pool, two restaurants, tennis courts, a nine hole golf course, and provisions at Little Circle, servicing the needs of both yachtsmen and tourists with an extensive selection of foods and wines.

Scuttlebutt Bar and Grill serves lunch only from 11am. Upstairs you will find the Callaloo Restaurant serving breakfast, lunch and dinner. Scuttlebutt is a casual restaurant whereas the Callaloo is a more elegant restaurant.

Baskin' in the Sun operate dive tours, rent and sell dive equipment and some clothes. Jim and Odile Scheiner's Rainbow Visions Photo Center sell and develop film, sell cameras and underwater cameras and will videotape you while you are diving. Hiho rent kayaks and windsurfers along with instruction.

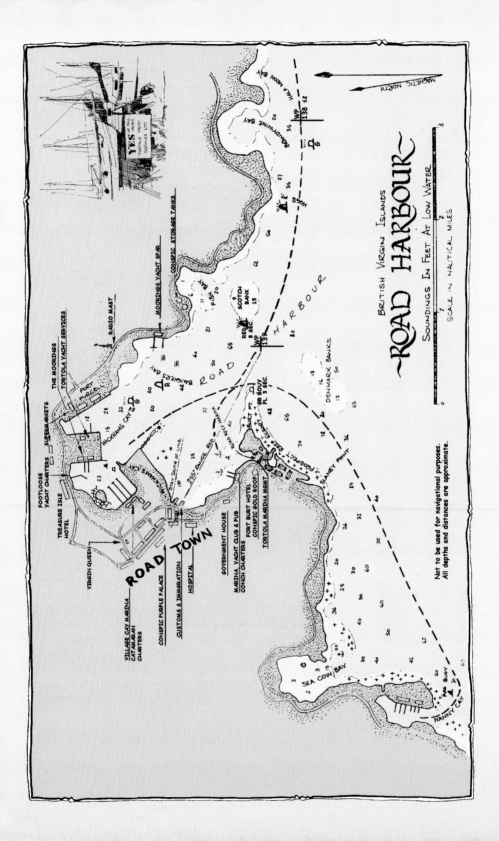

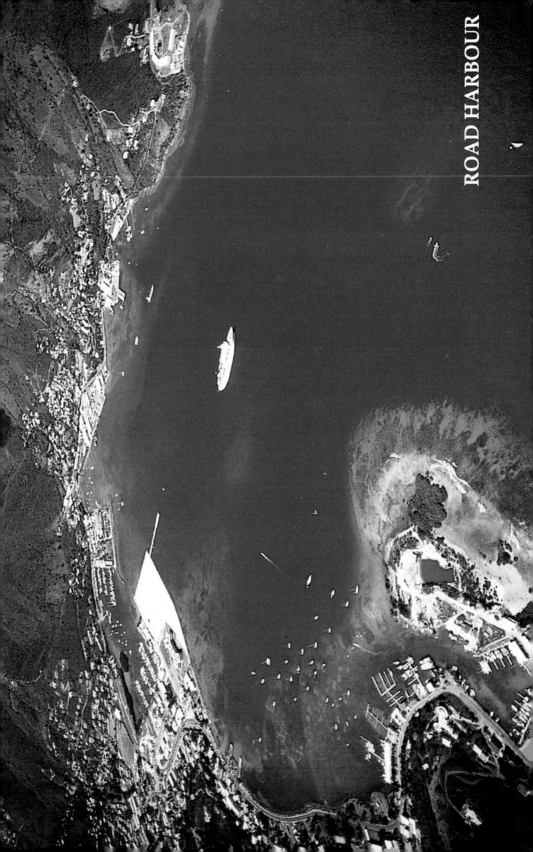

C13, C13a, C14

Road Harbour

Road Town, the capital of the British Virgin Islands, is the center of commerce, shipping and social activity. Over the past decade, tremendous development has taken place to enable it to better cope with the steady influx of cruising and charter boats. Now Road Town can boast some of the most sophisticated nautical facilities in the Caribbean chain.

Navigation
Approaching Road Harbour from the west, your first landmarks will be the fuel tanks located by Fish Bay on the eastern side of the harbor. The other is the dome shaped blue roof of the Fort Burt Hotel, located high up on Burt Point, the western side of the harbor entrance.

Locate the green sea buoy (FL green 3 seconds) marking the end of the reef, extending east from Burt Point and leave it to port. There is a red conical buoy (FL red 8 seconds) marking Scotch Bank on the eastern side of the harbor.

Fort Burt Marina
Once inside the buoys, it is advisable to head for the customs dock (approximately 292 degrees magnetic), until the Fort Burt Jetty is abeam. This will bring you clear of the reef that extends to the north of the mangroves. Anchor to the northeast of the docks about 300 feet out. Check the sketch chart for location of sandbars and anchorage.

Hundreds of sailors have found themselves aground on the sandbar that extends north of the mangroves because they rounded up too quickly. The situation is particularly embarrassing because of the proximity of the local pub which overlooks the anchorage.

If you wish to inquire as to services or docking, pull alongside and check with the dockmaster. Fort Burt Marina has been updated and refurbished with new docks and slips. They do accept transient boats and offer gas, diesel, water and ice as well as telephone and TV cable hook

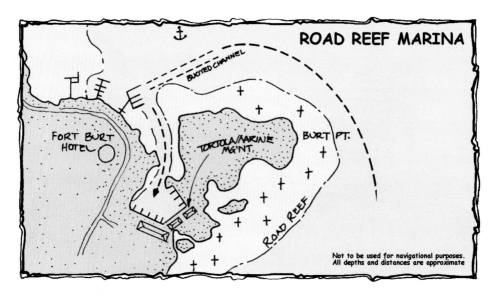

ROAD REEF MARINA

BUOTED CHANNEL

FORT BURT
HOTEL

TORTOLA MARINE
MG'NT.

BURT PT.

ROAD REEF

Not to be used for navigational purposes.
All depths and distances are approximate

up and of course, electricity. Call on VHF 12.

Paradise Pub is perched at the waters edge with a dinghy dock. It is open Monday through Saturday from 7am through 10pm; Sundays they are open for happy hour from 5pm. Dress is casual. On Friday and Saturday nights there is entertainment and Saturday night the Pub rocks! For supplies, Island Marine Supply has a well managed marine chandlery, and Riteway Supermarket operates a grocery in adjacent quarters from which you can resupply. Elm Sailmakers are also found in this complex should you require their assistance.

Road Reef Marina

A channel has been marked with red and green buoys into Road Reef Marina. Leave the green buoys to port to skirt the shal-

low areas with red buoys to starboard. You will be leaving Fort Burt Marina and Smith's Ferry dock to starboard.

There are a couple of shallow patches close to the roadside beneath Fort Burt Hotel, so favor the port side of the channel as you enter the pool of Road Reef Marina. Tortola Marine Management manages the complete marina; most services except fuel are available. Road Reef Marina monitors VHF channel 12, should you require their assistance. In the same complex that houses the marina office is the marine division of the Royal Police, the BVI Yacht Club, the office of VISAR, Doyle Sailmakers and Island Care Electronics. Road Reef Plaza next door to the marina has a variety of shops including a Riteway that sells provisions to yachtsmen.

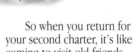

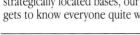

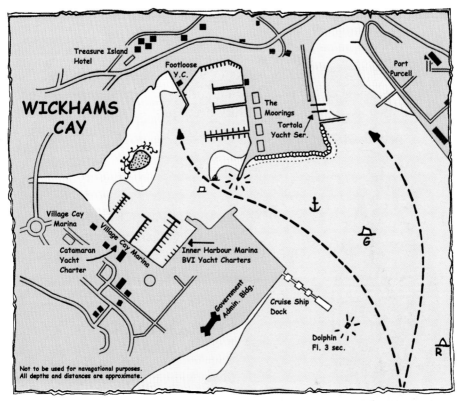

Treasure Island
Hotel

Footloose
Y.C.

WICKHAMS
CAY

The
Moorings

Tortola
Yacht Ser.

Port
Purcell

Village Cay
Marina

Village Cay Marina

Catamaran
Yacht
Charter

Inner Harbour Marina
BVI Yacht Charters

Government Admin. Bldg.

Cruise Ship
Dock

G

Dolphin
Fl. 3 sec.

R

Not to be used for navagational purposes.
All depths and distances are approximate.

The Government Dock

As the main port of entry to the British Islands, all vessels arriving from the U.S. Virgin Islands or other foreign ports must clear with customs and immigration before proceeding to a marina.

Anchor off the town dock, as it is not advisable to lie alongside; apart from the commercial traffic, the surge is often excessive. In landing the dinghy, use a dinghy anchor to keep the stern off.

Wickham's Cay

To the north of the government dock is the Wickhams Cay I and II Yacht Harbour and Marine Service complex. Approaching from seaward,

you will see the government administration building and cruise ship dock. There is a quick flashing 3 second light marking the dolphin off the cruise ship dock and numerous masts behind a stone breakwater. Head for the masts until you see the outer set of buoys marking the channel entrance. Leaving red to starboard, proceed through the breakwater entrance (80 feet wide by 10 feet deep). There is a quick flashing red light on the end of the breakwater.

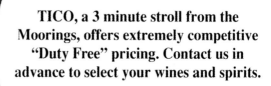
C13, C13a, C14

The Moorings / Mariner Inn

One of the Caribbean's most comprehensive facilities, the Moorings/Mariner Inn has been developed around the Moorings charter fleet of 160 yachts. The complex consists of 38 air-conditioned lanai rooms overlooking the harbor, a fresh water swimming pool, restaurant, gift shop, provisioning store and service facilities. Underwater Safaris operates its dive shop and tour business at the head of the dock.

For docking information it is best to contact the dockmaster via VHF 12.

Upon entering the harbor, there will be three docks. The first, "A" dock, is the one used for visiting yachts and returns and offers finger pier docking for 90 boats. Water is available, as is shore power of both 110 and 220 volts.

Any vessel needing diesel fuel should contact the dockmaster. "B" and "C" docks are reserved for the Moorings bareboat and crewed charter fleet.

Footloose Dock

In the center as you approach from the breakwater, directly in front of Treasure Isle Hotel, is the new home of Footloose Sailing Charters.

Treasure Isle Hotel, across the road, is one of Road Town's finer hotels, offering air-conditioned accommodations, fresh water pool with gardenside dining. The staff members are known for their friendliness, and often remember guests from previous visits.

Village Cay Marina

To your port when entering, Village Cay Marina can accommodate over 100 yachts of up to 150 feet in length. The slips offer metered water and shore power, phone service, and cable TV. Shower facilities, laundromat, ice and provisioning are also available. There is a fresh water pool, and a breezy waterfront restaurant and bar. Village Cay is the home of Southern Trades Yacht Sales and Yacht Charters.

No Shirts. No Shoes.

The Marina Hotel offers air conditioned rooms, all within short walking distance of the banks, shopping and other conveniences of downtown Road Town.

Near the complex, the Ample Hamper offers custom provisioning services and a fine selection of wine, cheese, paté and various other foods to tempt the palate. Near Ample Hamper is the Mill Mall home of one of the three Sea Urchin shops, carrying a collection of swimwear and casual clothes.

In Columbus Centre you will find outside dining at the Fish Trap seafood restaurant. Also in the Centre are Virgin Island Sailing, Girl Friday, DHL, Caribbean

C13, C13a, C14

Connections and several shops. Within a few minutes walk of the marina are several banking institutions including Barclay's, Chase Manhattan and Nova Scotia, and numerous business offices, gift shops and restaurants. Spaghetti Junction Restaurant combines Italian and Caribbean fare just a short walk from the marina. They are open Monday through Saturday for dinner with reservations.

The Inner Harbour Marina

Inner Harbour Marina is nestled alongside Village Cay to the south. Yachts can pay for their stay by the hour, day or month. The services provided include water, electricity, and convenient walking distance to the shops of Road Town. BVI Yacht Charters bases it's operation at the marina and monitors VHF 16. The Captain's Table, a congenial restaurant, overlooks the harbor and offers excellent food.

Tortola Yacht Services

Located on Wickham's Cay II behind the Moorings, Tortola Yacht Services owned and operated by Albie Stewart, is one of the foremost yacht care centers in the Caribbean. The shipyard has both tami lift and marine railway capabilities up to 80 tons, dry storage for up to 40 yachts, an awlgrip refinishing team, yacht brokerage and Golden Hind Chandlery.

Located conveniently in the immediate vicinity are Nautool Machine who do machining and welding, Omega Caribbean woodworkers, Clarence Thomas Plumbing Supplies (carrying plumbing, electrical and marine supplies), Tradewind Yachting Services, and Al's Marine.

DeliTICO, and TICO Liquors — just a short walk from the boatyard and the marina can help you stock the boat with liquor and get some goodies from the deli. You can also walk across the main street to Riteway, a complete market.

Baugher's Bay

On your starboard hand as you enter Road Harbour is a small bay with a marina that is occupied by the Moorings Yacht Spa, a full service marine repair facility welcoming cruising yachtsmen. The marina facilities include docking, electricity, fuel, water, ice and showers. Moorings are available and should be paid for ashore. Also located at the marina is The Woodshop for custom marine and domestic woodworking.

Ashore in Road Town

When going ashore in Road Town, it is important to observe the local dress code, which prohibits swimwear, brief attire and shirtless males. In order to avoid embarrassment, please cover up.

The ferry dock at the center of town houses customs and immigration, as well as an office of the B.V.I. Tourist Department. A taxi stand is right outside making it convenient to get anywhere.

Road Town has some beautiful old West Indian buildings, complete with red tin roofs and Victorian dado work around the porches. A walk down Main Street east from Peebles Hospital will reveal all sorts of delights tucked away behind newer buildings or squeezed shoulder to shoulder along Main Street. Most of the shops are clustered along Main Street from Peebles Hospital to the bottom of Joe's Hill. Stop in at Lady Sarah's across from the hospital, you can have English tea in their Parlour Cafe and browse through their collection of gift items.

A half block away towards the west on the waterfront is Richardson's Rigging, distributors of Harken rigging products.

A visit to the Philatelic Bureau of the post office across the street from the Sir Olva Georges Square should be a must stop for anyone who would like to take home a collection of the exotic and colorful stamps of this tropical country.

You may wish to get caught up on the news at home with a New York Times or a magazine from Esme's Shoppe on the Square. Get yourself a fresh baked treat at Sunrise Bakery while you read your newspaper. Visit the Virgin Island Folk Museum, situated in a quaint, West Indian building, and examine the artifacts from days gone by. On the water front have a snack, breakfast, lunch or dinner at Capriccio di Mare. They are serving from 8am. This is a great place to have a cappuccino while waiting for the ferry. The restaurant next door, Le Cabanon Cafe serves breakfast, lunch and dinner from 8am to 11pm.

Hand-crafted silver jewelry is a specialty of Samarkand. The Sea Urchin features island sports and beachwear, while Kaunda's Kysy Tropix carries film and camera accessories.

Kids in de Sun will help you outfit your children for life in the tropics. You can get your crew matching, embroidered shirts at Personal Touch. Ooh La La carries toys, games and assorted frivolities. Caribbean Handprints specializes in silk screened clothing and accessories.

On the waterfront and Main Street you will find the Pusser's Company Store and Pub. This is a delightful, air conditioned pub where you can cool down with a beer or lemonade and a deli sandwich or pizza. If you haven't tried a Pusser's Painkiller, this may be the time. Friday nights the pub is jamming at happy hour, it is the place to be. Thursday evenings stop by for "Nickel Beer Night".

C13, C13a, C14

Also on the waterfront to the east is the Seaview Hotel and Maria's By the Sea Restaurant which features local Caribbean cuisine and seafood overlooking Road Harbour.

Continuing down Main Street is Tavern in the Town, Flaxcraft jewelry store featuring hand crafted gold, silver and coral jewelry. Growing Things offers baskets, fresh floral arrangements and gifts. Sunny Caribbee Herb and Spice Company is located in a delightful old West Indian house, the shop carries specially packaged herbs and spices from the islands. Visit their air conditioned art gallery next door for art treasures displayed for sale. The Carifta Shop carries an assortment of clothing and accessories and fragrances for women.

Fort Wine Gourmet store has a wide selection of wines and liquors as well as a special selection of gourmet goodies. Not to be missed for the *gourmand*.

Little Denmark has a wide assortment

of things from jewelry and watches to fishing gear and china. Next door is Serendipity — Domino featuring handicrafts, jewelry, clothing and gift items. Caribbean Fine Arts offers custom framing with a selection of West Indian and local art and prints.

Smiths Gore Real Estate is perched on a huge boulder across from Little Denmark. Further down the street you will find Her Majesty's Prison, an old and interesting edifice, and one we hope you'll never have to see from the inside. St. George's Anglican Church is another lovely landmark worth a visit.

Continuing past the church on your left is the Joe's Hill which leads up to Mount Sage or over to Cane Garden Bay. At the top of the hill follow the signs to Skyworld Restaurant and Gift Shop. The panoramic view is breathtaking, the temperature cool and breezy. They serve lunch and dinner with reservations.

If you are still feeling energetic

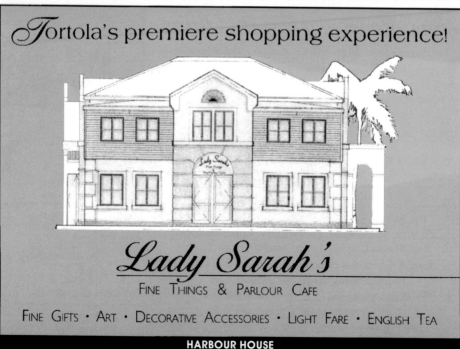

C13, C13a, C14

continue on Main Street past Sunday Morning well, past the high school to the J. R. O'Neal Botanical Gardens across the street from the police station. It is a refreshing stop away from the hustle and bustle of Road Town. The garden features a beautiful, exotic variety of lush, tropical plants.

Coming in to Road Harbour from the sea, you will see an old, purple Victorian building with white trim. This is the Bougainvillea Clinic, affectionately known to the locals as the "Purple Palace". Dr. Tattersall, who specializes in plastic surgery is well known for both his surgical skills and his sailboat racing skills.

Many other shops and services, too numerous to mention, are available in Road Town. Check with the tourist department, or even the yellow pages of the phone book to find what you are looking for.

BOAT BUILDING IN THE VIRGINS

Because of the scattered formation of the Virgin Islands, the inhabitants, by necessity, became expert boat builders, specializing in small, light craft that were ideal for these sheltered waters.

The unique skills that the West Indians learned from the 18th-century Navy have been preserved, virtually unchanged, to the present day, and "Tortolan Sloops" are still launched with regularity

C13, C13a, C14

Brandywine Bay

This lovely curve of a bay is carved out to the east of Road Harbour and provides a comfortable overnight anchorage in the usual east/southeast moderate trade winds, but can have a surge if the wind moves around to the south.

Brandywine Bay is tucked in behind a reef that extends out from both sides of the land. The opening between the two sections of reef is wide and safe for entry in the center between the two reefs, with a depth of at least 10 feet. The entrance is easy enough to see in reasonable light. As a landmark to locate Brandywine Bay, look for the "Greek Temple," an imposing building with a columned facade, situated on top of the headland, immediately to the east of the bay.

Anchoring

Brandywine Bay Restaurant, situated on the headland to the east of the bay, in front of the Greek temple, and overlooking the Sir Francis Drake channel, maintains three moorings for dinner guests. These moorings are located in the center of the bay directly in line with the entrance to the bay. The southern most mooring is in the deepest water, while the mooring closest to the northern shore

is in approximately 7-8 feet of water. The restaurant monitors VHF 16 after 2pm and is available by telephone all day for reservations and instructions for mooring. If you choose to anchor, select a spot in the center of the bay to the east or west of the line of moorings, beware of shoal water that extends from all shores. If there is a surge, usually caused by a southerly wind or generally very rough local conditions, you may want to use a stern anchor in order to keep the bow of your boat facing the entrance of Brandywine Bay.

Ashore

As you face the row of condominiums on the water edge on the eastern side of the bay, the dinghy dock is located about 50 yards to their right. Once ashore, follow the pathway to the left of the dock to where it meets the concrete road on Brandywine Estate, and then it's just a short walk up the hill to the restaurant.

For dinner only, Brandywine Bay Restaurant offers al fresco dining on cobblestone terraces. Davide and Cele Pugliese are your hosts in this international restaurant with a distinctive Florentine flair. Dinner reservations are requested.

A new era in the charter business has begun!

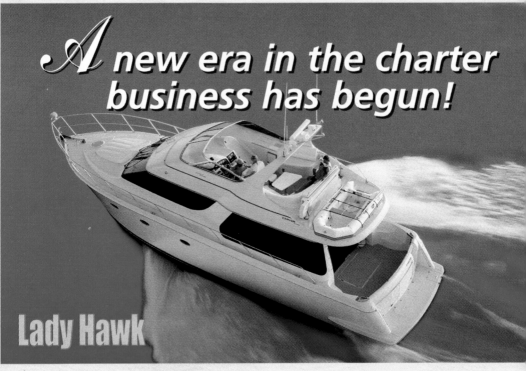

Lady Hawk

*N*ow you are able to charter one of the finest and most luxurio[us] yachts, the brand new Carver 530 Motoryacht "LADY HAWK" in th[e] Caribbean.

Take control of the yacht in the futuristic pilothouse with all th[e] electronics or at the spacious flybrigde. Make a good nights sleep in or[e] of the two great staterooms with innerspring double mattresses. Use the electric davit for the dinghy to take you to the beautiful beache[s]

Contact your Charter Yacht Agent, who will be happy to make you[r] reservation of LADY HAWK. Either as a bareboat or with our profession[al] captain.

We welcome you on board LADY HAWK.

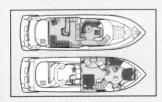

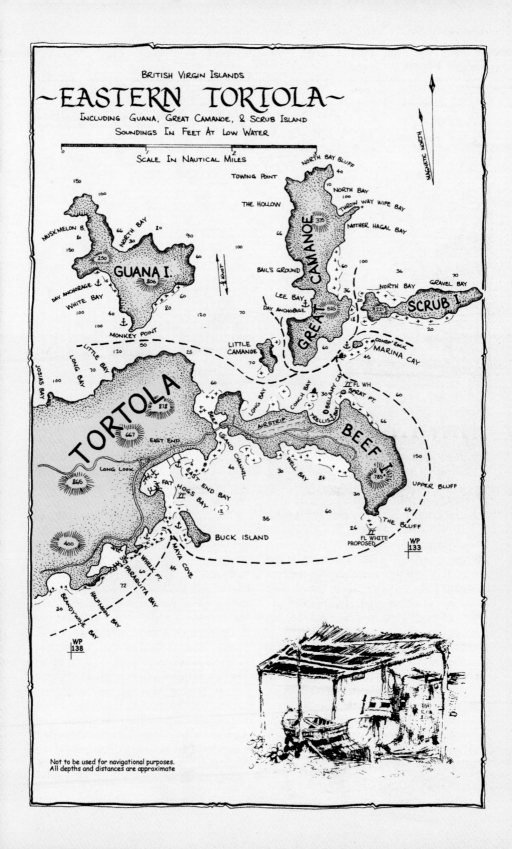

Maya Cove

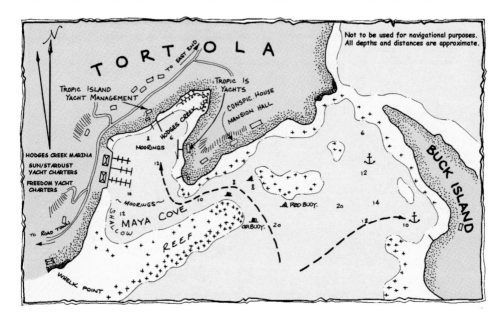

Maya Cove or Hodges Creek, as it is shown on the charts, is approximately a half mile west of Buck Island on the southeastern shore of Tortola. Sheltered by the reef, it is always cool and free of bugs.

Tropic Island Yacht Management, Sun Yacht Charters and Stardust operate their charter fleets from this protected haven.

Navigation

When approaching Maya Cove from the west, it is well to remember that the reef extends from Whelk Point to the buoyed entrance at the northeastern end of the reef. Entry should be made only under power.

The buoys are easy to see and are located under a promontory of land approximately 75-100 feet high. The channel is marked with red and green buoys. Proceed through the center leaving the red buoy to starboard. At the last green buoy you will be making a turn to port, which will lead you to the harbor.

Anchoring

It is imperative when anchoring that you do not obstruct the channel after entering. You may pick up one of the moorings operated by Tropic Island Yacht Management and pay for it ashore at their charter base.

The main anchorage is to the south of the channel. Don't go too far back into the Cove, as it shoals off rapidly.

Ashore

Immediately in front of you as you enter the Cove is the red roof of Hodges Creek Marina. Sun Yacht Charters operates the Hodges Creek Marina, the base for its charter fleet as well as that of Stardust Yacht Charters and Freedom Yacht Charters. This full service marina provides fuel, water, ice, laundry, and showers. Calamaya, the marina restaurant serves a variety of Caribbean and Mediterranean cuisine for breakfast, lunch and dinner. Bluewater Divers have a dive shop on the dock along with a gift shop and Ample

Hamper can take care of your provisioning needs from their new shop on the dock. Sun Yacht Charters monitor VHF 16.

Tropic Island Yacht Management operates their charter fleet from the Maya Cove Marina at the northern end of the Cove. This full service marina provides fuel, water, ice, laundry, and showers. The Pelican Roost Restaurant and Bar is open for breakfast, lunch and dinner.

Next to the fresh water swimming pool are the beautifully finished studio villas with kitchens which are available for long or short term rentals. Underwater Safaris, one of the oldest dive operations in the British Virgin Islands has a direct hot line from the marina for all of your diving requirements. Tropic Island Yacht Management monitor VHF 12.

Buck Island

There is a small anchorage in 7-10 feet of water on the western shore of Buck Island. Very few yachts anchor here. In certain sea conditions it can be very rolly, but most of the time is an ideal anchorage.

Take care not to go too far toward the northwest tip of the island, as the bottom shoals rapidly. There is no passage between Buck Island and Tortola except by dinghy with the engine tilted up.

Fat Hog's Bay and East End Bay

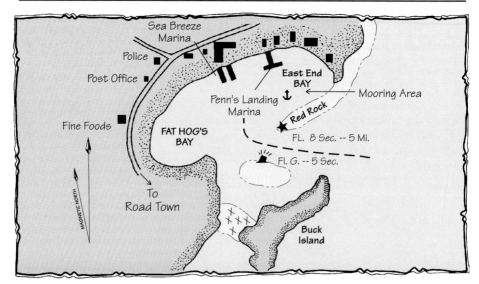

Fat Hog's Bay and East End Bay are located north of Buck Island between Beef Island Channel and Maya Cove. These beautiful, well-protected bays are conveniently situated in the middle of the cruising grounds and are perfect for overnight anchoring.

Navigation
Both anchorages are easily accessible

from Sir Francis Drake channel by leaving Buck Island to port and going between the green can and Red Rock. There is a buoyed unlit channel leading to Penn's Landing Marina or head directly to the Seabreeze Marina dock, Harbourview Marina, or pick up one of the white mooring buoys on the eastern side of the channel. Please do not anchor within the mooring area or obstruct the channel by anchoring inside it.

Average depth from Red Rock into East End Bay is about 9 feet with good holding ground and excellent protection behind the reef. Call ahead to either Seabreeze or Penn's Landing on VHF channel 16.

Ashore

Facilities at both Seabreeze and Penn's Landing include water, ice, fresh water showers, and overnight dockage. Moorings by Moor Seacure can be paid for at Penn's Landing. Penn's Landing Restaurant, which is open for lunch and dinner offers casual seaside dining with a cool breeze. The Sailor's Ketch Seafood Market supplies a wide variety of freshly caught local fish in addition to imported seafood.

Both Seabreeze Yacht Charters and Tradewinds Yacht Charters are housed at the Seabreeze Marina. The Bistro restaurant is open for snacks, drinks or full meals. A short walking distance down the road is the Virgin Queen Harbourview Restaurant across from Wheatley's Harbourview Marina. Hotel accommodations are available at the Seabreeze Marina. Two stores are convenient for stocking up on supplies, the Ritebreeze grocery store, Fine Foods market, and the Parham Town General Store.

Caribbean Flavas (upstairs) Restaurant and Bar is located between Penn's Landing and Seabreeze. Downstairs is the B & F Medical Complex, with walk in appointments available as well as it's own dispensary.

Trellis Bay, Beef Island

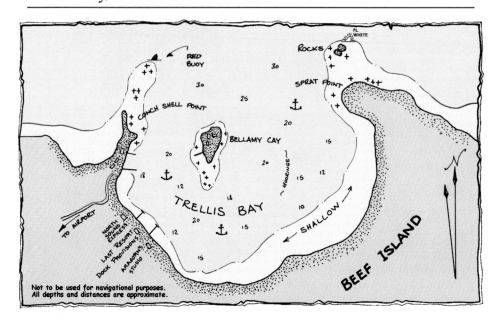

Not to be used for navigational purposes.
All depths and distances are approximate.

Located on the north shore of Beef Island, Trellis Bay was once a major anchorage in the B.V.I., with a hotel, large marine railway and jetty. The railway and hotel have since been abandoned, and the jetty is now used by the boats servicing Marina Cay. The anchorage is well protected even in adverse weather conditions, and its proximity to the airport makes it ideal for embarking and disembarking passengers.

Navigation

Entering Trellis Bay from the north, stay to the east of Conch Shell Point to avoid the submerged rocks. These rocks are marked by a red buoy, which should be left to starboard as you enter the bay.

If entering from the east, take care to locate the two rocks to the north of Sprat Point. The outside rock is marked by a white flashing light. Leaving them to port, enter Trellis Bay halfway between Bellamy Cay and Sprat Point.

Anchoring

Good anchorage is available off either side of Bellamy Cay in 10-20 feet of wa-

ter. Do not anchor within 200 feet of the western shore of the bay to leave a channel for the frequent ferry boats and cargo vessels. The holding ground is excellent in some places but poor in others. However, moorings are available throughout the anchorage. Beware of underwater obstructions in areas less than 10 feet deep (in the eastern and southern parts of the bay). The area south of Sprat Point is shoal and should be avoided. A sandbar extends due south of Bellamy Cay; take care when passing over in the dinghy.

Ashore

The Last Resort on Bellamy Cay is an absolute must on a cruise around the Virgins. Run by Englishman Tony Snell, his wife Jackie and donkey Vanilla, the Last Resort offers excellent value in buffet style food and Tony's own brand of entertainment. You will find this evening of hilarity and song unforgettable. Be sure to check out their gift shop on the island.

Ferry service to Bellamy Cay is available for those driving to Trellis Bay.

The Conch Shell Point Restaurant can be reached leaving your dinghy by the dock past the public phone, and walking up the small path to the right. Owned by the Dawson family, this restaurant has an excellent reputation for both the food (West Indian and continental) and the service.

Jim Scheiner

Trellis Bay

For those who wish to learn to windsurf, the BVI Boardsailing School is located on the beach to the south of Bellamy Cay. Windsurfing has become increasingly popular in the Virgin Islands. The steady winds combined with the consistency of the weather provide an excellent learning environment.

Located on the south shore of Trellis Bay is the Beef Island Guest House with bar and snack bar De Loose Mongoose.

Breakfast, lunch and dinner are served from 8:30am to 9pm. Try their rum punch called the "No-see-um".

Next to BVI Boardsailing, with the thatched roof, is Aragorn's Studio, a Tortolian born artist who works in copper, ceramics and silkscreen. Aragorn is famous for his copper sculptures and one of a kind woodcut and handpainted fish print t-shirts. Keep an eye out for his "boat shop" in the anchorage. He will

come by the anchorages of Marina Cay and Trellis Bay with his boat loaded with t-shirts, crafts, fresh bread and local fruits usually in the mornings. In the afternoons Anouk comes around in her dinghy with her handcrafted jewelry for sale.

Trellis Bay is the home of Gli Gli, the largest Carib Indian dugout sailing canoe in the Caribbean. Gli Gli is available for day charters, providing a unique and historical sailing experience.

On the beach near the government dock is Flukes Designs workshop and gallery. You are welcome to visit the artists at work, handpainting t-shirts, pictures and maps. Other local crafts are also on display.

If you find you are running out of supplies, provisions are available at the brightly colored Trellis Bay Market. The North Sound Express ferry shuttles guests to North Sound from their dock here convenient to the airport. The Marina Cay Pusser's ferry picks up at the government dock.

Eastern Tortola and the Camanoe Passages

When sailing around Tortola from the north side, several passages are available.

The passage between Monkey Point on the southern end of Guana and Tortola is plenty wide and free of hazards. The large rock on Monkey Point is your landmark. Once through, you may either bear off to starboard and negotiate the channel between Little Camanoe and Beef or continue due east, leaving Little Camanoe to starboard, making the transit between Little Camanoe and Great Camanoe.

The latter should be negotiated in good light and then only under power. There is a small reef on the northeast tip of Little Camanoe and the seas are usually breaking, making it easy to identify. When the ground seas are up during the winter months, the surf breaks heavily on this reef.

The channel, though narrow, carries adequate depth and is free of reef or other hazards. Once clear of the channel, the entrance to Marina Cay to the northeast and Trellis Bay to the southeast are before you.

The passage between Little Camanoe and Beef Island should be negotiated only in good light. Be sure to avoid the reef area that extends from the southwest tip of Little Camanoe. Another hazard in this area is the middle ground or reef that lies two thirds of the distance between the southwest tip of Great Camanoe and the rocks on the eastern end of Long Bay.

A red nun buoy marks the rocks that lie 100 yards off the westernmost point of Trellis Bay. This buoy should be left to starboard; from here you have good water to enter Trellis Bay or continue to the east.

Anchorages

All the anchorages listed below are recommended as daytime stops only. During the winter when the northerly ground seas are running, none of these are recommended even as comfortable lunch stops.

C13, C13a, C14

Photograph by Dougal Thornton

Don't Miss Marina Cay...

"A Flower covered tropical jewel"... secure moorings
in a sheltered lagoon, magnificent snorkeling & much more!

●**Casual dining on the Beach**–Enjoy dining on our beach verandah. We have very good food and drink! Choose from grilled lobster, fish, chicken, steak, or our chef's special.

●**Great Snorkeling & Watersports:** A special experience in the warm, shallow waters of the surrounding reef.

●**A Full service fuel dock,** including ice, water and free ferry service.

●**Laundromat:** Located alongside our spotless new bathrooms and showers.

●**A PUSSER'S Co. Store** specializing in tropical & nautical clothing, unique accessories and unusual gifts.

●**Spectacular 360° view.** Have a drink on the summit and enjoy the breathtaking view of the reef & surrounding islands.

●**Enjoy our Mini-Hotel.** 4 rooms and 2 villas overlooking the reef and the Sir Francis Drake Channel beyond.

●**Some Marina Cay history:** Inhabited occasionally by fishermen, in 1936 Marina Cay became the home to American author Robb White and his bride Rodie. Marina Cay also became the subject of White's book "Two on the Isle," which was made into a 1950's movie, actually filmed on Marina Cay and starring Sidney Poitier and John Cassavettes. The Robb and Rodie White House still stands on the summit, and is open for viewing daily. Robb and Rodie's story is told photographically on the wall of the restaurant and Robb White's book is for sale in the PUSSER'S Company Store.

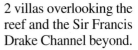

PHONE 494-2174 OR CALL MARINA CAY ON VHF CH 16

Marina Cay was recently chosen as the official home of the Republic of Cuervo..

Tortola / Little Bay

If there is no surf on the beach, this anchorage is a delightful stop. Anchor well off, make sure your hook is well set, then dinghy ashore.

Guana Island, White Bay, Monkey Point

White Bay is on the southwest shore of Guana Island and is easily spotted by its long white beach. The anchorage is 20-25 feet deep, and care should be taken not to swing into the coral heads inshore. The island was named for the rock formation to the north of White Bay, which resembles the head of an iguana.

This island is private, so exploring ashore is not permissible. Another day stop is in the small cove to the west of Monkey Point. The snorkeling is good and there is a small beach facing east. Power in slowly and drop anchor in 15-20 feet, taking care not to foul the coral heads, or pick up a National Park Trust mooring if you have paid your fee.

Great Camanoe / Lee Bay

Another little bay used infrequently is Lee Bay on the west coast of Camanoe. The anchorage is deep — 35 feet — but the snorkeling is good.

Marina Cay

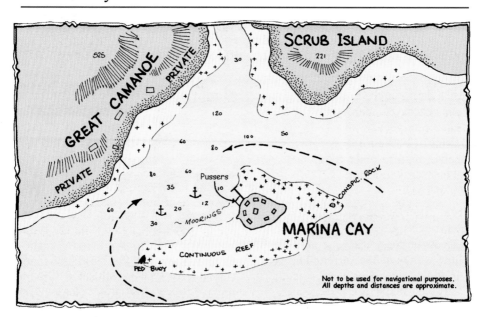

Not to be used for navigational purposes.
All depths and distances are approximate.

Marina Cay, nestled behind a reef and lying between the islands of Camanoe and Scrub, is easy to enter and provides the visiting yachtsman with good holding in an all weather anchorage. For those who have read Robb White's book *Our Virgin Island*, it was Marina Cay of which he wrote.

Navigation

Approaching Marina Cay from the east, you have two choices. The recommended route is to go around the north end of the island. There is good water up to the large rock that marks the northeast end of the reef. Leave it to port and pass between Marina Cay and Scrub Island into the anchorage.

Jim Scheiner / Marina Cay

Alternatively, approaching from the west, you should favor the southern tip of Great Camanoe. There is a red marker at the southwest end of the reef. Leaving it well to starboard, you will enter the anchorage. The reef extends south and west of Marina Cay and is highly visible in good light.

If the light is good, it is also possible to approach Marina Cay from the north between Scrub Island and Great Camanoe. There are reefs lining either side of the channel and you should favor the Great Camanoe side when entering. This anchorage should be negotiated only in good light under power.

Anchoring
Several fully maintained moorings are in place, and should be paid for ashore. The holding ground is reasonable for anchoring. Camanoe Island is private and off limits for visitors. Consideration should be given in the proximity of the homes to keep noise levels down and respect the privacy of the residents.

There is excellent snorkeling behind Marina Cay.

Ashore
Marina Cay has a full service fuel dock, offering ice, water, garbage disposal, laundry facilities and showers for yachtsmen. They monitor VHF 16. Pussers Marina Cay provides free ferry service from the government dock in Trellis Bay — check with them for the departure times.

Ashore you will find a Pusser's Company Store stocked with their nautical and tropical clothing, unique accessories and gifts. The Sunset Bar, at the highest point of Marina Cay is a great place for a drink with a spectacular view. The beach offers casual dining at the grill. The island even boasts six rooms for those wanting some time ashore.

Dive BVI offers dive trips and instruction daily. A new air station is in operation and ocean kayaks and Hobie Cat rentals are available. Dive BVI also offer day trips from the island to Anegada.

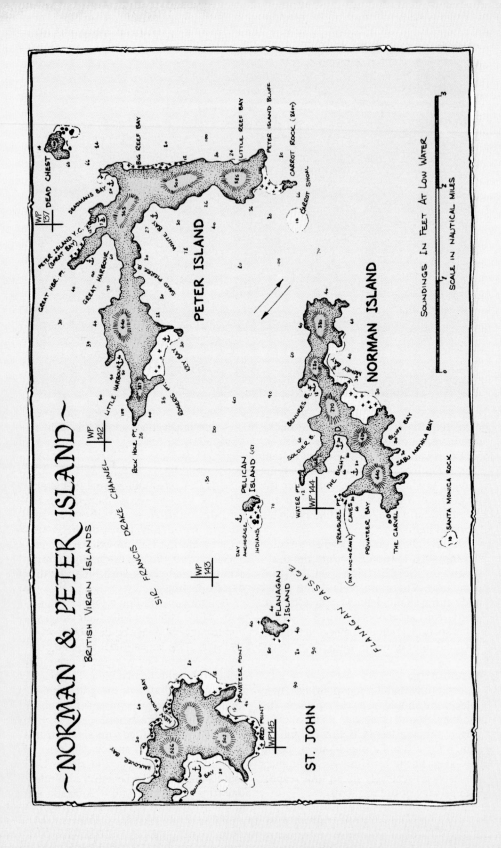

~NORMAN & PETER ISLAND~

British Virgin Islands

PETER ISLAND

NORMAN ISLAND

ST. JOHN

SIR FRANCIS DRAKE CHANNEL

FLANAGAN PASSAGE

DEAD CHEST

WP 137

Peter Island Y.C. (Great Bay)

GREAT HARBOUR PT.

DEADMANS BAY

BIG REEF BAY

LITTLE REEF BAY

PETER ISLAND BLUFF

CARROT ROCK (84ft)

CARROT SHOAL

WHITE BAY

SPRAT BAY

GREAT HARBOUR

LITTLE HARBOUR

KEY BAY

ROBBERS PASS

RECK HOLE PT.
26

WP 142

PELICAN ISLAND (21)

DAY ANCHORAGE

INDIANS

SOLDIER B.

SCRUB I.

WATER PT.

THE BIGHT

TREASURE PT.

CAVES

(DAY ANCHORAGE)

PRIVATEER BAY

THE CARVEL

BLUFF BAY

SABA MATHILA BAY

WP 144

FLANAGAN ISLAND

WP 143

FOOD BAY

PRIVATEER POINT

RED POINT

WP 145

MANACER BAY

ROUND BAY

SANTA MONICA ROCK

SOUNDINGS IN FEET AT LOW WATER

SCALE IN NAUTICAL MILES

NORMAN ISLAND
The Bight

Norman is the first island of any size that, together with the islands of Peter, Salt, Cooper and Ginger, form the southern perimeter of the Sir Francis Drake Channel. Often referred to by the locals as "Treasure Island", legends of Norman Island are resplendent with stories of buried pirate treasure. A letter of 1750 stated, "Recovery of the treasure from *Nuestra Senora* buried at Norman Island, comprising $450,000 dollars, plate, cochineal, indigo, tobacco, much dug up by Tortolians."

The main anchorage on Norman Island is the Bight, an exceptionally well sheltered anchorage.

Navigation
On making an approach to the Bight, the only hazard is the Santa Monica Rocks, which lie to the southwest of the Carvel Point. There is in excess of 6 feet of water over them, but watch out for sea swells. If your approach brings you by Pelican Island, remember that you cannot pass between the Indians and Pelican.

The entrance to the Bight is straight forward and without hazard. Enter between the headlands, keeping in mind that there is shoal water just off both points.

Anchoring
The best anchorage is well up in the northeast corner of the bay near Billy Bones or the southeast section. You will need to get far enough in to anchor on the shelf in 15-30 feet of water. Or there are many mooring buoys in place that you may pick up for the night. Someone will come by dinghy to collect the mooring fee usually in the early evening. If you anchor instead of picking up a mooring be sure that you are well clear of the moorings and have plenty of room to swing without fouling a mooring. Be aware that the wind tends to funnel down through the hills, giving the impression that the weather is much heavier than it is once you are outside of the bay.

Ashore
A dinghy trip to Treasure Point and the caves for snorkeling and exploring is a must. Take your flashlight and tie up your dinghy to the line strung between two small round floats. This avoids dropping an anchor and destroying coral. You may also take your sailboat and pick up a National Parks mooring during the day (with a permit). Good snorkeling also exists on the reef at the eastern end of the harbor just south of the beach. Please do not feed the fish at the caves, it tends to make them aggressive.

Jim Scheiner / The Caves

If you are in the mood for a hike, take the track from the beach by Billy Bones to the top of the hill. It should be negotiated only with adequate shoes and clothing to protect you from the brush. Caution is also advised when encountering the local population of goats or wild cattle. Stay clear of them.

Located in the Norman Island Bight, the William Thornton, a floating restaurant was christened in 1966. The new boat is a replica of a top sail lumber schooner, measuring 93 feet. Lunch is served from noon to 3pm and dinner from 7 to 10pm daily. Nicknamed the "Willie T," stories abound about many wild nights partying aboard. The ambiance is casual and often riotously fun! The "Willie T" monitors VHF 16.

New to the Bight is Billy Bones Beach Bar and Grill at the northeastern section of the bay. A delightful establishment, they are open from 9:30am until the last person staggers off to their dinghy at night. Both lunch and dinner are served in a casual atmosphere or drinks at the bar. This is a great place to watch the sunset and escape the boat for awhile. Reservations are advisable. They monitor VHF 16.

At around 5pm daily, the supply vessel *Deliverance* makes the rounds to the yachts in the Bight, Cooper Island, and Peter Island selling ice, water, fruit, veggies, booze and other goodies you may require.

Other Anchorages

To the west of Water Point (the northernmost point) is a small cove which provides an excellent lunch stop. Approach the anchorage under power and work up to the western end of the bay. Anchor in 25-30 feet of water with plenty of swinging room, as you are likely to be backwinded. If other vessels are anchoring in the bay, it may prove prudent to use a second anchor to reduce the amount of swing.

Treasure Point

Providing there is not much sea running, a delightful daytime stop can be had by anchoring approximately 300-350 yards south of Treasure Point. You will have to anchor in 30-40 feet of water,

avoiding damaging the coral bottom. Make sure the anchor is well set in sand before going ashore. You are likely to be backwinded, so don't be surprised if you end up lying stern to the caves. The National Parks Trust moorings are available here for your use during the day with a permit as mentioned above.

The snorkeling is excellent along the mouths of the four caves. Caution: Do not use the outboard engine in this area as there are always swimmers in the area — use your oars carefully.

Benures Bay (or Benares Bay)
When the wind moves around to the south, there is a protected anchorage on the north coast of Norman Island called Benures Bay. Anchor up in the northeast corner as close to the pebble beach as

possible. The bottom is sand and the holding is good. Snorkeling on the western end is pristine.

Pelican Island / The Indians
This would be considered a daytime stop only, but well worth the effort. Do not attempt to sail between Pelican Island and the rocks to the west called the Indians. Approach them from the north and anchor midway between in 10-15 feet of water avoiding coral or pick up a Parks Trust mooring.

A reef extends between the two and provides excellent snorkeling as does the area immediately around the Indians. As part of the National Parks Trust, this area is protected. You will find National Parks Trust moorings available for use with a permit.

PETER ISLAND

Sailing to the east, the next island is Peter. Captain Thomas Southey wrote his impressions of the island in his chronological history of the West Indies over 100 years ago:

"In May (1806) the author with a party

visited Peter's Island, one of those which form the bay of Tortola, a kind of Robinson Crusoe spot, where a man ought to be farmer, carpenter, doctor, fisherman, planter; everything himself."

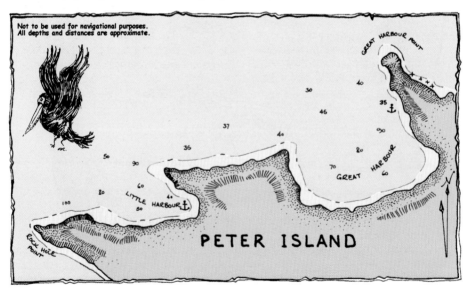

Not to be used for navigational purposes.
All depths and distances are approximate.

PETER ISLAND

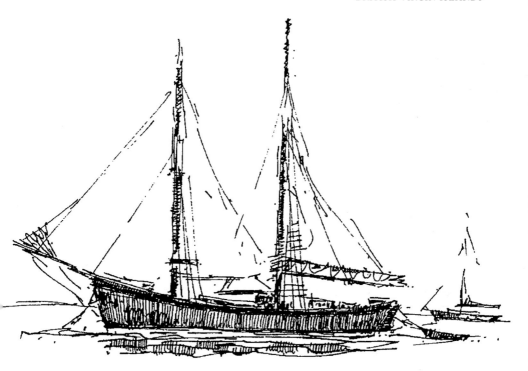

Little Harbour

There are several good overnight anchorages on Peter Island, the western-most of which is Little Harbour. Although it doesn't look it on the chart, Little Harbour is a well-protected overnight stop with good holding ground.

When approaching, the first landmark is a white house on the northwest point, which forms the east side of the harbor.

Anchoring

The best spot to anchor is well up in the eastern reaches of the bay, in 15-25 feet over a sandy bottom. You will be backwinded, so check your swinging room relative to other vessels and use two anchors if necessary. If the anchorage is crowded, anchor close to shore on the southern coast of the bay in order to stay in 25-35 feet of water. The center drops off rapidly.

Great Harbour

Great Harbour is considered too deep to make a worthwhile anchorage; however, if you can spend the time, there are two shallow areas and the rewards are those of private seclusion.

It is important not to get in the way of local fishermen who run their nets out into the bay each afternoon. For this rea-son, it is recommended that you find the 3 fathom spot on the northwest shore, about one third of the way in from the point. While the fishing is going on, the least amount of activity in the bay the better. After the fishermen have gone, you can bring the boat in closer to shore.

Sprat Bay

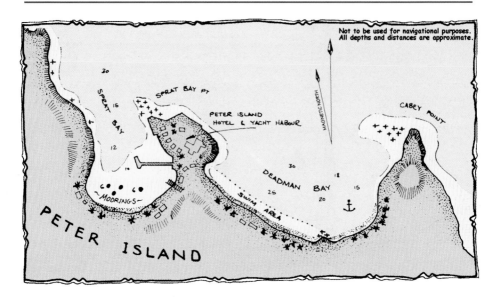

Peter Island Yacht Harbour

Sprat Bay is easy to spot from the channel by the row of roofs that comprise the accommodation section of the Peter Island Hotel and Yacht Harbour. The entire bay, Deadman's Bay and several beaches on the south coast are part of the complex.

Navigation

When making your entrance to Sprat Bay, it is important to familiarize yourself with the location of the reefs on either side of the channel. The main reef extends north and slightly west of the main bulkhead, so do not get too close to the western shore.

Entering on a heading of 165 degrees magnetic, you can either tie up to the dock, which now sports new finger piers or pick up a mooring. The dock has 20 mid-sized slips and 3 megayacht berths. Do not go too far into the southern end of the bay as it is shallow. Thirty moorings are now located in Sprat Bay, which allows for more boats than if they were anchored. After picking a mooring up, check in with the dockmaster ashore.

Marina amenities are water, fuel, ice, showers, and cable TV. The marina stands by on VHF channel 16. Dinner reservations should be made in advance.

Ashore

The Peter Island Yacht Harbour and Hotel complex was originally built by Norwegians and was done in excellent taste and it has recently been completely renovated. The 40 unit hotel and restaurant extends along the bulkhead. Reservations for breakfast, lunch and dinner should be made at the front desk, and yachtsmen are requested to adjust their attire to suit the tone of the hotel.

Dive BVI has a base here for those interested in diving and or airfills. The Beach Bar and Deadman's Bay are favorites of yachtsmen. In season, they often hold beach barbecues with bands and dancing.

There are numerous walks to take, but be sure to take the short walk to the top of the hill to the eastern side of the harbor for a delightful, panoramic view of the channel and Dead Chest Island.

C13, C14

Deadman's Bay

The easternmost anchorage on Peter Island, Deadman's Bay is a beautiful day stop, but you will feel the effects of the surge that makes its way around the northeastern point. Move right up into the extreme southeastern corner when anchoring. The bottom is grassy and it is sometimes difficult to get the anchor set, but the snorkeling is excellent and the ideal, white sand beach is fringed with palm trees.

The beach to the west is for the use of hotel guests only, and yachtsmen are requested to respect the line of buoys designating the swimming area.

The South Coast of Peter Island

There are two anchorages on the south side of Peter that are worthy of mention, but some regard to sea and weather conditions should be noted when planning the anchorage.

White Bay

Named for the white sand beach, White Bay is a reasonable anchorage when the ground seas are not running. Anchor close to shore, but be careful of backwinding.

Key Point

There is an excellent anchorage to the west of Key Point. Make your approach from the south, favoring the key side in order to clear the rock on the west side of the entrance. Anchor between the point and Key Cay in 18 feet of water.

The snorkeling is excellent and the anchorage is open to the prevailing breeze, keeping it free from bugs.

Dougal Thornton /Dive Boat at the Indians.

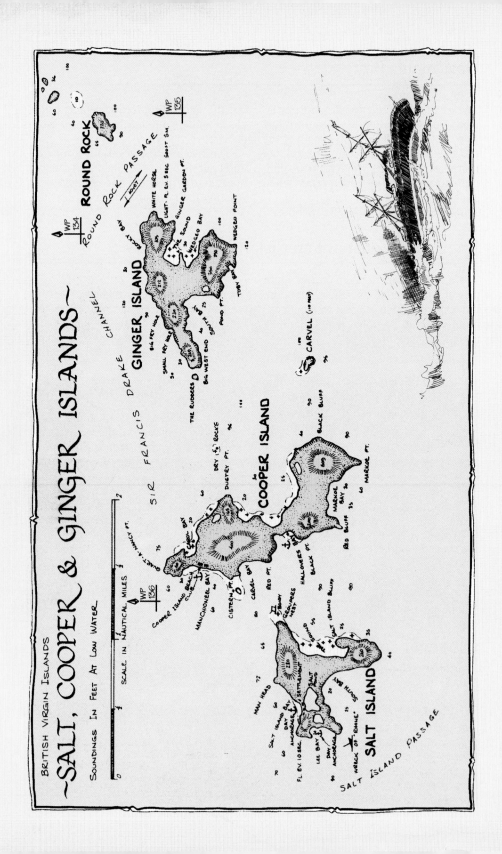

BRITISH VIRGIN ISLANDS

~SALT, COOPER & GINGER ISLANDS~

Soundings In Feet At Low Water

SCALE IN NAUTICAL MILES

ROUND ROCK

WP 134

WP 135

Round Rock Passage

1 KNOT

GINGER ISLAND

GINGER GARDEN PT.

LIGHT. FL EV 5 SEC 500T 5M

WHITE HORSE

GOAT BAY

THE SOUND

WEDGOO BAY

WEDGED POINT

TONY BAY

POND PT.

BIG WEST END SOUTH

SMALL FRY HOLE

BIG FRY HOLE

THE RUDDERS

SIR FRANCIS DRAKE CHANNEL

COOPER ISLAND

DRY ROCKS

DUSTLEY PT.

CARVEL (10 mi)

BLACK BLUFF

MARKOE PT.

MARKOE BAY

RED BLUFF

BLACK PT.

HALLOWE'ES PT.

RED PT.

CARZEL BAY

CISTERN PT.

MANCHIONEEL BAY

COOPER ISLAND BEACH CLUB

WP 136

SALT ISLAND

MAN HEAD

SALT ISLAND BAY ANCHORAGE

FL EV 10 SEC

LEE BAY

DINGHY ANCHORAGE

WRECK OF "RHONE"

2ND HILL

SETTLEMENT

SALT

TURTLE BAY

COLOURED NEST

SALT ISLAND BLUFF

SOUND

SALT ISLAND

SALT ISLAND PASSAGE

Salt Island

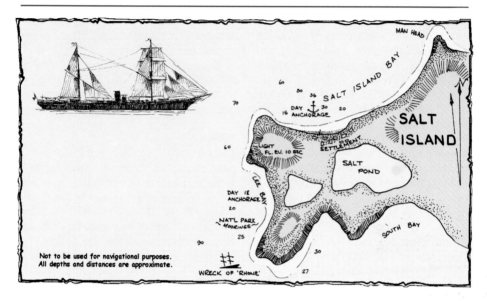

MAN HEAD

SALT ISLAND BAY

60
50   36   SALT ISLAND BAY
70
DAY   30   20
IS ANCHORAGE

60

SALT
ISLAND

LIGHT
FL. EV. 10 SEC

SETTLEMENT

SALT
POND

LEE BAY

DAY 18
ANCHORAGE
20

NAT'L PARK
MOORINGS
90   25

SOUTH BAY

30

Not to be used for navigational purposes.
All depths and distances are approximate.

WRECK OF 'RHONE'   27

Named for the island's three evaporation ponds, Salt Island was once an important source of salt for the ships of Her Majesty, the Queen. The island and its salt ponds, although belonging to the Crown, are operated by the local populace. Each year at the start of the harvest, one bag of salt is accepted by the Governor as annual rent. In 1845, a barrel was quoted at one shilling and, although inflation has taken its toll, salt is still sold to visitors. The settlement just off Salt Pond Bay, is deserving of a visit.

Local Salt Islanders will be pleased to show you around the salt ponds and explain how the harvesting is done.

Anchoring

Both of the Salt Island anchorages are affected by a surge and consequently should be considered day anchorages only.

Salt Pond Bay is clear of hazards, but the prudent skipper is advised to ensure that his anchor is well set before going ashore. Anchor in 10-20 feet of water.

Lee Bay is another alternative for those wishing to dive the

Rhone. Located on the west shore, Lee Bay is not very well protected. Moorings are available here for boats under 50 feet to pick up in order to dinghy over to the Rhone. Anchoring over the Rhone is strictly forbidden and is protected by the National Parks Trust. Constant anchoring by boats has destroyed the coral.

The National Parks Trust has installed moorings for the use of permit holders only, at the site of the Rhone.

It is suggested that you dinghy over from Lee Bay, drop off snorkelers and use the dinghy mooring line available.

Watch out for divers!

Cooper Island

As you sail between Salt and Cooper Islands, you will see a rock off the northeast point, marked by a green buoy with a red stripe. You can go to either side of the marker as there is 20 feet of water.

The principal anchorage on Cooper Island is Manchioneel Bay located on the northwest shore. When approaching the bay from the north, around Quart-O-Nancy Point, you will be on your ear one minute and becalmed the next. The point shelters the wind entirely, and we would recommend lowering sail and powering up to the anchorage.

Anchoring

There are several maintained moorings off of Cooper Island that are available for any vessel's use at the cost of $20.00 per night. You may pay ashore at the Beach Club.

If you are anchoring, the bottom is covered in patches of sea grass and, consequently, it is sometimes difficult to get the anchor set.

You can anchor almost the entire length of the beach in 10-25 feet of water, but it is advisable to minimize swinging room.

Ashore

There is a good, sandy beach fringed with palm trees with views of many of the islands to the west. Between the two main jetties is the Cooper Island Beach Club, managed by Steve Pardoe and Toby Holmes. The south jetty is for powerboats only, so dinghies should be tied to the north jetty when going ashore. The menu is varied and the setting unique. Both lunch and dinner are served daily. Reservations are recommended for dinner. Go ashore during the day, or call on VHF 16.

Island Wonders Gift Shop next to the jetty has local gift items for sale and is open from 9:30 to 5:30 daily. Underwater Safaris has an airfill station as well as a boutique filled with goodies. The hours are from 8:30 to 8:00pm daily. Underwater Safaris monitor VHF 16. They also run a boat to and from Road Town to Cooper Island and can be reached for a ride by phoning or on VHF 16.

Thirteen new beachfront efficiencies are available at very reasonable rates with great views of the islands and Sir Francis Drake Channel.

For some excellent snorkeling, take the dinghy to the south of Manchioneel Bay to Cistern Point. You can tie your dinghy off to the line attached to two buoys and snorkel around the rocks and reef.

Caution: Manchioneel Bay is named for the tree that grows there which produces a small, green apple. Don't eat the apples from the manchioneel tree — they are poisonous and will burn you from stem to stern.

Other Anchorages

If the sea conditions are light, there are two day anchorages just to the south of Manchioneel Bay: Carver Bay under Cistern Point; and Haulover Bay.

By tucking yourself in the southeast by the corner the surge will be minimal. The island of Ginger has no tenable anchorages.

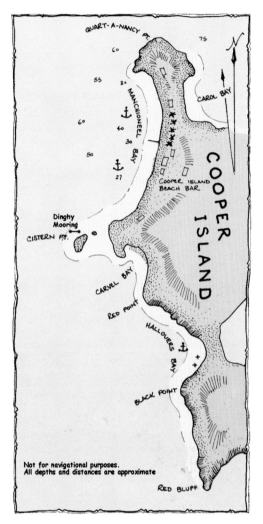

Not for navigational purposes.
All depths and distances are approximate

BRITISH VIRGIN ISLANDS

~VIRGIN GORDA~
(SOUTH)

SOUNDINGS IN FEET AT LOW WATER

SCALE IN NAUTICAL MILES

VIRGIN GORDA
panorama
British Virgin Islands

VIRGIN GORDA

The "Fat Virgin", as Columbus irreverently called it because of its resemblance from seaward to a fat woman lying on her back, was once the capital of the British Virgins with a population of 8,000 persons.

The island is approximately 10 miles long with high peaks at the north and central areas. All land over 1000 feet high on Virgin Gorda has been designated National Parks land to preserve its natural beauty.

Laurance Rockefeller built the Little Dix Bay Hotel, as well as the Virgin Gorda Yacht Harbour in St. Thomas Bay.

The Baths

When planning a trip around the island, it is essential to include the Baths. Located on the southwest tip of Virgin Gorda, the Baths are a most unusual formation of large granite boulders. Where the sea washes in between the huge rocks, large pools have been created, where shafts of light play upon the water, creating a dramatic effect. The beach adjacent to the Baths is white and sandy and the snorkeling excellent.

Navigation

When approaching from the Sir Francis Drake Channel, the first landmark will be the large rock formations. There are fine, white sandy beaches of varying sizes and the Baths are located at the second beach from the westernmost tip of Virgin Gorda. If there is a ground sea running, it is advisable to keep sailing into the Yacht Harbour and take a taxi to the Baths.

Anchoring

It is possible to anchor all along the coast, but the preferred spot for landing people ashore is directly out from the beach in 30-35 feet of water. The bottom is rock and coral, so check your anchor with a snorkel prior to going ashore, or preferably, to avoid damaging coral, pick up a mooring. If anchoring further north, be mindful of Burrows Rock, which extends 200 feet out from the small headland at the south end of Valley Trunk Bay.

Ashore

If there is any sea at all, landing a dinghy can prove tricky. Take ashore only those articles that you don't mind getting wet, and wrap cameras and valuables in plastic bags. The entrance to the Baths is unmarked but is at the southern end of the beach under the palm trees. Make your way in between the slot in the rocks and follow the trail. Do not leave valuables in your dinghy. There is excellent snorkeling around the point from the Baths south to Devil's Bay, but the beaches to the north are private. A fabulous trail leads inconspicuously between the Baths and Devil's Bay. Wear reef shoes — it can be slippery, but is well worth the challenge.

Colorful stalls on the beach sell souvenirs, crafts and t-shirts and it is also possible to get a cold, refreshing drink at the Poor Man's Bar. At the Top Of The Baths you can enjoy breakfast, lunch and dinner while enjoying the view of the

Baths and the channel to the west, or cool off in their fresh water pool. Meal service starts at 8:00am and dinner service stops at 10pm. Dinner reservations are recommended and they monitor VHF 16.

Spanish Town / Virgin Gorda Yacht Harbour

Once the capital of the B.V.I., Spanish Town is still the major settlement on the island. Although opinions vary, it is commonly thought that Spanish Town is so called for the number of Spanish settlers who came to mine the copper at Copper Mine Point early in the 16th century. The mines were still working until 1867, and it is estimated that some 10,000 tons of copper ore were exported.

The Virgin Gorda Yacht Harbour is located in the middle of Spanish Town (or the Valley as it is more commonly referred to) and is the hub of shopping and boating activity on the south end of the island. Misty Isle Yacht Charters makes its home in this marina complex.

Navigation

To enter the Yacht Harbour, you should familiarize yourself with the location of the reef that parallels the shoreline. Approach the harbor on a line with the prominent jetty in St. Thomas Bay. The first buoy will be on your port hand and will be green. Immediately to starboard, you will notice a red buoy. Leave it to starboard, as you would with the U.S. system of red right returning.

As you round the red buoy, you will turn approximately 90 degrees to starboard and pass between two more sets of buoys before entering the harbor. Once inside, you may dock at the fuel dock or pull into a slip and seek the dockmaster.

There is no anchoring in the Yacht Harbour.

When leaving the Yacht Harbour and St. Thomas Bay and heading north to Gorda Sound be sure to give Colison Point a wide berth, as the rocks extend well out from the land into the water.

Ashore

Customs and immigration services are available dockside from 8:30am to 4:30pm Monday through Friday and on Saturday from 8am to 12:30pm. Sundays

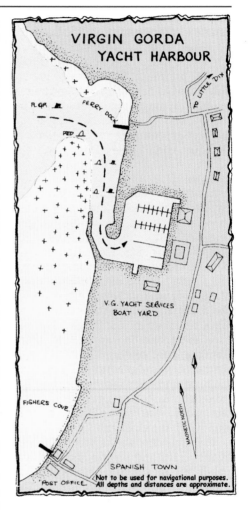

VIRGIN GORDA YACHT HARBOUR

V.G. YACHT SERVICES BOAT YARD

FISHERS COVE

MAGNETIC NORTH

SPANISH TOWN

POST OFFICE

Not to be used for navigational purposes. All depths and distances are approximate.

and holidays incur overtime fees.

The marina has dockage for 150 yachts up to 150 feet in length with water, fuel, ice, provisions, showers, and a marine chandlery. The maximum draft inside the harbor is 10 feet. Complementing the marina is a full service boat yard and dry storage facilities adjacent to the harbor, with a 70 ton Travel Lift. The facility has the capability to haul and store multihulls up to 40 feet with their submergible hydraulic trailer. The boatyard offers complete services including

awlgrip and osmosis treatment for boats. A commissary and the Spanish Town Cafe and Deli are conveniently alongside. You may call them on VHF 16.

The marina complex offers such facilities as a bank, drug store, Buck's Food Market with a complete range food and spirits, The Wine Cellar (including cheeses and baked goods), Thee Artistic Gallery and a few other shops. The Bath and Turtle Pub is open from 7am to 11 or 12pm daily where they serve breakfast lunch and dinner. On Wednesday and Sunday nights they have a live band to get everyone dancing.

For divers, Dive B.V.I. operates a full service dive shop offering daily tours as well as rendezvous dives from the yacht harbor. Power Boat Rentals have an array of boats to rent and Mahogany rents cars if you want to explore the island by land.

Little Dix Bay Hotel is a taxi ride away and those wishing to look around the grounds are welcome for drinks and luncheon. Reservations are required for dinner. Although jackets are not required, shorts are not allowed in the dining room after 6pm. Appropriate, casual attire is welcome.

The Olde Yard Inn is known for it's excellent cuisine and lovely garden. Their Sip and Dip Grill serves burgers and sandwiches at lunch from 11:30am to 3pm and dinner from 6:30pm daily. Dress is elegantly casual and reservations are requested. Monday, Friday and Saturday are entertainment nights.

Other restaurants in the area are the Crab Hole specializing in Creole dishes, Chez Bamboo specializing in bouillabaisse, and Fischers Cove where you can get breakfast, lunch and dinner from 7am to 10pm daily in a casual, friendly atmosphere. The Mine Shaft Cafe has an easygoing atmosphere and serves lunch and dinner from 11am to 11pm. Tuesday nights are steel band nights and Friday is ladies night with cheap drinks and live music.

Savannah Bay

During the summer months or when the ground seas are down, there is a very nice daytime anchorage in Savannah Bay. To enter the bay, just north of Blowing Point, you must have good light in order see the reefs. The entrance between the reef is at the southern end of the bay.

Watch for the small reef that extends from the headland on your starboard hand and work your way around the coral heads that comprise the center reef. Once inside, you can anchor in 15-25 feet of water and the snorkeling is excellent.

Giorgio's Table is a charming Italian restaurant located on the point between Pond and Tetor Bays. There is a jetty available for guests having lunch, dinner or drinks at the bar overlooking Sir Francis Drake Channel. They monitor VHF 16.

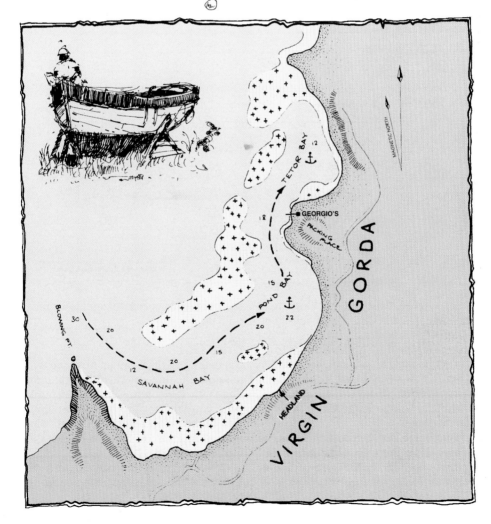

Long Bay

Long Bay is another day anchorage that is tenable only when there is no ground sea. Located just to the southeast of Mountain Point, this anchorage is easy to approach, and anchoring is on a sandy bottom in 15-25 feet of water.

The Dogs

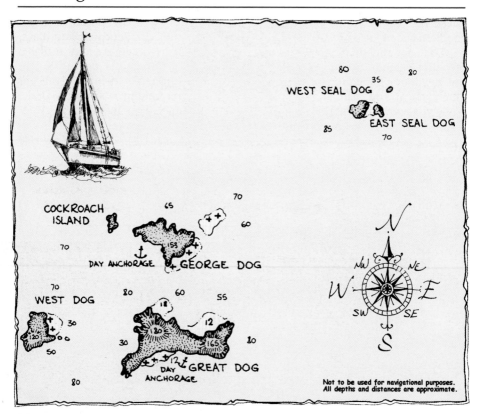

Not to be used for navigational purposes. All depths and distances are approximate.

Great, George, West and Seal Dogs lie to the west of Virgin Gorda, and have good water all around them. They are all in a protected area of the National Parks Trust. It is not possible to sail or power between West and East Seal Dogs. If there is not sea running there are two good daytime anchorages in the lee of Great Dog and George Dog.

On George Dog, the best anchorage is in the bay to the west of Kitchen Point. You will have to anchor in 25-35 feet of water and will probably be backwinded, so check your anchor carefully, or pick up a mooring.

Great Dog

Depending on the weather, there are two possible anchorages. The most common one is on the south side of the island. Here you will have to anchor in 20-30 feet of water on a rocky bottom. The second spot is off the beach on the northwest coast.

The snorkeling is excellent in both locations, but don't anchor here during ground seas.

LEVERICK BAY

Resort & Marina

- 10 slips and 36 moorings.
- 110 and 208 volt electricity.
- Fuel, Fresh water and ice.
- Freshwater showers and laundry facilities.
- Fresh water swimming pool and tennis.
- Pusser's restaurants, bar and Company store.
- Full service dive shop.
- Supermarket.
- Spa.
- Caribbean arts and crafts.
- Water sports instruction and equipment rental.

Photography by Dougal D. Thornton

Virgin Gorda Villa Rentals

- Air-conditioned guest rooms.
- Air-conditioned condominiums.
- Individually styled villas, many with pools at Leverick Bay and around the Island.
- All resort facilities available to villa guests.

For more information or to make reservations contact
1-(284) 495-7421
Fax: (284) 495-7367
e-mail: leverick@caribsurf.com

Visit us on the web at
www.VirginGordaBVI.com

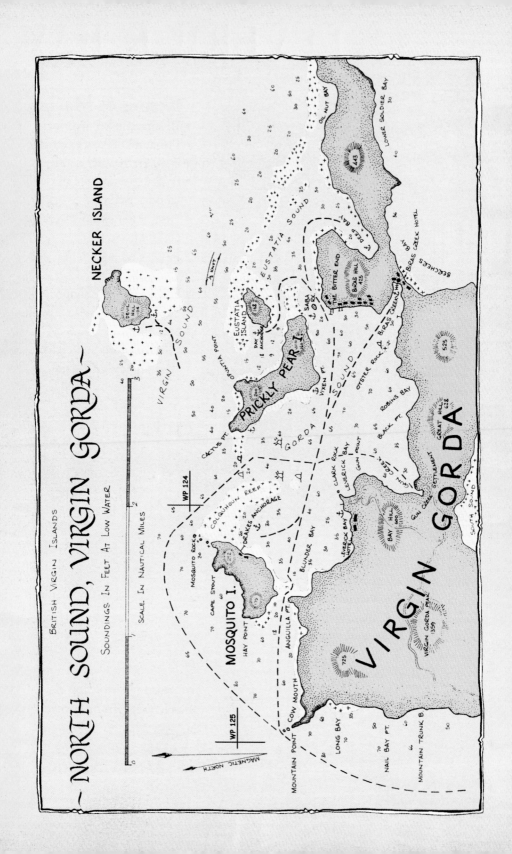

British Virgin Islands

~ NORTH SOUND, VIRGIN GORDA ~

Soundings In Feet At Low Water

Scale In Nautical Miles

NECKER ISLAND

VIRGIN SOUND

EUSTATIA SOUND

EUSTATIA ISLAND

DAY ANCHORAGE

SABA ROCK

THE BITTER END

BRAS HILL 415

DEEP BAY

BRAS CREEK HOTEL

BEECHES BAY

LOWER SOLDIER BAY

OIL NUT BAY

GORDA SOUND

PRICKLY PEAR I.

CACTUS PT.

OPUNTIA POINT

VIXEN PT.

OYSTER ROCK

BRAS CREEK

ROBINS BAY

BLACK PT.

GREAT HILL 628

525

COLQUHOUN REEF

DRAKES ANCHORAGE

MOSQUITO ROCKS

MOSQUITO I.

HAY POINT

BLUNDER BAY

CLARK ROCK

LEVERICK BAY

GUN POINT

LEVERICK BAY HOTEL

BAY HILL 600

GUN CREEK SETTLEMENT

SOUTH SOUND

WP 124

WP 125

ANGUILLA PT.

COW MOUTH

MOUNTAIN POINT

LONG BAY

NAIL BAY PT.

MOUNTAIN TRUNK B.

VIRGIN GORDA PEAK 1359

725

VIRGIN GORDA

MAGNETIC NORTH

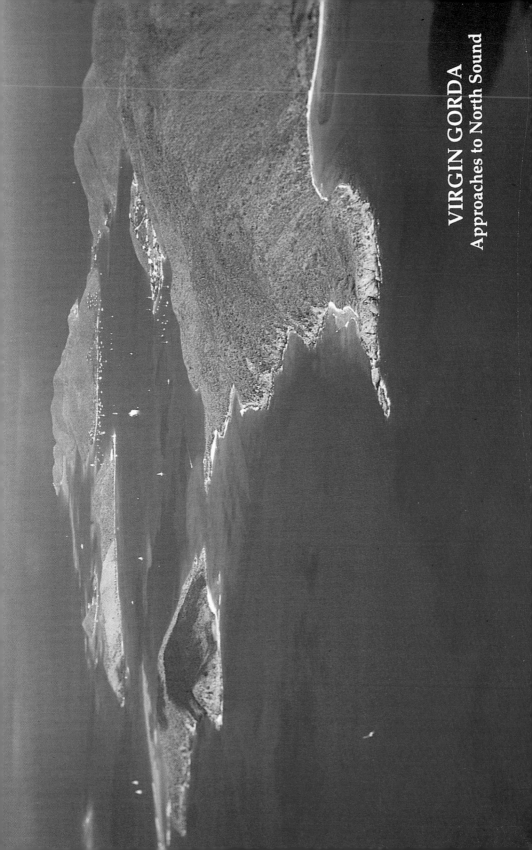

VIRGIN GORDA
Approaches to North Sound

North Sound

Located at the northern end of Virgin Gorda, North Sound or Gorda Sound as it is sometimes called, is a large bay protected all around by islands and reefs. It is an ideal place to spend several days exploring the reefs and relaxing. There are numerous restaurants and marina complexes here to suit all tastes.

Navigation
Northern Entrance Via
Colquhoun Reef
When making your approach to the Sound from the north, you will easily be able to recognize Mosquito Rock just to the north of the tip of Mosquito Island.

Leaving the rock well to starboard,

Saba Rock, the Bitter End and Biras Creek.

head for the green can buoy (Flashing green 4 seconds) that marks the port side of the channel when entering. This will keep you clear of both reefs. Leaving the green can to port, you will proceed past a red cone or nun (Flashing red 4 seconds) to starboard. Continue through the red and green buoys into the Sound.

If you are proceeding to Drakes Anchorage, there is another red buoy (Flashing red) marking the lower end of the reef. It is imperative that you leave it to starboard in order not to find yourself aground. Once past the buoy, you can proceed directly to the anchorage with clear water.

If you are heading for Bitter End or Biras Creek, continue into the Sound past the sandspit on Vixen Point and then head for the cottages on the hill that comprise the accommodations at the Bitter End.

There is one other navigational hazard in the Sound and that is Oyster Rock which is to the west of the Biras Creek anchorage. The rock is marked with a red cone buoy.

Anguilla Point Entrance

This entrance is tricky, but in fact can carry 6 feet; however, it is recommended that vessels of over 5 foot draft should use the northern approach, and *bareboat charters not use this entrance at all.* During ground seas and heavy swells, it is always advisable to use the northern passage.

Entrance from the west is recommended under power only. There is a reef extending from Hay Point on Mosquito Island, so make sure your course is laid a little south of east, or approximately 95 degrees magnetic, which should bring you in half way between Anguilla Point to starboard and Mosquito Island to port.

In order to stay in the deepest water, lay a course from the center of the cut to Gnat Point southeast until you clear the sandbar.

When leaving the Sound, there is a range that can be utilized. By placing the tip of Anguilla Point in the "Cows Mouth", a hollow in Mountain Point, follow it until clear of the point and shoal water to starboard and then head for Seal Dog Rocks.

Drake's Anchorage, Mosquito Island
Anchoring

Located on the east shore of Mosquito Island under Colquhoun Reef, Drakes Anchorage has long been one of the favorite North Sound stops. Anchor off the docks in 15-20 feet of water. The holding ground is good and the prevailing wind keeps the anchorage cool and bug free. Ten moorings installed and maintained by Moor Seacure are available for use. Payment may be made at the restaurant.

Ashore

Ashore, you will find an informal hotel and restaurant serving breakfast, lunch and a romantic five course dinner with a French flair. Dress is casually elegant. Call early on VHF 16 for reservations. Ice is available for yachtsmen. This is a private island with only 24 guests in 10 ocean front cottages and 2 deluxe villas. Facilities are reserved for the guests, however, you are very welcome at this superb restaurant.

There is excellent snorkeling on the reef west of Anguilla Point.

Leverick Bay
Anchoring

Several moorings are available to pick up or you may choose to stay in the marina for the evening. Check with the dockmaster ashore. If you are anchoring be sure to keep clear of the moorings.

Ashore

Located on the northern shore of Virgin Gorda, Leverick Bay is a great recreational center. The resort has restaurants, gift shops, Buck's Food Market, a women's salon, pool, beach, and a full service

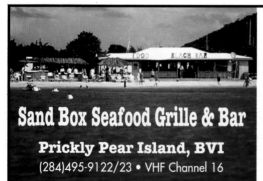

WELCOME
CRUISING YACHTSMEN

Visit The Bitter End Yacht Club
"A world class sailing resort!"

Join us for a meal...a day...overnight. We've everything for your enjoyment.

Excellent deep water anchorage. 70 moorings. Garbage pickup available. Deep draft dockage at our Quarterdeck Marina for yachts up to 150ft. 110 V hookups, or 208 V electricity. Showers on dock. Ice. Water. Gas.

Yachtsman's favorite rendezvous. Enjoy pina coladas on the Clubhouse Terrace or try our world renowned restaurants, the Clubhouse Steak and Seafood Grille or the English Carvery. Champagne breakfasts. Club lunches. Gourmet dinners. English Pub at the Emporium, draft beer and sandwiches. Evening entertainment with our own steel band, The Reflections, the reggae band, The Latitude Stars or mellow calypso music by Eldon John on guitar. Free TV and video movies nightly in the Sand Palace.

Shopping ashore. Browse and shop the Reeftique, "smartest little shop in the BVI" for gear, coverups and gifts. Visit Captain B's Trading Post for film, charts, snorkeling gear, Caribbean art. Stock your larder from the Emporium. Select from packaged liquor, wine, staples, fresh vegetables and fruit, eggs, ice cream, and our famous Entrees to go!

Activities! The Caribbean's Top Watersports Destination. Rent a Laser, Sunfish, Optimist sailing dinghies, Escape, Hobie Cat Wave, Rhodes 19, J-24, Boston Whaler, Freedom 30, Bradley 22, Mistral Sailboard, or join an excursion to one of the nearby islands. Book scuba with famed Kilbrides. Daily snorkeling trips. Excursions to Anegada. Freshwater pool with bar and luncheon service. Two beautiful beaches.

Luxury Accommodations. A full resort with 50 duplex cottages and fleet of charter boats. Ask for a room tour!

Come see us when island cruising. Register for a Bitter End Decal and pick up a copy of our latest North Soundings newspaper.

The Bitter End Yacht Club
North Sound, Virgin Gorda, BVI

Marina dockage or dinner reservations: 494-2746
or Standby VHF Channel 16

marina with fuel, ice, water, showers and a laundromat. A fuel fill up of 25 gallons will get you a free bottle of Pusser's Rum. Dive BVI operates a full service dive shop on the premises.

Pusser's Company Store and the elegant Terrace Restaurant with Victorian style bar offer a great view of North Sound and the surrounding island. Pusser's Leverick Bay is described as the "Gunkholing Headquarters" for North Sound. Use of the pool and showers for visiting yachtsmen are convenient and refreshing. Rental vehicles are available for exploring the island. The Beach Bar adjacent to the pool area serves pizza, hamburgers, ice cream and frozen drinks, as well as breakfast. Buck's Supermarket offers complete provisioning.

Weekends are fun at Leverick Bay with a band on Saturday and a beach barbecue, volleyball and steel band on Sunday.

Gun Creek

To the east Leverick Bay around Gnat Point, Gun Creek provides a protected anchorage. Ashore there is the local settlement of Creek Village. Should you need provisions check out the Gun Creek Convenience Center and Eatery. Scheduled for completion in February 1999 is a family style restaurant, a bed and breakfast inn, and a drop off laundromat as early as September of 1998. You may tie your dinghy up to the ferry dock and find the store about two hundred yards up the main road.

Vixen Point Anchoring

Several moorings are available off of the beach at Vixen Point on Prickly Pear Island. Register and pay for them ashore at the restaurant. This anchorage has fairly good holding on a sandy bottom, but be sure to avoid anchoring too close to the moorings.

Ashore

The Sand Box Seafood Bar & Grill serves lunch from 10:30am to 5pm daily and dinner from 6:30 to 11pm in a casual beach bar atmosphere. They also serve a mean margarita! The beach is good for swimming and you have a good view of the goings on in the Sound. The Sand Box monitors VHF 16.

Bitter End
Anchoring

Located on John O'Point, the Bitter End is a recreation center resort hotel, with restaurants and marina with overnight dockage, guest rooms and moorings. Visiting yachtsmen are welcome to pick up a mooring for $20.00

per night. Garbage pick up from your boat is available for a nominal fee.

If you are anchoring, please keep clear of the moorings (garbage collection may be available for anchored boats as well). There is room behind the moorings and to the northwest of Saba Rock.

There are two sets of buoys marking the approach for the North Sound Express ferry boat. Avoid anchoring near this channel to keep it clear for ferry traffic.

The Quarterdeck Marina has an 18 yacht capacity for yachts up to 100 feet in length and deep draft. Electricity, fuel, water, hot showers and ice are all available, as well as access to the resort facilities. The dinghy dock is located next to a mini shark cage. Watch your step!

Ashore

Visitors are welcome at the clubhouse restaurant for breakfast, lunch and dinner and may join the activities, windsurfing rentals and Anegada excursions, book dive trips with Kilbride's Sunchaser Scuba, and use the beach, bar, gift shop and Emporium bakery-deli with its English pub and complete package store. Telephones are located in the lobby for your use if necessary. Free launch service is available.

The Bitter End offers luxury shoreside accommodations, swimming pool, three beaches and boat rentals. Property tours can be arranged through the front desk.

Happy Hour is from 4-6pm. Dinner reservations are required and may be made via VHF channel 16. There is entertainment nightly from steel band, reggae, jazz to folk guitar. Nightly movies are shown for those with withdrawal from the movie and TV scene. The Bitter End is also headquarters of the Nick Trotter Sailing School. The resort is host to many and various sailing regattas and activities throughout the year.

The Moorings charter company has a service base at the Bitter End for Moorings charterers. They monitor VHF 12.

Saba Rock

Saba Rock is undergoing a major renovation and the planned opening will be during the 1998 winter season. The new resort will have two new bars, a restaurant, gift shop, dockage and hook ups for larger power boats, a long dinghy dock and overnight rooms will be available. Sailboats can anchor next to Prickly Pear Island facing Saba Rock or pick up a mooring.

Saba Rock will be participating and promoting sailing and water sport activities in North Sound. You may call them on VHF channel 16.

Biras Creek

A very protected anchorage fringed by mangroves, Biras Creek was developed by Norwegian interests who built a lovely resort complex at the head of the harbor. There are 11 moorings and capacity for 11 yachts up to 60 feet in length at the marina. Fuel, ice, water and showers are available.

Biras Creek Restaurant is noted for its fine cuisine and romantic atmosphere. The dress is elegantly casual, and men are requested to wear long trousers for dinner. Biras Creek monitors VHF 16.

On your starboard side as you enter Biras Creek are the buildings for the services for the hotel. This is the location of the Fat Virgin Cafe. You may tie up to the dinghy dock for lunch — the cafe is open from 10am to 6pm and serves sandwiches, burgers, chicken and roti. They will stay open for dinner if you make advance arrangements.

C12a, C13

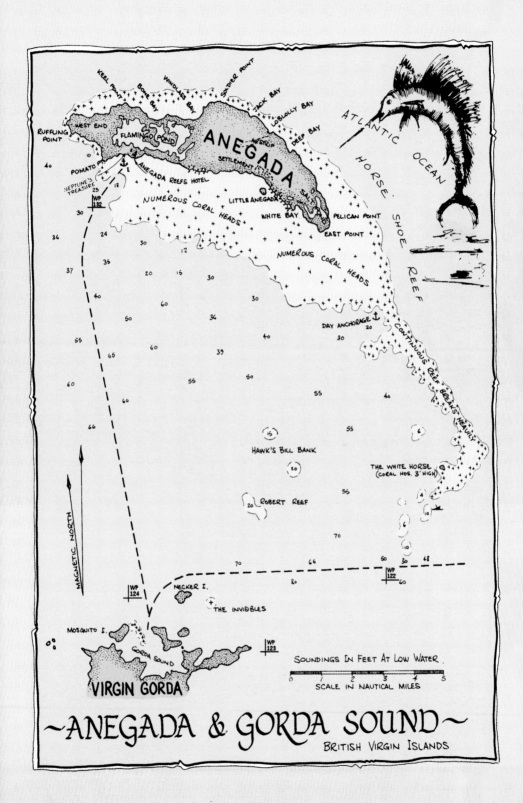

KEEL POINT BONE BAY WINDLAS BAY SOLDIER POINT PACK BAY LOBLOLLY BAY DEEP BAY

WEST END FLAMINGO POND ANEGADA MIDRIP SALT ATLANTIC OCEAN

RUFFLING POINT

40

POMATO PT. ANEGADA REEFS HOTEL SETTLEMENT

NEPTUNE'S TREASURE 25 18

WP 132

30

36 24 NUMEROUS CORAL HEADS LITTLE ANEGADA WHITE BAY PELICAN POINT

HORSE SHOE REEF

12 EAST POINT

37 38 30 NUMEROUS CORAL HEADS

40 20 15 30 30

50 60 36 30 DAY ANCHORAGE 20 30

55 65 40 39 40 CONTINUOUS REEF BREAKS HEAVILY

60 55 50 55 40

60 55 55

66 15 55 6

HAWK'S BILL BANK

10 THE WHITE HORSE (CORAL HDS. 3' HIGH)

20 ROBERT REEF 55 4

10 6

70 10

MAGNETIC NORTH

70 66 50 30 48

WP 124 80 WP 122 60

NECKER I.

THE INVISIBLES WP 123

MOSQUITO I.

GORDA SOUND

SOUNDINGS IN FEET AT LOW WATER.

VIRGIN GORDA

0 1 2 3 4 5

SCALE IN NAUTICAL MILES

~ANEGADA & GORDA SOUND~

BRITISH VIRGIN ISLANDS

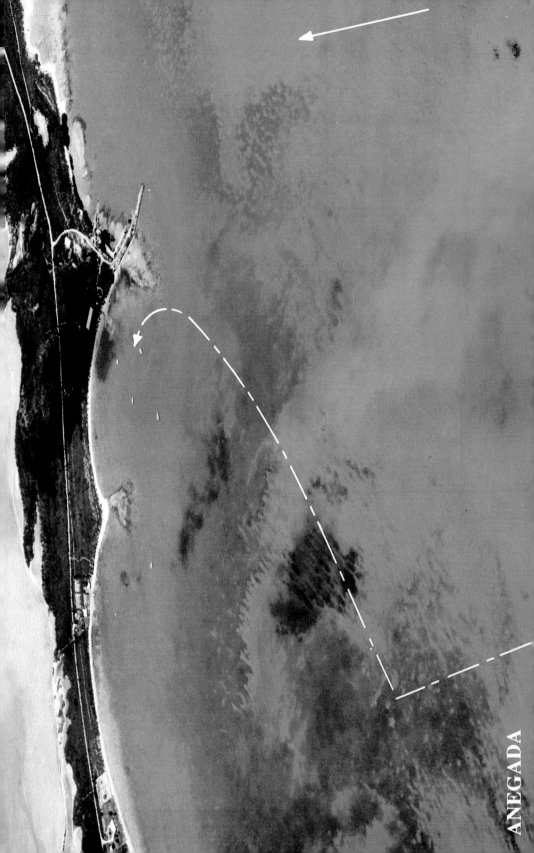

ANEGADA

ANEGADA, The Drowned Island

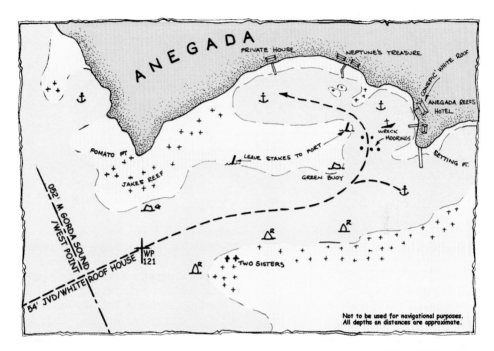

Not to be used for navigational purposes.
All depths an distances are approximate.

In contrast to the mountainous volcanic formation of the remainder of the Virgin Islands, Anegada is comprised of coral and limestone, and at its highest point is 28 feet above sea level. Created by the movement between the Atlantic and Caribbean plates, which meet to the northeast of the island, Anegada is 11 miles long and fringed with mile after mile of sandy beaches.

Horseshoe Reef, which extends 10 miles to the southeast, has claimed over 300 known wrecks, which provide excitement and adventure for scuba diving enthusiasts who descend on them to discover their secrets. The reef also provides a home for some of the largest fish in the area, including lobster and conch. The numerous coral heads and tricky currents that surround the island, along with the difficulty in identifying landmarks and subsequent reef areas, make it off limits to many charter companies.

Day excursions from Marina Cay, Leverick Bay and Peter Island locations

are also available aboard Dive BVI's high speed catamaran several times a week.

Navigation

Because of its profile and surrounding coral heads, Anegada should be approached only in good weather conditions and with the sun overhead in order to see the bottom. Leave North Sound between 8-9:30 am to arrive at the west end of Anegada with good light to see the reefs. Steer a course of 005 degrees magnetic which will take you from Mosquito Rock to Pomato Point. The 1-2 knot current will set you down to the west. Approaching the island, you will see coral patches, but if you are on course, they will have 10-20 feet of water over them. Owing to the low elevation of the island, the palm trees and pines will be sighted first. Do not turn off course until you have identified Pomato and Setting Points and located the red buoy marking the entry into Setting Point. When in line with the eastern tip of Jost Van Dyke head in

towards Anegada steering 050 degrees magnetic (no need to go further west).

There are five markers, 2 greens and 3 reds. As you approach the first red and green, go between them keeping the red to starboard and green to port maintaining 070 degrees. Follow the next two reds in keeping them to starboard. The last buoy is a green and this must be kept to port. Steer around this buoy and come into the anchorage on 015 degrees magnetic. If in doubt call Anegada Reef Hotel or Neptune's Treasure on VHF channel 16 for assistance.

Anchoring

Yachts drawing over 7 feet should anchor off the commercial dock which is in line with the green buoy in 10-15 feet of water. All others can make their way into the inner harbor, watching out for the coral heads that extend out from the small headland between the hotel and Neptune's Treasure and the coral off the dock (see chart). Drop the hook in 8-12 feet of water on a good, sandy bottom. If picking up a mooring buoy, the outer buoys are for boats of 7 foot draft and the inner ones for 6 feet and less. Please go into the hotel straight-away and pay the appropriate mooring fee. If anchoring do not foul the area for boats wishing to pick up moorings.

Ashore

Anegada has a lot to offer the visiting yachtsman. The hotel rents bicycles and vehicles and operates a taxi service which takes guests across the island to the great snorkeling beaches of Loblolly Bay. Flamingos, recently reintroduced to Anegada, may be seen on the salt ponds, and a nature trail has been opened around the Bones Bite area where you may spot some iguanas, also look for the wild orchids on the west end of the island.

If you want dinghy fuel, you can walk through the hotel gate to Kenneth's Gas Station. Ice is available at the Anegada Reef Hotel and there is also a fishing tackle shop which sells bait, lures, rods etc. for the enthusiastic fisherman, who wishes to fish the bonefishing flats. Don't miss going to the Soap Factory next to the hotel with all of it's exotic fragrances. There are several bars and restaurants in the village, known as the Settlement and on some of the beaches. However, most of the beaches are deserted and you need to take some cold drinks with you, some sunscreen and a t-shirt.

In the evening, a dinghy from Pam's Kitchen pulls into Setting Point anchorage selling delightfully fragrant fresh breads and cookies to the boats at anchor.

The Anegada Reef Hotel is owned and run by Lowell Wheatley and his wife Susan. There are 20 hotel units and an informal bar on the beach. Dinner is served by reservation, VHF 16. The food is excellent, and barbecued lobster is one of the house specialties. A 46-foot sportsfisherman is available for charter for those wishing to try some deep sea fishing. The hotel has a compressor for airfills, and tanks can also be rented.

Neptune's Treasure, a little farther along the beach, also serves breakfast from 8:30am, lunch from noon to 2:00 and dinner at 7pm. The restaurant specializes in lobster, conch and local grouper caught by the Soares family who own the restaurant. Please make your reservations by 4:00pm on VHF 16. Neptune's Treasure now has new guest rooms as well as a campground with tents and foam mattresses for rent. You may also buy souvenirs and local art at the gift shop while having a drink and enjoying the view. Public showers are convenient for those wanting a fresh water shower.

Pam's Kitchen and Bakery is open at Neptune's Treasure from 8:00am to 5:00pm with fragrant, freshly made muffins, cookies, pies, breads and she sells ice. At 5:30 she takes the goodies in the dinghy and sells to the yachts at anchor.

Whistling Pine, a new bar and restaurant is nestled amongst the pines to the west of Setting Point. They are open for lunch and dinner and monitor VHF 16.

Check for live music on Wednesday and Friday nights.

Also west of Setting Point is the Anegada Beach Club, open from 9am to 6pm daily unless dinner is served. If there are not enough people for dinner a taxi will drive you free of charge to the Pomato Point Restaurant. Jeep rentals and taxi service are available. No credit cards are accepted — cash only.

The Pomato Point Restaurant with a gift shop and museum are open from 9am daily. Dinner reservations are requested by 4:30pm. This restaurant overlooks an incredible beach and serves local dishes and seafood. Cash only accepted, they monitor VHF 16.

On Lower Cow Wreck Beach on the north shore you will find the Cow Wreck Beach Bar and Grill. They are open all hours and serve West Indian specialties and seafood. Further east to Loblolly Bay is the Big Bamboo, on the beach and open daily from 9am serving Anegada style

lunches and dinner on request only, with reservations in advance. The restaurant sports several hammocks in the trees where you can relax and contemplate the sea and sky. Flash of Beauty on the eastern end of Loblolly Bay serves drinks, sandwiches and seafood from 10am to 6pm. Reservations are requested for meals. All of the restaurants on the north shore only accept cash.

Pat's Pottery featuring hand-painted plates, mugs, t-shirts, ornaments and native dolls is open in the Settlement from 9am to 5pm Monday through Friday and from 9am to 2pm on Saturday. If you are there outside of those hours try knocking and if available they will open the shop for you.

For transportation call the Anegada Taxi on VHF 16 or at 495-0228 or DW Jeep Rentals who will pick you up and drop you off free of charge (495-8018). Daily, weekly or monthly rates for your convenience.

A youth examines the contents of a fish trap washed ashore on an Anegada beach.

The B.V.I.'s Offshore Financial Services Industry

By Julian Putley Author of *Sunfun Calypso*

The late Chief Minister, H. Lavity Stoutt, described the economy of the beautiful British Virgin Islands as having "twin pillars", meaning that the territory was financially dependent on tourism and offshore financial services. It is not surprising that tourism should be described in this manner. But many are surprised to learn that the other pillar is the offshore financial service sector for it is not immediately obvious and certainly not very outwardly visible. But in terms of government revenue earned, the twin pillars are on an almost equal footing.

It was the termination by the U.S.A. of its double taxation treaty with the B.V.I. in 1984 which led to the establishment of the International Business Company (IBC) as the foundation of the B.V.I.'s offshore financial industry. Now, around 40,000 IBC's are set up annually and government revenues from financial services this year should exceed $50 million. To date more than 210,000 IBC's have been incorporated in the B.V.I. and the jurisdiction has become the world's premier corporate domicile. The reason is plain to see: exemption from all local taxes and stamp duties, confidentiality and anonymity — no disclosure of directors' names or capital, flexibility and ease of operation. It costs $300.00 or $1000.00 depending on size to set up an IBC and the paperwork is processed quickly.

When Hong Kong returned to China last year about 35,000 IBC's were established in the B.V.I. These IBC's, in this case mostly trusts, were set up to escape Hong Kong estate duty and for the beneficiaries to avoid being taxed on worldwide income and assets when taking up

B.V.I. Government Building

Dougal Thornton

residency in other countries. Other IBC's may be set up to protect assets from lawsuits or to provide a means of doing business which may otherwise be denied. For example an IBC may be established by an import/export company to do business between two countries restricted by political sanctions. Capital gains taxes may be avoided too. An IBC that buys property overseas, develops the property or waits for it to increase in value and then sells it at a profit may benefit from tax advantages.

This may all sound as though the B.V.I. and its IBC's are specifically designed to cheat the taxman or other worthy beneficiaries of their rightful dues but this is clearly not the case. Just as a tax accountant will carefully evaluate and categorize a person's or company's earnings and expenses in a way that will be most beneficial to his client so an IBC and or trust can provide tax management and benefits for their principals. The B.V.I. owes its success as an offshore jurisdiction largely because of its integrity — regulation and legislation are constantly being passed in order to keep the destination clean. That and the fact that the territory is perceived as being politically stable under the British flag. The B.V.I. has managed to avoid any high profile money laundering schemes that have plagued other small offshore islands.

It seems to be the way of the world that sometimes a country's demise gives a boost to another, but such was the case with Panama in the mid 80's when the country was on the brink of disaster with

Dougal Thornton

Noriega as its leader. Wealthy but scared business people flocked to the newly formed IBC jurisdiction of the B.V.I. to take advantage of its services and protect their assets. Similarly Hong Kong residents have done likewise. These two countries along with Latin America appear to have provided the lion's share of the B.V.I.'s IBC business.

The B.V.I. is also a destination of choice for those well heeled individuals who wish to protect their assets for future generations by avoiding estate and death duties. Thousand of trusts are based in the island because it is a well run and secure jurisdiction with a solid base of professionals: law firms, trust company professionals, money managers and a government committed to a supportive role with the private sector.

Apart from the extremely successful IBC business, the B.V.I. is making a great effort to encourage insurance companies and mutual funds to base here. Already 1500 plus mutual funds controlling $55 billion are incorporated in the B.V.I. and the jurisdiction is courting new business with new flexibility and support services. In April 1996 the territory's first offshore bank opened its doors and a whole range of investment portfolios were offered. Previously the B.V.I. had been cautious in the realm of offshore banks because of the risks of money laundering and applications are rigorously scrutinised.

Now with such a solid foundation and extraordinary early success it seems that the B.V.I.'s finance industry can only go from strength to strength.

UNITED STATES VIRGIN ISLANDS

THE UNITED STATES VIRGIN ISLANDS

OFFICE OF THE GOVERNOR
GOVERNMENT HOUSE
Charlotte Amalie, V.I. 00802
340-774-0001

MESSAGE FROM THE GOVERNOR

On behalf of the people of the Virgin Islands, I extend a heartfelt welcome to you. It is my sincere hope that you will enjoy your visit to the United States Virgin Islands. May it be an unforgettable one.

Virgin Islanders are a sharing people. We know that we boast of breathtakingly beautiful crystal-clear blue waters and spectacular views to ensure a memorable visit. With our predictably warm and sunny climate, you are almost guaranteed good weather for sailing, parasailing, diving, snorkeling or just a relaxing and a healthy swim. Boating in our waters is sure to be a therapeutic experience.

Throughout the U.S. Virgin Islands, you are sure to find great duty-free bargains in jewelry, perfumes, electronics and liquor. And, you may retreat to many of our world-class resorts. This will complement your aquatic experience for a perfect land and sea get-away.

Once again, welcome and do enjoy your stay with us.

Roy L. Schneider, M.D.
Governor

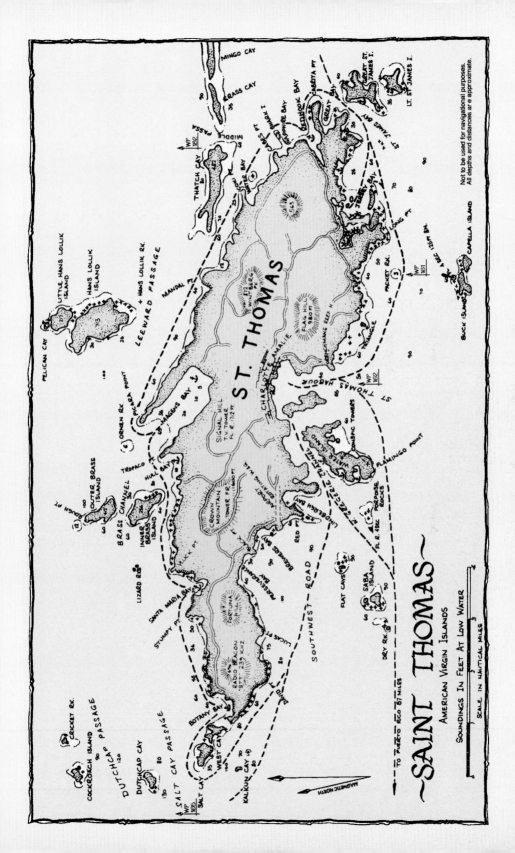

~SAINT THOMAS~

American Virgin Islands

Soundings In Feet At Low Water

SCALE IN NAUTICAL MILES

MAGNETIC NORTH

Not to be used for navigational purposes.
All depths and distances are approximate.

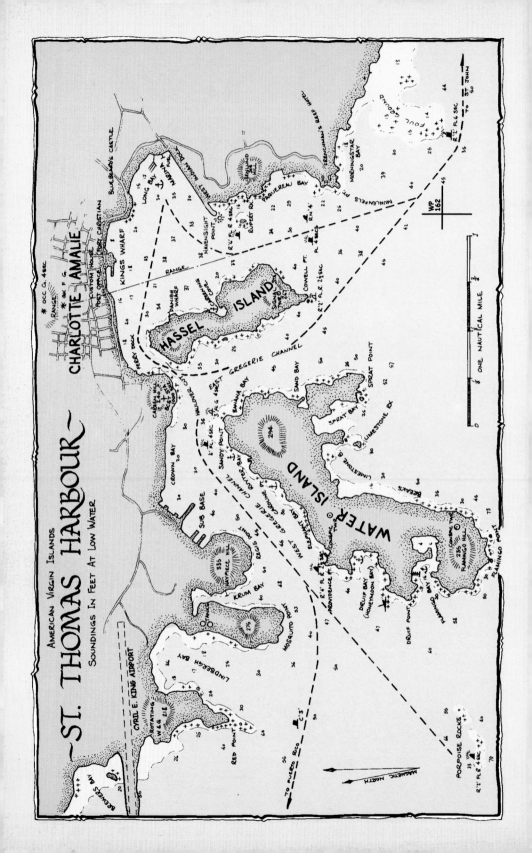

ST. THOMAS HARBOUR
U.S. Virgin Islands

Charlotte Amalie / St. Thomas Harbor

Named after a Danish Queen, Charlotte Amalie is the capital city of the U.S. Virgin Islands and a major seaport. Used extensively over the centuries as a haunt of pirates and privateers, St. Thomas was declared a free port by the Danes; thus enabling the sale of goods, livestock and ships acquired in honest trade or under the flag of piracy.

The town still has many of the original Danish buildings and mansions on the hillside overlooking the harbor. Picturesque alleys and stairways will lead you from large

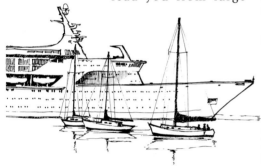

mansions to traditional West Indian houses surrounded by gardens.

Sheltered in all weather, St. Thomas Harbor tends to have a surge, especially when the wind moves around to the south, making it uncomfortable for small boats. Since it is a commercial harbor, swimming is not recommended.

Navigation

If you are making your approach from the east, you will pass the red nun buoy marking Packet Rock, which lies due north of Buck Island. It is best to stay well off the coast.

Another red nun "R2" marks the shoal ground that lies to the south east of the harbor entrance. You will also be able to see the Frenchman's Reef Hotel that sits atop Muhlenfels Point.

As you continue in, you will pick up two more red buoys marking Rupert Rocks. Leaving them to starboard, you can head directly for the anchorage.

Once inside the harbor, you will note several buoys off the West Indian dock. These designate the turning area for the many cruise ships that come and go on a daily basis and the anchorage lies to northeast of them.

Anchoring

The traditional anchorage for yachts is off the Safehaven Marina and Hotel complex, now under construction. Take care not to foul any of the private moorings that have been laid down by the charter yachts operating out of the harbor. If you wish to tie up to the dock, contact the dockmaster via VHF or pull up to the fuel dock for slip assignment.

It is not recommended to tie up to the quay in Charlotte Amalie as the surge is both dangerous and uncomfortable.

Ashore/Safe Haven Marina (formerly Yachthaven) and Surrounding District

Customs clearance can be carried out wharfside at the ferry dock at the west end of the harbor; the hours are from 8am to noon and 1pm to 5pm Monday through Saturday with no fees for clearance. Sundays and holidays they are open from 10am to 6pm and carry an overtime fee of a maximum of $25.00 per boat. This is the only customs and immigration facility on St. Thomas for clearance. Cruisers planning to stay on the east end of St. Thomas may find it easier to clear in at Cruz Bay, St. John. They do not monitor the VHF radio.

There is a dress code, you must wear a shirt and shoes, not just a bathing suit. U.S. Virgin Island Customs and Immigration law requires all people on board to accompany the skipper while clearing. Non U.S. citizens arriving by private or chartered boat must have a visa in order to clear U.S. immigration. U.S. citizens must have proof of citizenship: a passport, voters registration, or birth certificate plus a photo I.D. to check in to the U.S.V.I. from the British Virgin Islands. For questions call immigration at 340-774-4279.

Yacht Haven Marina was sold in February of 1998 and became known as Safe Haven Marina. The old Ramada Hotel which was damaged during hurricane Marilyn will be torn down and there are plans to build a large resort and condominium complex with restaurants and shopping. The land based tenants will have to relocate during the construction. There are plans to add an additional 500 slips to the marina. It is uncertain whether the docks themselves will be closed down during the rebuild.

The marina monitors VHF 16 and the office is open from 8am to 5pm, 7 days a week. There are presently 130 slips up to depths of 30 feet and they can

C16, C16a

accommodate lengths of up to 300 feet. The marina offers ice, showers, electricity, water and dinghy dockage. When the new facility is complete they will also include telephone and television service along with other amenities.

At present Wok on Water is the only restaurant currently open on the property. Island Marine Supply, Reefco and

Underwater Safaris are located at the marina. Island Marine Supply is open from 8am to 5pm Monday through Friday and from 8 to 11am on Saturday. Reefco is a marine refrigeration and air conditioning business. They also work on reverse osmosis and desalination systems, electric motors and pumps. They are open from 8am to 5pm Monday through Friday and monitor VHF 16. Underwater Safaris is a dive shop open from Monday through Saturday from 8am to 5pm. They monitor VHF 7.

Nearby in Vitraco Park is Lighthouse Marine with marine hardware and rigging for sale as well as repairing and servicing Honda engines and parts.

A cable car near Safe Haven will carry you to the top of Flag Hill to Paradise Point presenting incredible vistas of Charlotte Amalie and the harbor. You can get a variety of tropical drinks and food as you gaze out on this spectacular view.

Charlotte Amalie

Main Street, or Dronningens Gade (which means Queen Street) with its Danish buildings and stone alleys is laced with shops and restaurants. Known as a free port, St. Thomas bustles with shoppers from the cruise ships, and visitors from all parts of the Caribbean and many other parts of the world.

U.S. citizens are allowed a $1200 duty free exemption on imports purchased on imports purchased in the U.S.V.I. Excellent values can be found on such luxury items as perfumes, camera gear, liquor, jewelry and other treasures.

Many attractive gift shops offering attractive prices line Main Street. Be sure to stop in at the Leather Shop, A.H. Riise's, Cardow Jewelers, Royal Caribbean, Little Switzerland, and Colombian Emeralds, all in the Main Street area.

Charlotte Amalie has many historical buildings steeped in a myriad of cultures. A tour of the town will take you through

many fascinating labyrinths of old stone buildings and wooden houses.

The Hospitality Lounge on Tolbod Gade, one building up from the waterfront, is a good place to rest your feet and get your bearings. A checkroom for parcels is provided, along with a hostess or host from 9am to 5pm, Monday through Saturday. The Tourist Board of the Virgin Islands maintains an office in that same area near the waterfront across from Emancipation Park, as well as another office at the West Indian Company Dock.

Emancipation Park named for the freed slaves, borders the vendors market on the seaside of the park. You can easily find it by looking for the rainbow of umbrellas with vendors selling local handicrafts and assorted other mementos. Next to the park is Fort Christian, now a museum, it is the oldest building in St. Thomas having been built in the 1600's.

Market Square, just west of the busy shopping district of Main Street, was a slave market in earlier days, and later became a market for local farmers. Note the wrought iron roof, which came from

a European railway station at the turn of the century.

The second oldest synagogue in the United States is located on Crystal Gade. It is open from 9am to 4pm, Monday through Friday, and 8:30am to 11:30am on Saturday. The sand floors in the synagogue are characteristic of Sephardic Carib Synagogues.

On Norre Gade stands the Frederick Lutheran Church, the official church of the Danish Virgin islands. It was rebuilt in 1826 after a fire. You may visit the church Monday through Saturday from 8am to 5pm and on Sunday from 8am to noon.

Above Main Street is the Governor's House and other government buildings, painted with traditional bright red roofs to be easily spotted from sea. This lovely building has housed both the governor's residence as well as his offices. The spacious second floor reception room can be viewed by appointment.

Bluebeard's Castle tower guarded the harbor and the Danish settlers, with the help of Fort Christian and Blackbeard's. The hotel and grounds command an excellent view of the harbor.

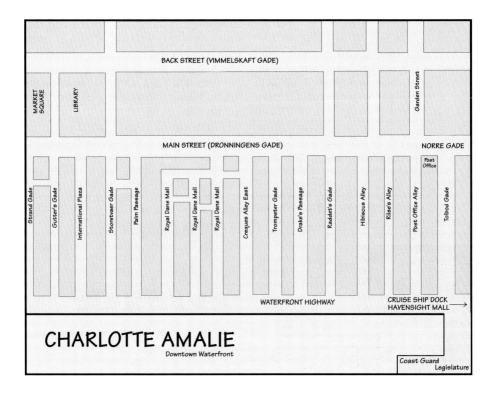

BACK STREET (VIMMELSKAFT GADE)

MARKET SQUARE

LIBRARY

Garden Street

MAIN STREET (DRONNINGENS GADE)

NORRE GADE

Strand Gade
Gutter's Gade
International Plaza
Storetvaer Gade
Palm Passage
Royal Dane Mall
Royal Dane Mall
Royal Dane Mall
Creques Alley East
Trompeter Gade
Drake's Passage
Raddet's Gade
Hibiscus Alley
Riise's Alley
Post Office Alley
Tolbod Gade

Post Office

WATERFRONT HIGHWAY

CRUISE SHIP DOCK
HAVENSIGHT MALL →

CHARLOTTE AMALIE
Downtown Waterfront

Coast Guard
Legislature

Beaches

Charlotte Amalie offers a central location from which to either rent a car, join a tour or hire a taxi to tour the island. Remember if you will be renting a car to drive on the left hand side of the road.

There are many beautiful beaches that should be visited, some with restaurants and dressing rooms. Magen's Bay Beach is located on the north side of the island in the curve of a sparkling bay. Small sailboats and snorkeling gear can be rented, changing rooms and showers are available. There is a nominal charge for admission. Hull Bay Beach, also on the north shore, offers some wave action for surfing and a snack bar.

Bordeaux and Stumpy beaches are on the western end of the north shore, but are accessible only by a rough road, and then a long walk.

Brewers Beach is near the University of the Virgin Islands. Lindbergh Bay is near the airport and three hotels.

Morningstar Beach, next to Frenchman's Reef Hotel is close to Charlotte Amalie, and offers dressing rooms and a restaurant.

Secret Harbour is a great beach for windsurfing, as is Sapphire Beach Resort on the eastern end of the island. Sapphire Beach Resort provides rentals of beach chairs, rafts, snorkel gear, sunfish, and jet skis. A restaurant is convenient and there is live music on Sunday afternoons.

Coki Beach on the northeastern part of the island has rentals of snorkel gear, floats and chairs and a small snack bar. You can also take time to visit Coral World at Coki Point.

These are just some of the highlights of the sights to see in St. Thomas. Pick up one of the tourist publications such as *St. Thomas this Week* or *Virgin Islands Playground* or pay a visit to the Tourist Board of the Virgin Islands for more details of what to see and where to go.

Crown Bay

Located immediately west of the Charlotte Amalie Harbor and north of Water Island is the Crown Bay Marina. Enter via West Gregerie Channel or East Gregerie Channel; both channels are well marked. Avoid the reef (which is well marked by a lighted tower) extending northward from Water Island.

While in Gregerie Channel, approach Crown Bay Marina by leaving the cruise ship dolphin piling to port. The entrance to Crown Bay Marina is immediately north of the northern most cruise ship dock.

You will find ample maneuvering room inside the basin. The controlled depth is 20 feet.

Upon entering, the marina's 315 foot fuel dock with high volume pumps lies hard to starboard. Water, diesel and gasoline are available.

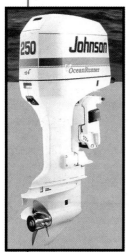

C16, C16a

Situated on 4-1/2 acres of landscaped grounds, the facilities at Crown Bay Marina are exceptional. There are 96 slips available ranging from 25 to 200 feet, all with dockside water, power, phone and cable TV hook ups. The marina offers daily, weekly, monthly and annual rates. Security is provided 24 hours a day.

Dockside retail shops, include Tickles Restaurant and Bar, with casual atmosphere is open daily until 10pm with the bar staying open for late night drinks. Gourmet Galley provides provisioning and sells ice, Marine Warehouse is a chandlery and also fills propane tanks. Sea Trade Dive Shop can take care of your diving needs. Swash It Laundry will take care of those dirty, salty clothes and sheets. St. Thomas Communications is an excellent place to go for essentials like phones, fax, secretarial and mail services as well as crew placement and car rentals. Crown Bay Maritime repair diesel engines and outboards. Monica's Salon and Bodyworks (massage therapy) offer amenities for those missing the finer things of shoreside life. Cellular One, BC

Travel, and the Atlantis Submarine maintain space at Crown Bay.

Also located in the harbor is The Think Tank the retail outlet for the Virgin Island America's Cup Challenge. Team Caribbean America's Cup Challenge docks their IACC training yacht, the former Stars and Stripes '92 at Crown Bay Marina.

A variety of support services are located within minutes away, as well as several beachfront hotels and guest houses. Bayside Canvas is located by Radio One and monitors VHF 16. Bayside Canvas does custom marine (and home) canvas and upholstery work. Island Marine has a store near Crown Bay with a large inventory of marine items in stock. The Crown Bay Marina complex is located about 5 minutes from the airport. Crown Bay Marina can be reached on VHF 16 or by calling 340-774-2255.

Haulover Marine Yachting Center

On the western side of Crown Bay is the Haulover Marine Center and Shipyard, providing a complete repair facility including yacht repairs, painting, fiberglass work, electrical and carpentry shops, as well as a sail loft and rigging facility. The Marine Center consists of Offshore Marine, Banks Sail Loft, V.I. Power Systems, and Island Rigging & Hydraulics. They are open from 8am to 5pm, Monday through Friday and on Saturday as needed and they monitor VHF 16.

C16, C16a

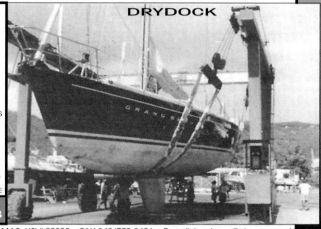
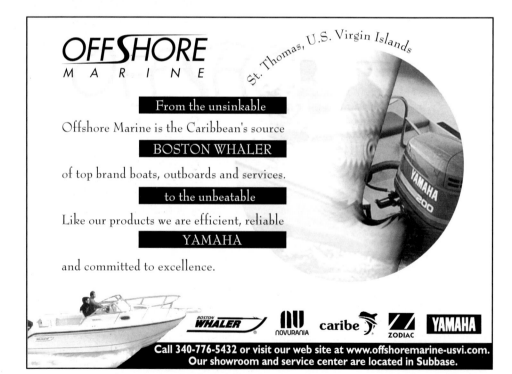
C16, C16a

Water Island

Water Island is among the largest private islands in the U.S. Virgin Islands. The island, once a military base, is owned by the U.S. Department of the Interior, and is leased to a private individual.

Water Island is two and one half miles long and one half mile wide. It can be reached via the ferry that leaves from the Sub Base on St. Thomas.

Water Island divides the east and west Gregerie channels. On the southern most part of the island is an old lookout tower on the top of Flamingo Hill.

Flamingo Bay

Flamingo Bay is a daytime anchorage in Water Island. The bay can develop a surge and therefore is not recommended for overnight anchorage.

Honeymoon Bay

Honeymoon Bay, or Druif Bay, slightly to the north of Flamingo Bay, is a favorite anchorage in normal weather. A beautiful white sand beach attracts swimmers.

The designated swimming area is well marked so you can avoid motoring through. Dinghies may be beached on either side. The anchorage has a sandy bottom in 15 to 20 feet of water. Good snorkeling can be found along the southern shore.

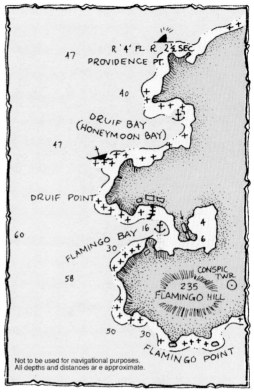

Not to be used for navigational purposes. All depths and distances ar e approximate.

Hassel Island

Hassel Island, just minutes from the Charlotte Amalie waterfront, is under the domain of the National Park Service. You can still see some 18th and 19th century fortifications, as well as some private homes and a shipyard.

The park has a limited trail system at this time, amongst the cactus and orchids. Green iguanas can be spotted from time to time. There is a small anchorage in the Careening Cove on the eastern side of the island, often full of local boats.

The Lagoon

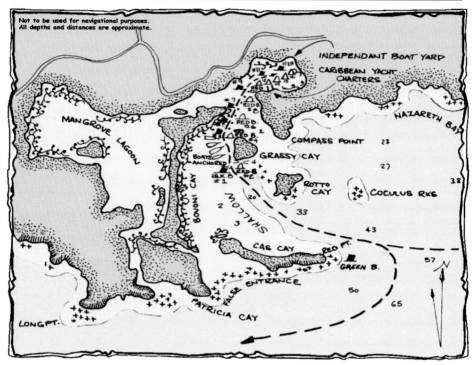

Not to be used for navigational purposes. All depths and distances are approximate.

Yachts drawing up to 7 feet have access to the Lagoon, the best hurricane shelter on the island of St. Thomas.

Navigation

When making your approach to the Lagoon, it is imperative that you not confuse it with the tricky "False Entrance" to the west. As its name implies, there appears to be a direct passage when approaching from the south or west, and boats at anchor can be seen at the head of the bay, but beware — there is a reef extending all the way across the false entrance.

A good rule of thumb would be to say: if you can't see a green can buoy on the port side of the channel, don't go in!

The channel into the Lagoon is well marked and provides no problems once you have identified Rotto Cay and its relationship to other landmarks. Leaving the green buoy on the tip of Cas Cay to port, and Coculus Rocks to starboard,

C15, C16

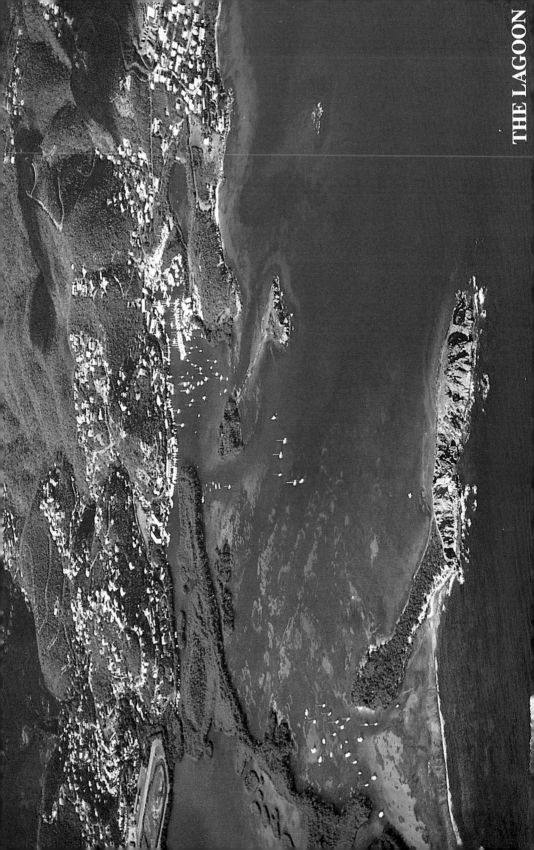

proceed to Grassy Cay. You will pick up a green buoy on your port hand and red nun marking the southern tip of Grassy Cay. Leave it to starboard. Take Grassy Cay to starboard by 25 feet, and round the red buoy on the northwest side. Leave the anchored boats to port and follow the channel. The channel is marked with red and green buoys and is easily followed leaving the red nuns to starboard when entering from the sea.

Ashore

Independent Boat Yard and Marina provides a full-service boat yard, complete with a 30 ton travel lift and 15 ton crane. The boat yard maintains a group of private contractors to accommodate boats requiring services, including: Bruce Merced (marine repair), Carpentry Plus, Electro Nautical, Mike Sheen's Fiberglass Shop, Island Rigging, Tim Peck Enterprises (awl grip work), and Mace of Arts, which does boat lettering.

Bottoms Up, a very casual bar and grill,

serves breakfast, lunch and dinner daily.

The marina includes 85 slips, with full services for both transients and live aboards. The depth is 7 feet. Daily hours are from 8am to 5pm.

Compass Point Marina across the Lagoon has 96 slips with electricity, water, showers, storage, marine services and dockage for transient and long term yachts. Hours are from 8am to 5pm daily except Sunday. The marina monitors VHF 16. The marina is headquarters for Caribbean Yacht Charters (CYC), St. Thomas Yacht Sales and Charters, Dave's Diesel Marine Services, Water Wizard (water makers), Chris Sawyer Dive Shop, Compass Canvas, Scott Schoeller Woodshop, Compass Point Boatworks (fiberglass repair), Tropical Refrigeration, Skip's Rigging, and Coki of St. Thomas (custom cushions and curtains). A pump out station is located at this marina.

For dining try Finn McCools, Raffles, and Dotties Front Porch.

East End Boat Park is a dry storage

ST. THOMAS AND ST. JOHN
PUBLIC MOORINGS INFORMATION

The Reef Ecology Foundation in an effort to further protect the coral reefs in St. Thomas and St. John have installed 45 public moorings for public use. The following are the guidelines and locations of these moorings:

- Moorings can be recognized by a vertical blue stripe around buoy.
- Moorings are for public use on a first come basis.
- Moorings are for day use only, with a three hour time limit.
- Use of the moorings is limited to vessels 60 feet or less.
- No fees will be charged for use of the moorings.
- Mooring use is at your own risk and therefore you must inspect the mooring to see that it is securely fastened to the mooring buoy and is

holding the vessel as intended. It is your responsibility for the safety of your own vessel.

- After picking up the mooring line, please run your bow line through the loop on the mooring line to tie off.
- Not to be used overnight or in storm situations.
- Moorings are maintained by the Reef Ecology Foundation for the preservation of the coral reefs.

Locations of Moorings:

Thatch Cay, Grass Cay, Congo Cay, Carvel Rock, Great St. James, Little St. James, Cow and Calf, Capella Island, Flat Cay, and Saba Island. For more details call the Reef Ecology Foundation at 340-775-0097.

and cruising guides of the Caribbean for sale.

Fish Hawk Marina in the Lagoon has 4 slips with up to 6 foot depths. They are open from 7am to 5pm daily. Tropical Marina maintains 18 slips with 6-1/2 foot depth. Ice, water and electricity are available. They sell and service Mercury marine products, do boat repairs, lift up to 40 feet, and have storage for boats up to 40 feet.

The Little Porch Bar and Restaurant is a casual restaurant located here serving lunch and dinner.

Saga Haven Marina has 36 shallow slips for long term dockage. There are no slips for live aboards. The two main power boat charter companies are based in Saga Haven; VIP Yachts, and Trawlers in Paradise as well as Island Trader. Wrapped and Ready sell ready to heat and eat meals. This is a convenient location with a secure parking garage and shops.

boat business in the Lagoon. They are open from 9am to 5pm daily. Also, located here is Caribbean Divers for dive gear rental, sales, and service. They are open daily from 9am to 5pm. Howe Marine Surveys have an office here open Monday through Friday from 8:30am-5:30pm. Caribbean Inflatables not only sell and repair inflatables and liferafts, but have an extensive collection of charts

Nazareth Bay (Secret Harbor)

From Christmas Cove, head towards the entrance to the Lagoon. Look for the white buildings of Secret Harbour Beach Hotel on the right.

The east side of the bay is full of coral heads, so head to the west side and anchor in about 20 feet of water. Do not use the moorings as they are private.

Do not attempt to bring your boat in to the dock as it is extremely shallow. You may tie your dinghy up to the hotel

dock. The dock to the right of the hotel dock is private.

Ashore

The Blue Moon Cafe and Aqua Action Dive Center are located on the property of the Secret Harbour Beach Hotel. The restaurant, with a stunning view of the sea, is open daily and serves breakfast, lunch and dinner with reservations.

Christmas Cove / Great St. James

A well protected, all weather anchorage, Christmas Cove is a first and last night stop for may of the charter boats operating out of St. Thomas.

Navigation
Making your approach to Christmas Cove, you will notice it is divided by Fish Cay. There is a reef extending from the Cay northeast to the shoreline of St. James.

Current Cut
Approaching Christmas Cove and the south shore of St. James from the north you will have to negotiate Current Cut. Current Rock sits astride the channel and is marked with a light. The eastern most channel is recommended, although the other can carry 8 feet.

As the name implies, there can be a strong current of up to 4 knots running in either direction depending upon the tide. If approaching from the west, start your engine in advance, as the island of Great St. James tends to blanket the wind. The Cow and Calf, a group of rocks awash to the southwest of Current Cut, are easy to see.

Anchoring
Anchor on either side of Fish Cay in 15 feet of water. Do not anchor too far out as the wind tends to become erratic. Do not pass between Fish Cay and the shore. If anchoring to the north of Current Cut, ensure that you are anchored close enough to the shore in order to be out of the current flow.

Ashore
There is good snorkeling toward the southern tip of the island. When the weather is calm, take the dinghy and explore the waters and reefs around the south end of St James Island

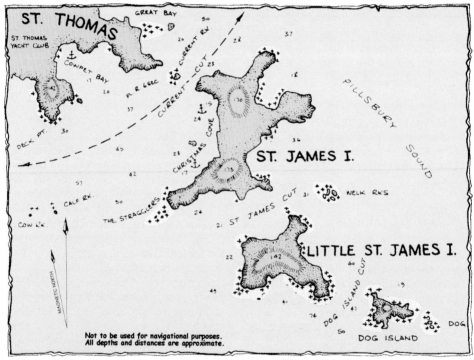

Not to be used for navigational purposes.
All depths and distances are approximate.

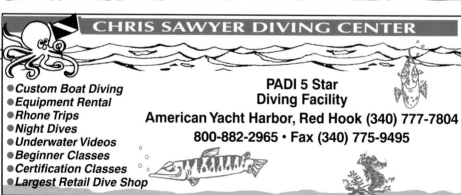
C15, C16

Red Hook

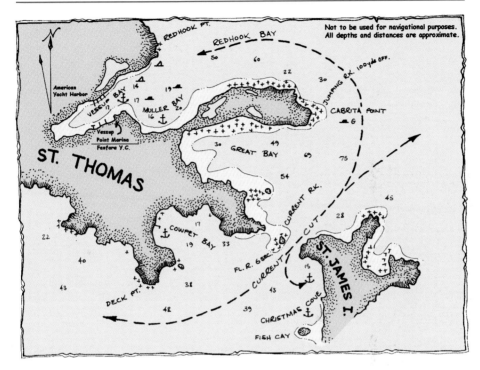

Just to the north of Cabrita Point on the eastern end of St. Thomas, Red Hook is a busy harbor with ferries departing for Cruz Bay, St. John on the hour. American Yacht Harbor, on the north side of the bay and Vessup Point Marina in the south side, provide yachtsmen with all services. Because of its exposure to the east, Red Hook is often a choppy anchorage.

Navigation
Once around Cabrita Point, favor the northern side of the bay where the water is deepest. Keep an eye out for ferry traffic and stay out of its way. There is a marked channel into Vessup Bay.

Anchoring
As there are numerous private moorings and a considerable amount of ferry, and other traffic, it is recommended Muller Bay on the southern side of Red Hook be used for anchoring. Stay clear of the channel and ferry dock and don't go too deep into the bay, as it shoals off rapidly past the last set of docks.

Care should be taken when laying an anchor not to foul a vacant mooring.

Ashore
American Yacht Harbor has all the basic yacht services including dockage, ice, water, fuel, electricity and showers. There are 98 slips in depths up to 10 feet. The marina complex includes a shopping village, and marine related businesses such as The Charterboat Center, All Island Machine (metal works), Chris Sawyer Dive Shop, Associated Marine Surveyors, and Neptune Fishing Supplies. If you want to explore the island you can get a car from Tri-Island Rent a Car located in Red Hook. Across the street is Red

Jim Scheiner

Red Hook

Hook Plaza with a grocery store, mail services, and two restaurants and bars. Marina Market is a block away and is a very well stocked market with an excellent selection of wines and champagne, meats and seafood. The Color of Joy sells original art and crafts by local artisans including jewelry, oil paintings, batiks and ceramics. You will certainly find something you cannot live without.

For those nights and days ashore try the Deli open 7 days a week from 6am to 6pm. MacKenzies Harborview for steak and seafood serves dinner from 5pm to 11pm. Gunther's Spot is a bar with a view of the harbor on the top floor of American Yacht Harbor and is open daily from 4pm until. It's a good way to end a day of duty free shopping, or grab a cool one while you wait for the ferry to St. John or Tortola. Cafe Wahoo at the Piccola Marina is open for dinner at 6pm next to the ferry dock right on the harbor.

American Yacht Harbor is home to

C15, C16

Island Yachts and Nauti Nymphs power boat rentals as well as numerous day charter and fishing charter vessels.

On the southern side of the harbor is the Vessup Point Marina. The marina, home to and managed by Fanfare Yacht Charters' fleet, has dockage for yachts up to 120 feet with drafts up to 15 feet. The marina provides electricity, water, and ice. Food, drink, and live entertainment are provided by Latitude 18 Restaurant and Bar.

Red Hook is a busy center for bareboat charters, crewed boat charters, fishing charters and many other marine oriented businesses. For more information and

directions, check ashore with the marinas. The ferry to St. John leaves from Red Hook every hour and the ferries from the British Virgin Islands stop here as well. Rental cars and taxis are readily available.

Coki Point around the corner from Red Hook is the home of Coral World Marine Park. Situated on 4 beautifully landscaped acres, this marine park offers incredible views of the ocean coral reef life 20 feet below the sea through a unique underwater observatory. Feedings for the fish and the sharks are scheduled during the day. The park is complete with gift shop, dive shop, ice cream shop and restaurant. It is well worth a visit.

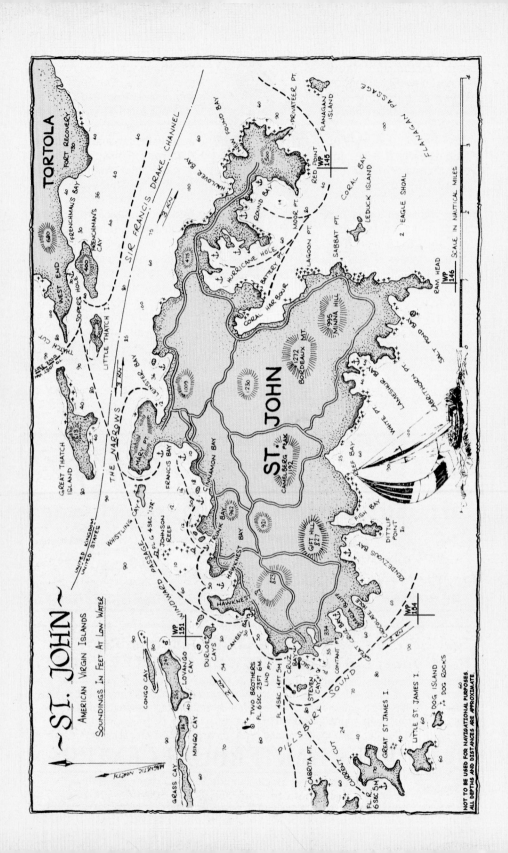

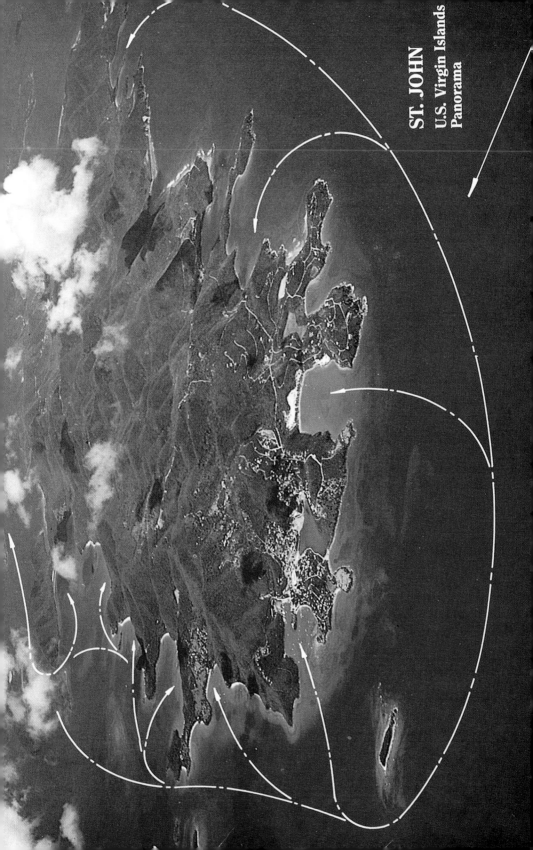

ST. JOHN

U.S. Virgin Islands
Panorama

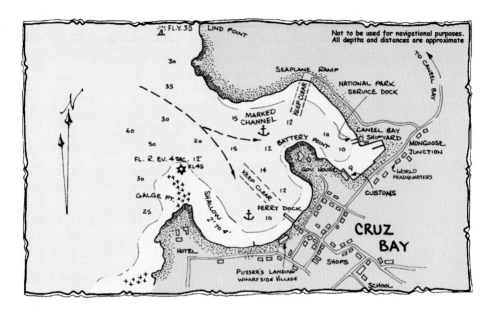

St. John / Cruz Bay

Cruz Bay, a port of entry, is the main town on St. John and, without doubt, the best place to clear customs. Serviced by ferries to St. Thomas on an hourly basis, many charters elect to leave their vessels in Cruz Bay and take the ferry to Red Hook.

Cruz Bay offers the yachtsman all of the basic services, including banks, post office, grocery markets, etc. Often crowded, the anchorage, though protected, is not necessarily a good overnight stop, as the movement of the ferries tends to make it uncomfortable.

Navigation

Approaching Cruz Bay from the southwest or Great St. James, it is not recommended to go between Stephen Cay and St. John, as there are numerous coral heads. Leave Stephen Cay to starboard.

Two Brothers Rocks are always visible in the middle of Pillsbury Sound, and have good water all around.

Entering Cruz Bay, there is a reef extending out from Gallows Point, marked with a flashing marker. Stay well to the north of it, as it is in very shallow water.

A flashing buoy to the south of Lind

C14, C15

Point marks the port side of the channel.

There are two marked channels within the harbor, one servicing the ferry dock to starboard and one servicing the National Parks dock and customs to port.

Anchoring

Shoal water extends from the marker on the end of the reef about 50 to 60 feet toward the ferry dock, so be careful when anchoring. Be sure to avoid obstructing both channels or you will incur the wrath of the ferry boat captains. Do not tie up to the dock as it is reserved for commercial traffic. A public dinghy dock has been built on both sides at the base of the pier.

Tie up on the west side of the dock using a short scope so that the dinghy doesn't get caught under the dock. Dinghies are not permitted on the beach.

All moorings in Cruz Bay, Great Cruz Bay and Coral Bay are private and subject to stiff fines for unauthorized use.

Ashore

The customs house is on your right in the northern section of the bay known as the Creek. Vessels clearing into the U.S.V.I. may tie up to the dock or they may clear in by dinghy as the dock is often full. The depth at the dock is 9 feet. There is a dinghy dock pier off the ferry

dock for those anchored out in the bay who are coming ashore to clear customs. If coming ashore this way, turn left along the waterfront to the customs building.

Caneel Bay Shipyards, across from customs, is a full service facility offering repair services for fiberglass, sails, refrigeration, woodwork and storage, as well as ice, fuel and water.

Several shops and offices are located within the waterfront area. Jeep rentals are available and a tour of the islands is highly recommended. Try Spencer Jeep Rentals and visit some of the beautiful beaches St. John has to offer. Caribbean Connections offers mail and telephone answering services both in Cruz Bay and in Coral Bay. Islandia Real Estate can make your dream come true if you are ready to trade it all in and move to the islands. They are located on Centerline Road.

For medical emergencies dial 911. There are doctors and clinics in St. John.

To replenish the galley Starfish Market is open daily from 7:30am to 8:30pm and they do provide provisioning. Check out their wine room and the walk in humidor. Marina Market is open from 6:30am to 9pm Monday through Saturday and 8am to 8pm on Sunday. Jyma Groceries is also open daily.

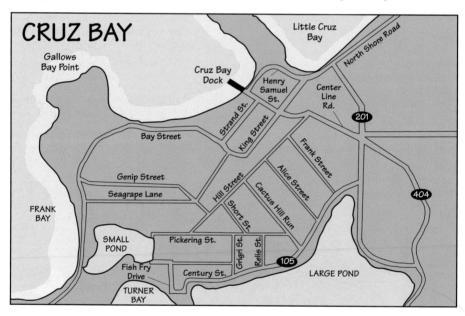

C14, C15

Cruz Bay

Steve Simonsen

St. John is an artistic community boasting painters, musicians, song writers and writers. For information on art galleries, restaurants, accommodation and happenings contact the Tourist Office near the post office, which is open on week days only. The last Saturday of every month is St. John Saturday with music, crafts, special food in the park, and other activities.

Scheduled taxi buses leave from Cruz Bay to many of St. John's exquisite beaches. You can also ride the new Dollar Buses. Round trip to anywhere on the island is $1.00 each way — a great bargain.

The National Park Service

One of the first stops you should make is to visit the National Park Service

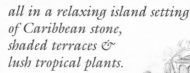

C14, C15

Visitor's Center next to Caneel Bay Shipyard. There are many new rules and regulations that you should be familiar with before spending time sailing and boating in the park. Besides the boating you should also familiarize yourself with the fishing and diving regulations. See our section on National Parks at the front of this book for many of these important regulations.

Almost two thirds of the island of St. John is protected as a National Park. Park rangers schedule hikes and tours throughout the park lands on both land and sea trails, identifying flora and fauna. Annaberg Sugar Mill can be toured on your own with the assistance of a pamphlet.

Any beach in the U.S.V.I. can be used by anyone according to U.S.V.I. law. However, you cannot gain access to that beach by crossing private property, or go beyond the beach onto private property. Some beaches therefore, are accessible only by sea.

Mongoose Junction

Just past the Park Service Center is a charming shopping arcade built of natural stone, known as Mongoose Junction. Visitors should stop by and browse in the quaint, interesting shops. You will find it hard not to part with some money here.

Mongoose Junction is the home of Proper Yachts, a charter company of both crewed and bareboats. The Mongoose Junction restaurant is open for breakfast, lunch and dinner, in an informal open air setting. Visit Mapes Monde, Island Fancy Gallery & Gifts, Bamboula, Bougainvillea Tropical Resortwear, Big Planet Adventure Outfitters, R & I Patton Goldsmithing, Caravan Gallery, The Best Of Both Worlds, Bajo El Sol Studio and Art Gallery, The Fabric Mill and Wicker, Wood & Shells, St. John Books & Cafe,

Holiday Homes of St. John and more. Try Morgan's Mango for a Caribbean culinary experience, just across from the National Park Dock.

At the base of the ferry dock you will find many wonderful shops and restaurants all within easy walking distance. There is tourist information available to guide you to all of the wonderful activities St. John has to offer. You can easily walk to the Fish Trap Restaurant for lunch and dinner located at the Raintree Inn.

Wharfside Village

Adjacent to the ferry dock is a wonderful collection of shops and restaurants overlooking the action in Cruz Bay. From clothing to fine jewelry it is a

great place to poke around if you've got some time and a bit of pocket money.

Pusser's St. John offers a picturesque view of the anchorage from their terrace restaurant, or upstairs in the Crow's Nest — a good place for a frosty beer or a Pusser's Painkiller. You can dinghy up from the anchorage; Pusser's is now three floors of fun.

The TV Sports Bar serves fresh shellfish and chowders daily, as well as the current sporting events on three color televisions. Pusser's Company Store in the Village features the company's own line of their nautical and tropical clothing, sport watches and chronometers, ship models, antiques of the sea, handmade luggage, unusual giftware and nautical accessories.

Stop by Shady Days for designer sunwear, Jewelers Warehouse, Isola (home accessories and gifts), American Paradise Real Estate, Moda, Verace for fantastic jewelry, Cruz Bay Clothing, Cruz

Bay Photo Center, Freebird Creations, Blue Carib Gems, Lowkey Watersports for dive and snorkel adventures and gear, Caribbean Villas & Resorts and Sting Ray Deli and Cafe for breakfast and lunch beachside...are all located in the Wharfside Village. Ellington's Restaurant is a little further along at Gallows Point with superb views of Pillsbury Sound. Cruz Bay and surrounding area has some wonderful restaurants and bars. Most of the details are in the restaurant section of the directory in the back of our book.

C14, C15

Caneel Bay

Traveling north from Cruz Bay, you will pass several beautiful white beaches, but they represent marginal anchorages because of the surge.

Caneel Bay is the home of the resort of the same name, which is built on the site of an 18th century sugar plantation. The property extends to the east side of the bay, to Turtle Bay, including the Durloe Cays.

Visiting yachtsmen are welcome in the bay, but are requested to keep noise to an acceptable level and to refrain from hanging laundry on the lifelines.

Anchoring

There is a ferry channel marked that services the small jetty in the middle of the bay. Stay well clear when anchoring. Stay outside of the line of buoys off the beach that designates the swimming area. There is an excellent holding in 15-30 feet of water on a sandy bottom.

Ashore

During the day visitors may go ashore, and are welcome to visit the gift shop and the Beach Terrace. Outside guests may make reservations for lunch and dinner at the Equator Restaurant. There may be times when the hotel must request that outside guests return at another time if the hotel management feels their visitor capacity has been reached. Uniformed hosts and hostesses are stationed throughout the complex to give directions and answer questions.

Eastbound

If you are sailing east, care should be taken negotiating the channel between the Durloe Cays and St. John. The wind can change around the headland and strong currents can create a choppy sea. On occasion, it is prudent to start the motor while negotiating this passage.

Hawknest Bay

The majority of this bay has been designated a swimming and snorkeling area by the National Park Service. There is a small anchorage to the northeast of the bay that is away from the posted area.

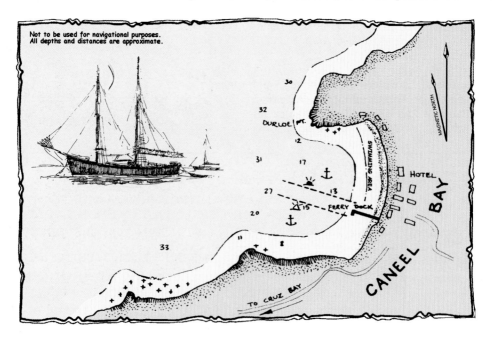

Not to be used for navigational purposes. All depths and distances are approximate.

ST. JOHN N.W. COAST

Johnson's Reef, Trunk Bay & Francis Bay

Trunk Bay / Johnson's Reef

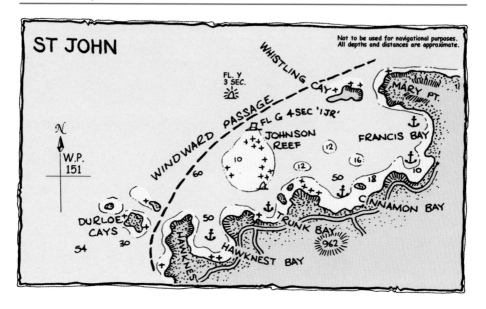

ST JOHN

Not to be used for navigational purposes.
All depths and distances are approximate.

WHISTLING CAY

FL. Y
3 SEC.

WINDWARD PASSAGE

FL G 4 SEC 'IJR'

MARY PT.

JOHNSON
REEF

FRANCIS BAY

(12)

N

W.P.
151

10

(12)

(16)

50

18

10

60

CINNAMON BAY

DURLOE
CAYS

54   30

50

HAWKNEST

TRUNK BAY

962

HAWKNEST BAY

One of the more spectacular beaches in the Virgin Islands, Trunk Bay is the site of an underwater snorkel trail for beginners. During the winter months or when a ground sea is running, it is not recommended as an overnight anchorage because of the bad swell.

Johnson's Reef

A large reef 1/2 mile to the north of Trunk Bay, Johnson's Reef, although well marked, continues to claim its share of wrecks due to negligence. The reef is marked at the northern end by a flashing yellow buoy (National Park Boundary Bouy) every three seconds and a lighted green buoy. At the southern extremity of the reef is a white buoy. The reef extends a considerable distance to the east and west of the buoys, and care should be taken to give it a wide berth.

Navigation

The approach to Trunk Bay is straight forward with the exception of Johnson's Reef, as previously noted. If approaching from the west, there is a small cay off the headland to watch for.

When leaving for the east, you can proceed between Trunk Cay and the white buoy marking the southern tip of Johnson's Reef, taking care to stay at least 200 yards off the shoreline.

When a ground sea is running, there will be considerable surface action and it is recommended to go around the outside, once again giving the reef a good offing.

Anchoring

There will be a line of marker buoys off the beach, which indicates the swimming area. Dinghies going ashore must use the channel marked with red and green buoys toward the western end of the beach.

During ground seas, the surf on the beach can make the landing of dinghies a difficult, if not a dangerous, task.

Ashore

The National Park Service maintains an underwater snorkel trail that extends around Trunk Cay. Picnic grounds and facilities are also maintained by the Park Service and snacks and cold drinks are available. There are also garbage facilities ashore.

Cinnamon Bay

The site of the National Park Campground, Cinnamon Bay provides a good daytime anchorage. Being exposed, it can be uncomfortable during ground seas. Stay outside the buoys when anchoring.

Accommodations include cottages, tents and bare sites. The watersports center offers snorkel gear and beach chairs for rent, as well as diving, sailing and windsurfing.

Maho Bay

Like Cinnamon Bay, Maho Bay is another nice day anchorage in calm weather. Maho Bay Camps welcomes boaters and has a well stocked store, as well as showers. Camping accommodations include canvas covered cottages hidden on a hillside in the National Park. A restaurant is open for breakfast and dinner. Dinghy in from Maho Bay or Francis Bay.

Francis Bay

Located on the northern shore of St. John, Francis Bay is the large bay extending to the southeast of Whistling Cay. All vessels over 125 feet in length must anchor in Francis Bay.

The National Park Service limits the length of time anchoring in Francis Bay to two weeks.

Navigation

If you are making your approach from the west, you will be rounding Johnson's Reef. Favor the northern end leaving the large green buoy to starboard. There is also a channel between Trunk Cay, and the white buoy (leave to port).

If you are approaching from the north, there is plenty of water through the Fungi Passage that lies between Mary Point on St. John and Whistling Cay. A small shoal area extends south from Whistling Cay, where the decaying ruins of an old customs house can still be seen.

Anchoring

Favor the eastern side of the bay and anchor in 20-30 feet

of water. When the wind is light, do not anchor close inshore because of the bugs. A small sandbar lies in the northeastern corner. Stay outside the buoys designating the swimming area.

Ashore

For those who feel like taking a healthy walk, the National Park Service maintains a trail that extends from the picnic site to an abandoned plantation house. From there you can follow the road to the Annaberg Ruins. The National Park Service maintains garbage facilities ashore.

Departing

If you are heading east, you will find yourself in the Narrows with the wind and current against you. Many of the local skippers prefer to lay a tack toward Jost Van Dyke. Then tacking back through the cut between Great Thatch and Tortola, rather than fighting the Narrows with its strong adverse currents.

Leinster Bay

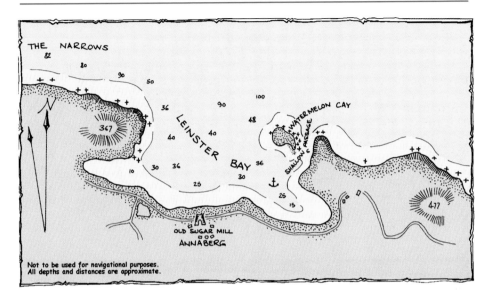

THE NARROWS
82
80
90
50
36
90
100
367
LEINSTER
40
40
48
WATERMELON CAY
40
30
36
BAY
36
10
30
25
30
25
15
477
OLD SUGAR MILL
ANNABERG

Not to be used for navigational purposes.
All depths and distances are approximate.

Located on the north coast of St. John, Leinster Bay lies directly to the south of the western most tip of Little Thatch. The anchorage is well protected and quite comfortable.

Navigation

Leaving Waterlemon Cay to port, work yourself up into the eastern end of the bay, known as Waterlemon Bay. It is not recommended to go between Waterlemon Cay and St. John leaving Waterlemon Cay to starboard from the north.

Anchoring

Anchor in the southeastern corner of the bay in 20-30 feet of water. The holding is good, but expect to be backwinded when there is no ground sea. There is a delightful anchorage in the lee of Waterlemon Cay.

Ashore

Aside from snorkeling around the cay, there are one or two interesting walks ashore. In the southwest corner of the bay, there is a trail that leads to the Annaberg Sugar Mill, the ruins of which have been restored by the Park Service.

If leaving your dinghy, please make sure that it is well secured. If the nature of the sea is such as to make it difficult, land it on the sandy beach back up in the bay and walk along the beach to the foot of the trail.

Carol Lee

Coral Bay and Hurricane Hole

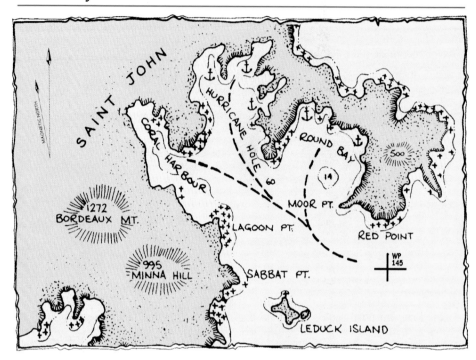

Comprised of a series of bays, coves, and fingers of land, Coral Bay and Hurricane Hole are located on the southeast corner of St. John. Hurricane Hole is the name given to the northern and eastern portion of the bay, where it is possible to tie up to the mangroves to gain protection from storms. During the rainy months, the area can be very buggy.

At the time of the slave days, when the sugar mills were at their peak, Coral Harbor was the main anchorage on St. John. There are some interesting ruins still in existence.

Navigation

If you are approaching from the east, the route is straight forward. Leave Flanagan's Island to port. Make your entry midway between Red Point on St. John and Leduck Island. It is wise to give all headlands in this area a wide

berth as most have rocks extending out from them.

If you are approaching from the south or west, then care must be exercised to avoid Eagle Shoal, which is very difficult to see. When rounding Ram's Head, it is possible to hug the shoreline, passing midway between Sabbat Point and Leduck Island, but the safer route is to stay south of a line drawn between Ram's Head and Water Point on the northern tip of Norman Island until Leduck Island bears northwest. Then enter midway between Leduck Island and Red Point.

Anchoring
Round Bay

Once around Moor Point, Round Bay will open up to starboard. There is a reef extending out from the shoreline (see sketch chart). Anchor to the right of the reef in 15-25 feet of water. The holding is good, but occasionally, a swell works its way around the point. If this happens, it is recommended to set a stern anchor.

Hurricane Hole

There are five separate anchorages comprising Hurricane Hole; the holding is good in all of them. The water for the most part is deep, too. But beware of bugs when the wind is light or after a rain.

Coral Harbor

The entrance is straightforward. Stay mid-channel until the stone house on the eastern side of the bay bears northeast. The channel is marked by red and green buoys that are privately maintained. You should then be able to anchor in 15-20 feet of water. Keep the channel clear for fishing boats, and do not pick up the private moorings you will see here.

Ashore

There is no customs service at Coral Bay. There are a number of buildings left over from slavery days, including the Moravian Mission and the ruins of an old sugar mill and a fort. Coral Bay has become the place to eat in St. John. Try the Shipwreck Landing, Sera Fina and Skinny Legs Bar and Grill. The Seabreeze is the only Coral Bay restaurant open for breakfast. The Jolly Dog Island Outpost at Shipwreck landing has "stuff you want".

Coral Bay Marine monitor VHF 16 and provides engine repairs. Coral Bay Watersports is a dive company renting dive equipment.

Coral Harbor is home to some wonderfully eccentric and dedicated cruising sorts. It is considered more of a haven from the tourists, rather than a tourist destination.

South Coast Bays of St. John

Beyond the point of Ram's Head, there are a number of bays, less frequently visited by the cruising yachtsman. We have listed below several of these anchorages, along with any pertinent information. In the south bays no anchoring is permitted by the National Park Service, however, there are some moorings available to pick up that are maintained by the park service.

Salt Pond Bay

Salt Pond Bay is an excellent anchorage. It is easy to enter, although there are rocks awash at the entrance. You can pass on either side of them; however, there is more room if you leave them to starboard.

When approaching and leaving, Booby Rock is easy to see (35 feet) with good water all around. Anchoring is forbidden, but the Park Service has provided moorings. The snorkeling around this anchorage is excellent.

A word of caution is that this bay has been subject to some petty thievery. Sunbathers, rental cars and boats all seem to be fair game.

Great Lameshur Bay

Another well protected anchorage, Great Lameshur Bay is easy to gain access to. Once inside, pick up a Park Service mooring. Anchoring is restricted.

Little Lameshur Bay

To the west of Great Lameshur, Little Lameshur offers good protection except when the wind is in the south. This is another bay with restricted anchoring. Pick up a mooring and head for the water. Snorkeling here is excellent.

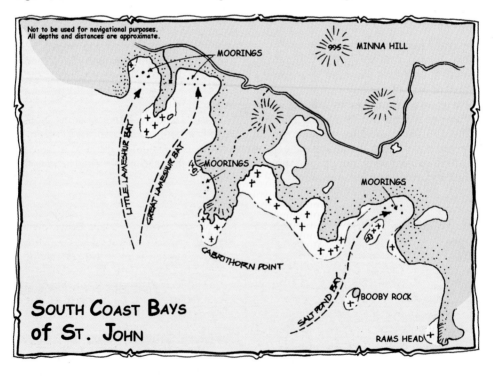

Not to be used for navigational purposes. All depths and distances are approximate.

MOORINGS

MINNA HILL

995

MOORINGS

MOORINGS

LITTLE LAMESHUR BAY

GREAT LAMESHUR BAY

CABRITHORN POINT

SALT POND BAY

BOOBY ROCK

RAMS HEAD

SOUTH COAST BAYS of ST. JOHN

Carol Lee

SHOPPING

Duty-free shopping, and a wealth of shops that are unrivaled in many other Caribbean destinations, make the U.S. Virgin Islands a shoppers' "mecca." Since the islands are outside the U.S. Customs Zone, the duty-free shopping can amount to significant savings of 20 to 50 per cent on a wide variety of items. Plus there is the advantage of a duty-free $1,200 per person allowance on purchases. This is higher than many other destinations in the world.

Variety is what shopping is all about on St. Thomas and St. Croix. Downtown Charlotte Amalie boasts such a wide range of stores and boutiques that it staggers the imagination.

Jewelers offer bargains on dazzling diamonds, emeralds and other precious gems, as well as buys on fine watches, gold necklaces, bracelets and other jewelry.

Savings can also be realized when purchasing cameras, liquors, fine china, silverware, perfumes and crystal. Many shops offer art and crafts, and other items created by island artists.

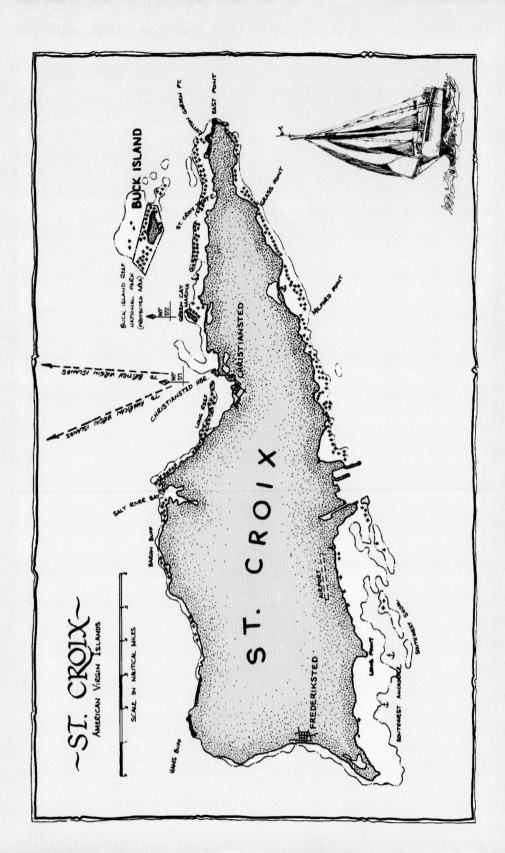

ST. CROIX
Christiansted

Lying 35 miles south of the other Virgins, St. Croix is the largest island in the group, approximately 26 miles wide. The island has retained more of its Danish character than the other U.S. islands, and many of the original *great* houses have been restored as have some of the historic sights.

daylight and therefore, in order to allow for delays, it is prudent to depart at first light and no later than 8am.

Navigation

When the weather is extremely clear, it is possible to see St. Croix from either St. Thomas or Tortola. But during hazy

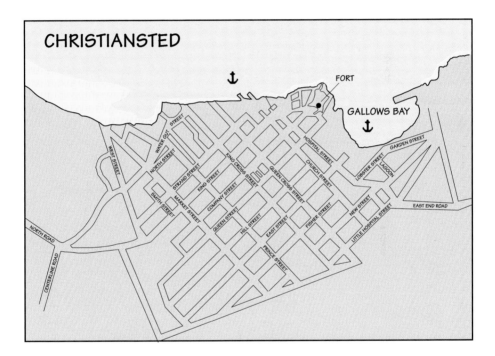

In order to preserve such dignity, portions of Christiansted have become national trust in order to preserve the original building facades characteristic of the early Danish architectural style.

When planning your trip to St. Croix, allow yourself a minimum of three days; one day to sail there, one day to sightsee, and one to sail back. Try to depart from either the eastern end of St. John or Norman Island in the B.V.I. for a better point of sail, either a close or beam reach.

It is imperative that the entrance into Christiansted Harbor be made only in

periods, you won't be able to see the hills until you are two hours out.

When laying off a course, it is wise to allow for a 1/2 knot westerly current. Therefore, as a rule of thumb, lay your course for the eastern end of the island in order to be set down onto Christiansted.

As you start to approach Christiansted, keep to the eastern side and correct your course accordingly. The saddle formed by Lang Peak and Recovery Hill makes an easy landmark. Head for a point midway between them until you pick up the

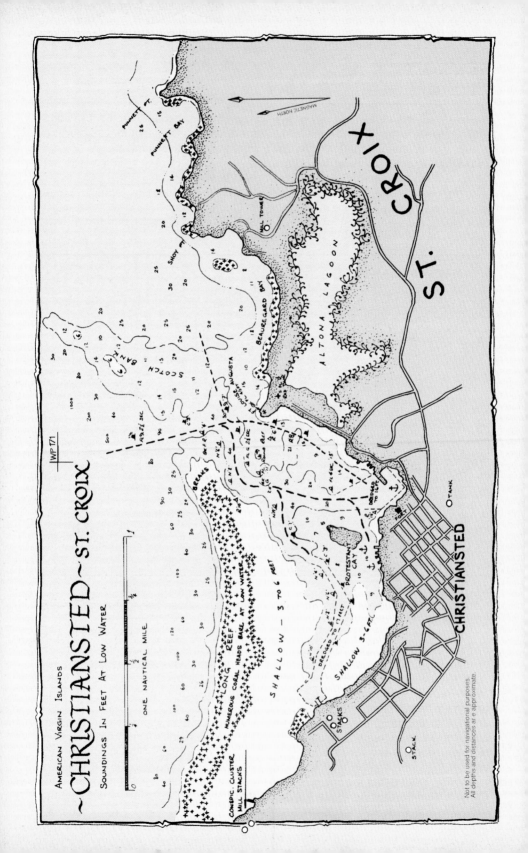

radio tower on Fort Louise Augusta.

You will pass the first green buoy to port and then line up the radio tower between the channel markers. This should be approximately 170 degrees magnetic.

Long Reef, which extends across the harbor entrance, will be seen breaking to starboard. On your port hand is Scotch Bank and, although the charts indicate that parts of it are covered with adequate water depth, it is wise to stay clear, as it breaks in a ground sea.

Although the entrance to Christiansted Harbor is well buoyed, it should be noted that Round Reef, which lies to the west of Ft. Louise Augusta, represents a major navigational hazard. You may go to either side of it if you draw under 10 feet.

The schooner channel can be negotiated by leaving the channel dividing marker to starboard, then leaving Round Reef to starboard, passing midway between the reef and Ft. Louise Augusta,

and then directly to the anchorage. This channel is for yachts carrying less than a ten foot draft.

Taking the deeper channel entails leaving the fixed marker to port and passing to the west of Round Reef, following the channel markers.

Anchoring

Most yachts use the anchorage in the lee of Protestant Cay. Head for the fort, which lies to the east of the Cay, round the Cay to the south and anchor off the southwest end in approximately 10 feet of water.

Do not anchor too far to the west as the water shoals off, and do not be tempted to utilize a mooring buoy that is currently vacant. The moorings are all private and, unless you know what is on the other end, prudence should dictate your using your own ground tackle.

It is a good policy to set two anchors to restrict swinging room as this anchorage

C17, C17a

is both crowded and prone to a current at certain times, which affects different boats in various ways.

Vessels of over 50 feet should anchor off the St. Croix Marina or may tie up dockside if so desired.

Ashore

Vessels sailing from the B.V.I. must clear customs and immigration, located to the south of St. Croix Marina or call them at 773-1011 for instructions.

Skippers should bring their identification and ship's papers ashore. If any crew member is not a U.S. citizen, you are required to take that member and his or her passport and visa with you to immigration (telephone 778-1419). All non U.S. citizens are required to have a visa with the exception of Canadians.

St. Croix Marina is a full service marina offering discount fuel, dockage for vessels up to 200' with 10' draft, showers, laundry, restaurant/bar, and ice. The boatyard offers long and short term storage, a 300-ton railway, 60-ton Travelift, fiberglass repair, USCG and ABS certified welding, custom painting, mechanical and electrical repairs, refrigeration and air conditioning service and much more. It is operated by Larry and Ginny Angus and can be reached by phone at (340) 773-0289 or VHF channel 16.

Nearby is Chandlers Wharf with restaurants and shops. The post office and

many shops are also located nearby and the assistance of the marina to point you in the right direction will help you find what you are after.

Silver Bay dock is located in downtown Christiansted and has transient space available with electricity and water for boats to 70 feet. Additionally there is parking at the dock. The maximum draft is 9 feet. The dock is located next

to the Caravelle Hotel and dockage can be obtained on site or by calling 778-9650.

The town of Christiansted is an easy walk from St. Croix Marina. This island is also one in which you are allowed a generous $1200 duty exemption on imports.

Christiansted is a charming town with many of the old buildings still intact. The shops are tucked inside many of these carefully rebuilt edifices, along with quaint restaurants in breezy courtyards.

The National Park Service maintains

five historic sites within walking distance of the waterfront. Fort Christiansvaern offers a self guided tour following numbered rooms and reading the history in a well written pamphlet by the Park Service. This fort was begun in 1734, and while it never engaged in battle, the view from the battlements affords a great panorama of the harbor. Don't miss seeing the dungeons. The fort is open daily and park rangers are on duty from 8am to 5pm.

The Scalehouse, location of the Visitors Bureau, has been restored to its original mid 1800 condition. It was used originally to check merchandise, with a scale built into the floor. This is a good place to get general information and directions for the island of St. Croix.

The West India and Guinea Company Warehouse holds the Post Office opposite the Steeple Building. U.S. Customs is on the second floor. Built in the mid 1700's, the building also houses public restrooms.

The Danish Customs House houses the National Park Service's offices. The building has been renovated and is open weekdays from 10am to noon.

The Government House was once the capital of the Danish West Indies. It is now used by various government departments. Parts of the complex date back to the mid 1700's. An interesting staircase leads to the ballroom on the second floor.

Downtown Christiansted is full of wonderful shops. The main streets for shopping are Company Street, King Street, Queen Cross Street, Strand Street, and the Caravelle Arcade. Crucian Gold on Kings Wharf sell Crusian bracelets exclusively designed and manufactured by a Crucian — a great memento of your trip to Christiansted.

There are many wonderful restaurants in Christiansted tucked in amongst the shops. Don't miss the lobster at Stixx on

C17, C17a

the Waterfront or the crab races. The Buccaneer Hotel has a calypso or steel band on Friday nights. The Commanche Restaurant on Strand Street is upstairs with a view of the harbor and has been around for years. Kendrick's has distinguished itself amongst St. Croix restaurants and is worth a visit. For a more extensive listing check the restaurant directory.

To tour the island of St. Croix you may want to take a bus tour, or rent a car from Thrifty Car Rental who will pick you up from your hotel to get you organized with one of their cars.

Cramer Park, a cove on the East End of the island, overlooks Buck Island. The park has a beautiful beach, picnic area, bar and restaurant.

The eastern most point of the island is also the eastern most part of the U.S.

Altoona Lagoon is a park and beach near the Fort Louise Augusta radio tower, right in Christiansted Harbor.

Don't miss the St. George Village Botanical Gardens, a restoration of an old sugar plantation. The gardens have plants and flowers indigenous to St. Croix.

Near the airport, on the south western part of the island is the Cruzan Rum Distillery. You can visit the distillery and watch the workers making the rum. A tour is available, along with a tasting bar concocting a rum drink every day.

Heading toward Frederiksted is the rain forest, with a 150 foot dam. Mahogany Road is lined with mahogany trees, yellow cedar and Tibet trees. The St. Croix Leap, also located in the rain forest is a group of woodcarvers and sculptors. You can order items to be shipped to you on completion.

Whim Greathouse, near Frederiksted, is not to be missed. It is a restored greathouse from the late 1700's which houses a museum and gift shop. It is open daily from 10am to 5pm. There is a small charge for admission.

Buck Island

Lying some 4-1/2 miles northeast of Christiansted Harbor, Buck Island is a national park and its surrounding coral reef is marked with underwater sign.

Numerous day sailing boats make the trip from Christiansted and Green Cay Marina daily, and anyone wishing to go along should contact the appropriate vessel at dockside. Although not recommended as an overnight anchorage, Buck Island provides an excellent day's diversions of sailing and snorkeling.

Navigation

Leave Christiansted Harbor the way you came in until you reach the sea buoy. Proceed northeast toward Virgin Gorda for 2 miles along Scotch Bank, and then head for the prominent point on the south end of the island.

An alternate route is to proceed out of the harbor to buoy C7 (see chart) off Fort Louise Augusta. Do not go further inshore owing to two shoal areas that have taken their toll in the past. Leaving Green Cay to starboard, stand out for the white beach on the western end of Buck Island.

There are two white buoys that mark the western extremities of the reef.

Anchoring

The best anchorage is directly off the white, sandy beach at the western end of Buck Island in approximately 15 feet of water on the sandy bottom.

Boats drawing less than 5 feet may use another anchorage inside the reef. Proceed eastward along the island, keeping the white buoy to port, until you see a large brown sign, placed by the Park Service.

You will also see red and green buoys that mark the entrance through the reef. Follow the passage to the eastern end of the island and pick up one of the National Park Service moorings.

If you have to anchor, please keep well clear of the reef and set your anchor only in sandy areas.

Ashore

The Park Service maintains picnic chairs and tables, as well as barbecue grills on the beach at the western end. A picnic pavilion is located east of the small pier on the south shore for your convenience.

There is a marked underwater trail here, which has been designated as a National Park. The snorkel trail starts at the southeast corner of the island, and those wishing to explore it should dinghy through the passage described above and moor at the start of the trail. Snorkeling here is spectacular, but do not touch the coral.

For those wishing to get some exercise, an overland hiking trail will provide an interesting walk among prickly pears, cactus and wildflowers.

Green Cay Marina

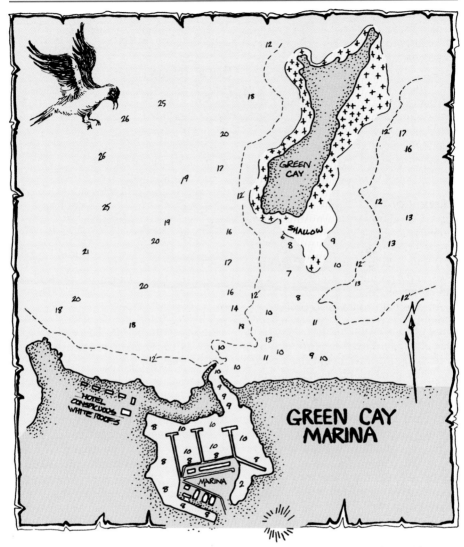

Green Cay Marina is a full service, well protected marina on St. Croix's northern coast. Located east of Christiansted, it should be approached from the western side of Buck Island, from which you will see Green Cay.

Leave Green Cay to port and head for the rock jetty. You can see yellow buildings with white roofs as a landmark from three miles offshore. The marina monitors VHF 16. If you call ahead, the dockmaster will meet you at the fuel dock and lead you to a slip. The marina carries 8 to 10 feet of water and is very well protected.

Ashore

The marina is well kept and has all of the amenities including showers, laundry, water, electricity, fuel, and ice. There is also a restaurant and a 46 room hotel, tennis and croquet courts, beach, gift shop and meeting facilities.

St. Croix Yacht Club / Teague Bay

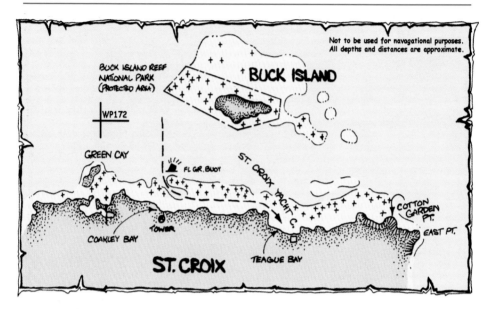

Not to be used for navagational purposes. All depths and distances are approximate.

BUCK ISLAND REEF NATIONAL PARK (PROTECTED AREA)

WP172

BUCK ISLAND

GREEN CAY

FL GR. BUOY

ST. CROIX YACHT C.

COTTON GARDEN PT.

EAST PT.

TOWER

COAKLEY BAY

ST. CROIX

TEAGUE BAY

Navigation

South of Buck Island, protected by a reef, is Teague Bay. There are two entrances to the bay, the first being the Coakley Bay Cut, marked by a lighted green marker. Leave the marker to port, go well into the bay towards the windmill, then head east, favoring the shore side. This entrance is good for 12 foot depths.

The second entrance, the Cotton Valley Cut is good for 7 foot depths. It is unlit and marked by privately maintained white buoys which are difficult to see. Head in between the buoys, watching for patch reefs east/ southeast of the Cut. Once inside stay to the center of the shore and the reef and head towards the Yacht Club.

Anchoring

There is good holding in sand, but take care to avoid fouling the private moorings which you will see here. Do not get too close to shore, as it shoals to 5 feet. There may be as many as 75-90 boats moored here during the busy season.

Ashore

The St. Croix Yacht Club extends a friendly welcome to visiting yachts. There is a small dinghy dock to the east, where you can tie up and go ashore. The restaurant an bar are open from 11:30am to 6pm. The Club is open Wednesday through Sunday and holidays year round. Duggan's Reef nearby can be reached by dinghy for dinner. Showers are available, ice may be purchased, and garbage may be left. However, no fuel, laundry, or provisions are available. Reciprocal use is offered to yachtsmen of recognized yacht clubs and other yachtsmen may request a guest pass. The Yacht Club stands by on VHF 16. There is a convenience store at nearby Duggan's Reef open until 7pm. Rental cars are available upon request.

Salt River

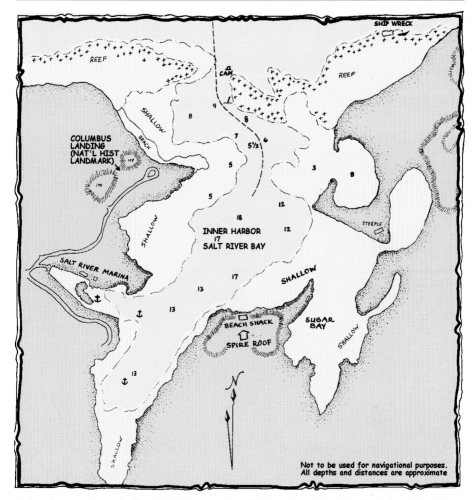

SHIP WRECK

REEF

CAN

REEF

SHALLOW

8

9

8

BEACH

COLUMBUS
LANDING
(NAT'L HIST
LANDMARK)

7

6

5½

5

3

8

100

5

12

STEEPLE

SHALLOW

18

12

INNER HARBOR
17
SALT RIVER BAY

SALT RIVER MARINA

17

13

SHALLOW

13

SUGAR
BAY

13

BEACH SHACK

SHALLOW

SPIRE ROOF

13

N

SHALLOW

**Not to be used for navigational purposes.
All depths and distances are approximate**

Columbus anchored off of Salt River and sent a party ashore in search of water. An unfriendly reception by the local Indians sent him sailing off. Salt River has been given National Park status to further insure its future will remain protected and much as it was when Columbus first saw it.

Navigation

This is a tricky anchorage to get to, but one which provides a very safe anchorage once you are in. Local knowledge is a big help for picking your way in. If you are approaching from the east avoid the White Horse Reef off of the Salt River Point; it usually breaks even during calm weather.

Find the break in the reef. Once inside White Horse Reef, turn to port, paralleling the inside of the reef and head towards the steeple. Align can 1 with the beach shack and spire roof and turn south. This can is privately maintained and, with no official support, can not be guaranteed that it will always be there. It is strongly advised that you call Salt River Marina for advice, and feel your way carefully with a depth finder.

In the west section of the bay is Salt

River Marina, which provides all services to dockside customers; fuel requires 24 hour notice. The Marina boasts a fine island setting, restaurant, marine supply store and dive shop. Salt River Canyon is rated as one of the ten best dive locations in the Caribbean. The marina office and restaurant are open 7 days a week. They monitor VHF 16 during daylight hours. Because of limited space available, advance notice is recommended when possible.

You should be able to take 6 feet into the harbor. This is a well protected and interesting anchorage, although not convenient to any shore based amenities; taxis are easy to access and rides to town can be arranged.

Frederiksted

This is a harbor used by large ships. It is seldom used by yachts as an anchorage, as the water is extremely deep.

The town does have some interesting old buildings, and is worth a visit if you are touring the island.

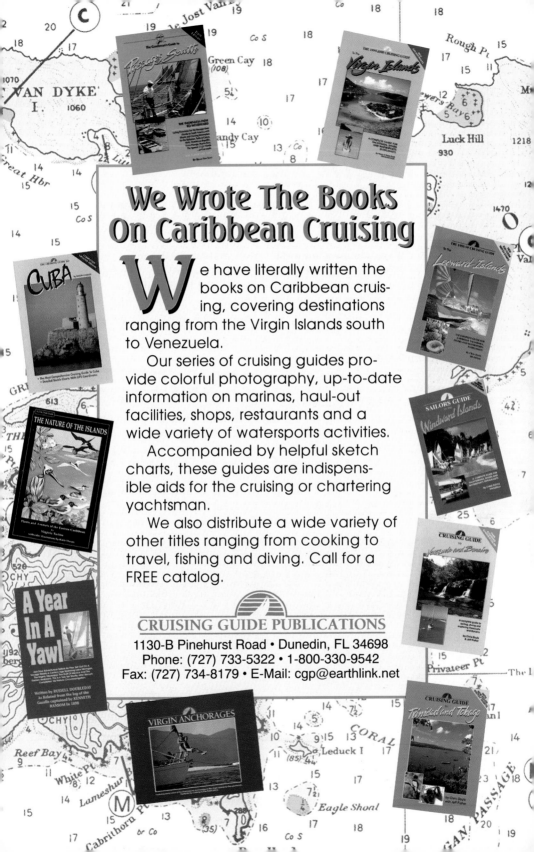

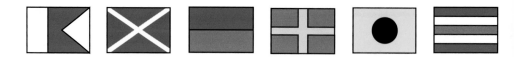

The Virgin Island America's Cup Challenge

*E*rnest Matthias, a native Virgin Islander of West Indian descent, has always been comfortable around the water. "As kids we used to take discarded sheets of "galvanized" (corrugated tin roofing material), pound them flat, and bent 'em up into crude metal canoes," reports Ernest, "We called these razor-sharp metal craft "bateau boats." They were tippy and difficult to handle, and if you made the slightest mistake — they'd sink like a stone."

Ernest was soon looking for bigger, faster craft to play on. Larry Best, skipper of the 60 foot ketch *Perseverance of Boston,* quickly signed Ernest aboard as crew.

"We were leading our class during one Thanksgiving Regatta," recalls Captain Best, "when our starboard jib sheet came untied. I figured we'd lost the race, because we'd have to drop the headsail to reattach the jib sheet during a tack, but I forgot about Ernest being aboard. He put the loose jib sheet in his teeth, and climbed hand over hand up the remaining sheet until he was about 20 feet above the water. Then, hanging by one hand above the lumpy waves, Ernest calmly tied a perfect bowline with the other!"

After that Ernest had no problem finding crew positions.

In addition to sailing big boats, Ernest started board sailing as well, He soon won a number of local board sailing competitions, and started up his own watersports rental company in Cinnamon Bay, St. John. "Competitive sailing

Anthony Blake

opened up an entirely new world of opportunities for me," he said. "But as a native Virgin Islander, I wondered just how far I could take it."

The answer is, amazingly enough, straight to the top. The very top. The *ultimate* top!

In mid-1998, Ernest Matthias was crewing aboard an International America's Cup Class (IACC), training vessel in New Zealand match racing against the Italians and the French for the right to challenge Russell Coutts and Team New Zealand during an informal Mini-America's Cup race.

Ernest hopes to return in 1999 for the real thing, and to be a member of the winning America's Cup crew against New Zealand in the year 2000.

Representing who? "Team Caribbean and the Virgin Islands America's Cup Challenge," said Ernest pridefully.

"At first, a lot of people thought I was either joking or nuts," admits Michael Bornn, co-founder of Team Caribbean and the Virgin Islands America's Cup Challenge (VIACC). "To put the best possible spin on it, there was a 'bit of initial skepticism' to put it mildly."

Michael, like Ernest, is another high achieving Virgin Islander. An investment counselor by profession and a community activist by inclination, he traces his family roots back to the Arawak and Caribe Indians — as well as Europe and Africa.

"I figured that since we have some of the finest sailing grounds in the world, as well as some of the best competitive sailors, that we should bring the America's Cup back to U.S. soil to focus the world's attention on both."

One fellow Virgin Islander who wasn't skeptical that the Virgin Islands could successfully challenge for the "Holy Grail" of yacht racing was Olympic medalist and international yacht racing champion Peter Holmberg, an old high school chum of Michael's.

"It was immediately apparent to both of us," said Peter, "that we'd need the support of the entire community — rich and poor, sailor and landlubber, black and white, continental and West Indian — everybody! And we also quickly realized that we'd need a group of very creative, hard working supporters to get our fund-raising efforts off the ground as quickly as possible. One of the first things we did was go to the St. Thomas Yacht Club."

"I must admit I, too, was taken aback," confirms Peter Stoeken, current commodore of the STYC. "We asked Michael and Peter how much it might cost to be competitive, and one of them mentioned the sum of 30 million dollars. Frankly, our jaws hit the yacht club's patio deck."

But the more the V.I. marine community considered such a unique and unlikely challenge and its many potential benefits for the people of the Virgin Islands the more the V.I. Challenge began to make some wonderfully audacious sense.

It was obvious that the positive international publicity the challenge could generate for the V.I. would be priceless. The last America's Cup series was the third most watched sporting event in the world, right behind the Olympics and World Cup Soccer and that's the real reason why so many millions of dollars are poured into it.

Plus, the America's Cup is truly an international icon of sporting excellence — exactly the right upscale image to link with a pristine tourist destination such as the Virgins.

And a tiny nation like the Virgin Islands

had never challenged for the Cup especially with a multi-national, multi-racial, multi-cultural crew. The international media was bound to fall in love with such a David and Goliath concept.

"It was just a natural idea," said Peter, " and the more we considered it, the more we became convinced it could actually happen."

The first challenge of the V.I. America's Cup Challenge was to make sure there would be across the board support for such a Herculean effort. In May of 1996, Peter and Michael went public with their plans, and immediately attracted 25 local founders to provide seed capital for the syndicate.

"Our economy is based almost solely on tourism," said Michael, "particularly water-related tourism. This 30 million dollars, most of which will come from corporate American, will be, in essence, the largest advertising fund the Virgin Islands could ever hope to have access to."

That's only part of it," chimes in Peter. "Our marine and chartering industries were badly affected by hurricanes Hugo and Marilyn. This will be an excellent opportunity to show the world how vibrantly these industries have rebounded."

"...and," continued Michael, "At the same time we can involve more of our local youth in the marine industry via our America's Cup Marine Training Facility."

"...and there is a national sports angle as well," said Peter.

"...yeah," agreed Michael. "Dallas has the Cowboys, Chicago has the Bulls, New York has the Mets. Why can't St. Thomas have a major, world class professional sports team as well?"

Why not indeed?

Within the month, 1996 STYC commodore Carol Hindels officially challenged for the America's Cup on behalf of the V.I. America's Cup Challenge — the first female yacht club commodore to ever do so.

The rest, as they say, is history. Almost immediately, a used 75 foot multi-million dollar International America's Cup Class (IACC) training vessel was purchased (from Team Dennis Conner), and VIACC crew training began. John Culter, a veteran of two previous America's Cup campaigns, was signed aboard. A local retail outlet for VIACC merchandise was opened in Hibiscus Alley in Charlotte Amalie, and numerous local corporations reached into the coffers to help jump-start the Challenge.

Perhaps the most heartening aspect of the Challenge was the breath of its local support. Initially, there was a worry that the average man on the beach wouldn't support such a costly sports endeavor, but that worry proved unfounded.

Everyone jumped on the band wagon. Local radio stations held "live on the air" fund-raising marathons during which taxi cab drivers donated their fares, waitresses pledged their tips, and even school kids promised a portion of their lunch money.

In January 1997, over $2,000,000 was raised locally within 30 days.

"We've been just amazed by our local support," admits Michael Bornn. "That's right," says Peter Holmberg. "Virgin Islanders of all walks of life have given us their full backing and that's truly amazing!"

The next hurdle was securing the services of a top yacht designer, only a handful of which are America's Cup caliber.

The VIACC stunned the yacht racing world by securing the services of famed naval architect David Pedrick of Newport. Two of his previous designs had won the Cup, and he was the only American designer to have a boat recapture the Cup from a foreign power.

"What really convinced me was the concept behind the team," said Pedrick. "They're people determined to win and at the same time they want to help their islands and their people. I find this highly admirable, and I'm glad to be a part of it."

Of course, the entire V.I. America's

Cup Challenge would be meaningless unless there was a local sailor with enough talent to steer it into the winner's circle.

Olympic silver medalist (Finn class) Peter Holmberg, Michael's co-founder and the VIACC's designated skipper, is clearly that man. He's won, or almost won, virtually every major regatta in the world. At one time or another he has beaten every top ranked sailor in the world.

But, skeptics asked, could Peter keep his competitive edge on the race course while immersing himself in the myriad organizational details of the America's Cup?

Peter Holmberg

Anthony Blake

"Well, its a challenge," admits Peter with a shy smile, "But once I'm out on the water, all the other stuff fades away. It's just me, the crew and the boat."

That's obviously true. In 1996 when the VIACC was being formed, Peter was ranked sixteenth by the International Omega Match Racing rankings. Throughout the next two years while energetically heading up the challenge on a 24/7 basis, Peter competed in numerous match races around the world. He won many of them, including such prestigious regattas as the Golden Gate Invitational, the Commodore's Cup and the Congressional Cup. His Omega Match Racing World Ranking had climbed to fourth in the world by mid 1998.

"This has made my job considerably easier," said Steve Morton, the main fund-raiser behind the VIACC. "There are currently 16 teams from 10 countries competing for the right to consistently moving upwards. For Peter, with his limited resources to be ranked fourth in the world is, well, WOW!"

Of course, the America's Cup is primarily a money/design game until the very end. The VIACC had great fundraising success in the Virgins, and thus quickly expanded its focus to include the entire region with its Team Caribbean concept.

The St. Thomas Yacht Club is still the challenger of record," says Peter, "and when we win the Cup it will come back home to St. Thomas. However, we think that, in a promotional sense, a rising tide lifts all boats and thus we're reaching out to Puerto Rico and the rest of the Caribbean for support."

In March of 1998, the Club Nautico (yacht club) of San Juan pledged its complete support to Team Caribbean, and allowed a full time fundraising center to be opened on its premises.

At almost the same time, Team Caribbean attracted its first major sponsor which was not Caribbean-related, Gant USA clothing.

"GANT has previously sponsored America Cup winners Ted Turner and Dennis Conner," said Peter Holmberg, "and this time they decided that Team Caribbean offered the best sponsorship package for their money. This is highly significant, especially in light of their past successful sponsorships."

By June of 1998, the VIACC was in the final stages of deciding which of five U.S. boat builders to contract to construct their hull, as well as finalizing their design and compiling a long list of needed building materials.

"We're going to be in New Zealand in 1999 for the challenger series, and hopefully, still there in the year 2000 for the Cup itself," says Michael Bornn.

"And we're going to be fast!" concludes a confident Peter Holmberg.

THE SPANISH VIRGIN ISLANDS

SUPPLEMENT:

by Bruce Van Sant

INTRODUCTION

The following information has been gathered painstakingly by cruising author Bruce Van Sant, author of *A Gentleman's Guide to Passages South,* now in it's sixth edition. Bruce Van Sant has spent many years cruising between Florida, the Bahamas, the Dominican Republic, Puerto Rico and the other islands of the Caribbean. Eastern Puerto Rico and the Spanish Virgin Islands have been a favorite cruising area of his and consequently he produced the *Cruising Guide to the Spanish Virgin Islands.* We added this supplement to our Virgin Island guide to extend the information in the total Virgin Islands cruising area for those who want to explore a pristine area with a Spanish influence.

Belonging to the Commonwealth of Puerto Rico, these islands lie between the U.S. Virgin Islands and Puerto Rico, both of which are territories of the United States. They were discovered by Columbus on his second voyage to the New World in 1493.

Columbus named the main island, called Borinquen by the Tainos that lived there, San Juan Bautista to honor Prince Juan, the son of Ferdinand and Isabela. Ponce de Leon, who explored the southeast United States, founded Puerto Rico's first settlement and was its first governor.

Many of the smaller islands were alternately ignored or disputed by the European powers during the four centuries in which the main island of Puerto Rico was a colony of Spain. They were ceded by Spain to the United States with the Treaty of Paris in 1898. Puerto Ricans are U.S. Citizens and half are bilingual.

The population is the most affluent in Latin America, but in 1995, 62 percent of the population was on welfare. Expect to be boarded by the U.S. Coast Guard. In 1995, 25 percent of the illegal drugs entering the U.S. did so through Puerto Rico.

The Spanish Virgin Islands embrace approximately 400 square sea miles to the west of the U.S. Virgin Islands. Unlike the U.S. Virgin Islands, Puerto Rico has an extensively developed industrial and agricultural infrastructure.

The Spanish Virgins, like the U.S.V.I., are entirely dependent on tourism, yet they are many years behind in the development of tourism infrastructure. This is bad for the typical resort tourist, but great for the getaway cruiser and diving enthusiast.

It means unaffected townspeople, undisturbed anchorages, pristine beaches and productive fishing (with a year-round lobster season).

Ashore, the Spanish Virgins offer immersion in the Spanish Caribbean with the escape clause of bilingualism and the convenience of U.S. institutions.

There are four cruising areas in the Spanish Virgins:
- Puerto Rico's East Coast
- La Cordillera
- Culebra
- Vieques

Be sure to schedule ample time to enjoy each of these very special areas.

ASHORE IN PUERTO RICO

Touring by Rental Car

Like in North America, one must have access to a car in Puerto Rico. If you decide to rent a car to tour the country, get a road atlas and follow the purple lines, the *Ruta Panoramica*, through the mountains and small towns, staying at designated Paradors, usually historic or otherwise noteworthy inns. A good rule to use while driving: stop at every lechón (roasting pig) at the roadside, buy a beer and rip off a piece of the *lechón*. It's delicious, you'll meet many good Puerto Ricans, and in this manner you'll only make about 20 miles a day on weekends and holidays.

Touring by *Público*

It is still possible to backpack Puerto Rico like you can in the Dominican Republic. There is not, however, the elaborate public transportation system found in the DR. Like North America, nearly everyone has access to a car, and for those that don't, there is still a good *público* system which has been waning as the island affluence waxes.

Carros Públicos are automobiles that travel specific routes between towns. They wait in ranks around the town square, or at terminal facilities in cities, until enough passengers have signed up to nearly fill the car. If you wish depart earlier or to travel in comfort, you may buy any unfilled seats. For best results, buy the 3 seats next to the driver. While públicos always gather and start from the same place, they deliver passengers to wherever, within reason, they wish to go at the destination town.

In Puerto Rico they are large honky old American cars with about the same interior space as Japanese ones used in the DR. The *públicos* in Puerto Rico cost much more than they do in the DR, but they only cram in 5 instead of 6, and like in the DR, you can always buy vacant seats for more comfort. Every small town has público ranks around the town hall square, except Boquerón. Larger towns have elaborate terminal buildings.

Fiestas Patronales

If you do Puerto Rico in the summer, take lots of time and hit every port. Summer in Puerto Rico is the season of the *Fiestas Patronales* [fee-ACE-tahs pah-tro-NAHL-ace]. These are celebrations each town throws for itself (and theoretically its patron saint) as a way to liven up the summer and the business doldrums.

The *Fiestas* are sequenced to permit the traveling entertainers, rides and food concessions to appear at every one. Yet each *Fiesta* has its own atmosphere as the town turns on for a full week. The *Fiestas* in the smaller towns will bring back the Fourth of Julys of 50 years ago for older cruisers from Main Street, U.S.A. The larger towns and county seats, such as Fajardo, often have fiestas which ring the central plaza for 3 and 4 blocks deep. Each port in Puerto Rico is either at or within a *público* ride from at least 3 *Fiestas*. Some of the entertainment provided at these festivals is world class. You may find yourself face to face with Jose Feliciano or Yolandita Monge.

237

WEATHER

Weather in the tropical tradewinds belt is seasonally predictable, permitting somewhat reliable cruise planning. Wind strength and direction, and possible swell, are factors to consider in setting a ports and diving itinerary, especially when choosing day anchorages. To help you plan your cruise, here are the annual cycles you can expect.

Winter Months

December through March, distant northern gales often create swell in exposed northern anchorages, and some day anchorages might be untenable. Fortunately, the lovely harbors of the south coast of Vieques and the reef anchorages of Culebra, Icacos and Palominos are unaffected. Cold fronts that make it this far south are often stalled or have dissipated into troughs which persist for several days. While not good for the avid sailor, these conditions make for fluky winds which in turn create diving and snorkeling opportunities across La Cordillera, in Culebra's outlying keys, and on Vieques' north coast.

Summer Months

From late July to early September there may be some "bloom" in the water which can restrict visibility for divers. Sailing is great in the cooling summer trades which make these islands cooler and less humid than most of North America at this time of the year. Long hauls to windward are pleasurable, and anchorages are often empty. Like fronts in the winter, summer tropical waves create breaks in the tradewinds, and otherwise exposed diving sites become open to exploration.

The Between Months

April to June is usually too late for strong fronts and too early for organized tropical waves. October and November are, conversely, too early and too late; trade winds moderate and days are clear and sunny. Northerly swells are infrequent

and there is minimum chop on Vieques Sound. Diving sites and day anchorages have their highest availability during these months.

AM/VHF Weather Forecasts

Local meteorological and marine reports are given hourly after the news on WOSO San Juan, 1030 KHz Am standard broadcast band. WVWI broadcasts a brief "Sailor's Report" on 1000 KHz AM, at 6:30am, Monday through Friday. This includes the short range NOAA coastal report and the next 12 hours of the National Weather Service's Offshore Report. NOAA broadcasts a continuous Weather Channel on VHF from San Juan, but it is of limited use to the cruiser more than three miles east of the Puerto Rico mainland. V.I. Radio, however, broadcasts a complete summary of the meteorological, coastal and offshore reports, as well as the Tropical Weather Outlook and Tropical Weather Discussion during hurricane season. This is also continuous and on a VHF Weather Channel which is received in eastern Puerto Rico.

While the coastal reports are fine for most islands and anchorages, if you are out on the open Sound in the daytime, or anywhere east or south of Vieques, you must listen to the Offshore Forecast for the Eastern Caribbean on WVVI's Sailor's Report or on V.I. Radio's VHF Weather Channel; no other report will do.

SPANISH VIRGIN ISLANDS FACTS

Airlines

There are direct flights to Puerto Rico from many U.S. cities. Luis Miñoz International Airport in San Juan, the capital, is the hub of the Americas and serves Europe as well. There is an inexpensive air service to Vieques and Culebra (known as "Isla Nena") from Fajardo and San Juan.

Ground Transport

Driving is on the right hand side of the road. The road signs are in Spanish, the distance markers are in kilometers & the gas is sold in liters. Temporary license/permit requirements usually depends on the car rental company's policies. Normally a valid driver's license from your home country will do.

Local services — Regularly scheduled city buses and metered taxis operate through metropolitan San Juan. Intra-island buses also run between San Juan, Mayaguez and Ponce. Inter-island flight service is available from San Juan, Ponce and Mayaguez to Vieques and Culebra.

Ferry

Old San Juan to Cataño: every half hour between 6:00am to 9:00pm
Fajardo - Vieques - Culebra: passenger and car.

Taxi Fares from San Juan Airport

Taxi fares are metered. It is not necessary to agree fares before hand but it's best to ensure the rates before the cabbie starts the meter.

Telephones

Puerto Rico has modern, reliable United States style telephone service (area code 787). A local call costs 10 cents.

During 1996 the area code of Puerto Rico was changed from 809 to 787. The country code is 1. Local information is 411; from outside Puerto Rico dial 1-787-555-1212. For directory assistance to others parts of Puerto Rico, dial 0. Person-to-person, collect and calling card calls are easy to place. At the center of the phone book are blue pages in English.

PUERTO RICO FACTS

Puerto Rico Profile

Geography

Situated between the Atlantic Ocean and the Caribbean Sea, Puerto Rico is the easternmost of the Greater Antilles. The 110 by 35 nautical mile island has a central mountain range which reaches an altitude of 4,389 feet at Cerro la Punta. Numerous rivers flow down the mountains to surrounding coastal plains. The island is approximately 1,000 miles southeast of Miami and about 40 miles from the U.S. Virgin Islands.

TIME — EST + 1. GMT (UTC)-4.

CLIMATE — Temperature -
High: Summer - 98 degrees.
Winter - 60 degrees.
Low: Summer - 60 degrees.
Average Humidity - 55% day -
80% night.
Average coastal daytime temperature 73-85 degrees, in the mountains, 5-10 degrees cooler; annual rainfall 62 inches.

History

Puerto Rico was discovered by Columbus in 1493 when the Taino Indians lived on the island. Its present capital, San Juan, was established in 1521. Puerto Rico is now a Commonwealth of the United States. The island's culture is a blend of Indian, African and Spanish and American.

Language

Spanish and English are the official languages.

Population

3.5 million with one third of the population concentrated in the San Juan-Bayamon-Carolina metropolitan area.

Money & Business

BANKING HOURS:
Monday to Friday 0830-1430.

BUSINESS HOURS:
Monday to Friday 0900-1700.
Shopping: 0900-1800 — Except the malls which are from 1000-2100 daily.

CURRENCY & CREDIT CARDS:
The U.S. dollar. Credit cards and Traveler's checks are widely accepted for all places, dining, nightclubs, resorts, and shopping. Major Cards such as American Express, Visa, Diner's Club, Discovery, Mastercard, and other Bank Credit Cards are accepted everywhere.

TAXES & SERVICE CHARGES:
Departure tax - None
Hotels & Casinos - 9%
Hotels - 7%
Service charge - 15%
Import Duty - 6.6%

CUSTOMS AND IMMIGRATION

The sailor travels in and out of the U.S. Virgin Islands and Puerto Rico as one might between New York and New Jersey. You are in the United States of America, with one exception: since the U.S.V.I.s are considered a duty free port, one must clear in to Puerto Rico upon arriving from the U.S.V.I., but not upon arrival to the U.S.V.I.s from Puerto Rico.

If arriving from either the U.S. or the British Virgin Islands, it will be necessary to clear customs. From Culebra, call 742-3531 or take the five minute walk to the airport. At any of the marinas in Fajardo, call the harbormaster on VHF channel 16.

In Fajardo, during regular working hours, call customs at 863-0950/0102/3250. Outside of regular business hours, call 253-4533/34/37/38 at the San Juan airport. Customs in Fajardo is located at the old customs house on the waterfront by the ferries in Puerto Real (see chartlet). Vessels not sporting a valid customs entry decal shall be asked to pay $25 for a new one. See the section on Culebra for more details.

Non-U.S. vessels, and vessels with nonresident *aliens* aboard (what Americans call foreigners, I'm afraid), must check into Puerto Rico at official ports of entry, which means Culebra or Fajardo on the east coast.

U.S. vessels can clear customs in Puerto Rico by phone from their landfall.

Customs will advise if they want your boat present when you call them. Customs requires a current sticker (*a cruising permit* for *citizens!*) in both the U.S.V.I.s and Puerto Rico. They'll tell you where and how to buy one if you don't have one.

Tips on Clearing Customs Easily

I am convinced the customs and immigration officials of the world meet every February in Den Hague to formulate plans for confounding guide writers. They get merit points for attending seminars in changing procedures rapidly. Find a good bartender or a cheap gourmet cafe and they'll be around at least six months, long enough to make the final proofs. Then the bartender will run off with the cook the day you go to press. Customs, however, has a plan. They change it every ten boats that enter. If someone tells you, "Here's how you clear customs in Gerfunknik!" you are probably better off doing the opposite of that which is suggested. That said I'll try my best to ease the experiences for you, but you won't get temporal detail.

In general, your experience with clearance officials will be dependent on your presentation. Have your boat and yourselves presentable. Have your papers in order: ships papers, passports and clearance out (*despacho* or *zarpe*) from your last port. Crew lists should be prepared with the name, address and passport number of each member of the crew.

Smile, be honest, friendly and courteous. Don't ask questions. Look bored.

The customs guys all over the world are trained to use their sixth senses. If you're tired from the trip and harried by the hassle of mooring in a strange place you may give odd responses to them. Get some sleep before dealing with guys who are just doing a job. Clear into ports which "specialize" in yachts, or anchor around the corner with your yellow Q flag flying, and get a good night's sleep before entering.

Boat and Dinghy Registration

Vessels remaining in Puerto Rican waters more than 60 days must register in Puerto Rico. Fees are similar to Florida, e.g. a couple of hundred dollars for a 35-foot boat, plus registration for a dingy with a motor.

COMMUNICATIONS

Mail

It is always best to use *general delivery*. Cafés, bars and marinas go out of business, change owners and policies. It is best to let the official postal system hold your mail for pickup. They are generally incorruptible, provide sorting and secure warehousing services which are their business. They are reasonably conscious of an obligation to you with respect to your mail. These things can not be said about a bar, restaurant or hotel where your mail will be pawed over by hundreds of cruisers, each one dripping wet and anxious to get to the bottom of the pile.

Your mail will be more conscientiously looked for by postal officials around the world if you follow this simple routine the first and every time you ask for it. Face the clerk squarely and look directly into his or her eyes. Smile brightly. Say "Good morning. How are you?" Pause and look like you're about to say goodbye, that you had only come there to make them happy. Then, with a shrug, remember you had minor business and, regretfully, wonder if they couldn't help you find your mail. Give them a card with your name written in large block letters. If your name is Van Somethingorother, tell them sometimes it's filed under Ess. This gambit works miracles everywhere. Even in the U.S. Virgins.

In Puerto Rico use "General Delivery". Since P.R. is bilingual the clerk will be scanning for General Delivery not Lista de Correos after he sees your gringo face.

Reckon with U.S. to Puerto Rico, four days. The USPO General Delivery.

How to Send the Mail

A tip about avoiding local taxes on parts shipped into Puerto Rico: send it *Priority*

Mail or *Air Parcel Post* to *General Delivery* to small locations that have presort delivery. Examples are Boquerón, PR00622; Salinas, PR00751; Fajardo, PR00740; or Culebra, PR00735. Uncle Sam refuses to collect local taxes, but large traffic points like San Juan, Mayagüez and Ponce have resident PR tax men who whomp you with 6.6% and delay delivery. Priority Mail may also help ensure delivery.

UPS is notoriously difficult for transients to deal with throughout the Caribbean.

Federal Express bends over backward to help in any way. FedEx is at 793-9300 in Puerto Rico. With FedEx you can call collect for pickup or inquiries to a *real person* who *can* answer your question. It may sound nautical to address yourself as:

— Captain John J. Courageous
— Aboard S/Y *Chicken Little*
— General Delivery

Your mail will almost certainly be stacked under <u>Captain</u>, or <u>Aboard</u>, or sent to the Little's household. Try this for better results:

— John Courageous
— General Delivery

Aside from the pretentiousness of such nautical addressing it makes you an easy mark. What do yacht people ever get except checks and bills? Their kids never write.

As you paw through the mail boxes yourself at the various bars and hotels along your route you will notice how nonuniform all those yachtie addresses are and how difficult they are to sort sensibly.

In Spanish countries, the middle name is often the main name for sorting. So leave out middle names unless you are John X. Smith.

Telephone

It's usually easiest and cheaper to call collect or with credit card. You can dial direct from any street booth. Multiple use credit cards are on sale at many tourist locations for various denominations. It is also possible to obtain telephone credit cards in the U.S. without having a permanent home phone installation. You are billed according to usage, but there may be monthly limits, such as $100. This is sufficient for most cruisers unless, like Superman, they're running a business from the phone booths of the world.

The area code in Puerto Rico is 787 and the country code is the North American code: 1. If you start speaking in English they will answer you in English. The booths in Puerto Rico have instructions in English.

LANGUAGE

Don't let the myth of language barriers undo the enjoyment of your cruise.

I remember turning an aisle in a Caribbean supermarket. Across the room were two gaily dressed old geezers by the fruit shelves. They were waving at me. One had a camera around his neck. Half way across to them I realized they were a clever life-sized cardboard cutout advertising something. I felt quite foolish. Most of us cruising the world see local life as these two dimensional cutouts unless, with luck, something occurs to get us involved. In non-English speaking countries, cruisers seldom get to read local newspapers. Uninterested in any subject outside their immediate yachtie environment, local language, newspapers, politics and so on lack reality and can't interest them.

In non-English speaking countries many cruisers excuse the lack of any but superficial interest with the old *language barrier*. Most, in fact, stay aboard waiting for weather rather than discover what's going on ashore or traveling inland. Many pay too much for everything and later whine they were "cheated". These cruisers never fulfill a good piece of their cruising goals.

With most of my adult life spent outside English speaking countries I think I have a qualified viewpoint on the matter. Simply put, *you erect your own language barriers.* Here's my experience. I have lived or worked in many countries where I did not speak the language. I have studied seven languages, and I came to live and work in four countries where I had to use the language well. Yet I always got along *best* in the countries where I didn't know the language!

If you don't do the local language, people expect less of you and help you more. They have more patience with you, going out of their way to guide you. People are more interested in you. If you speak their language, you are more of an interloper in their society, not a visitor. Yes, humans practice prejudice everywhere. Parents show great interest when daughter brings the foreign exchange student home for dinner, but the excitement really gets big when she brings one home to marry! As a visitor not able to use the language at all, you have *privilege.* As a visitor trying to pick up a few words, you have sympathy, and honor as well.

If you seriously want to talk well in a foreign language, go ahead and make a serious try. Be prepared for a mind wrenching, personality bending experience. Yes, languages carry culture, and learning them requires personality change. Acquiring language often causes physical pain. It takes a long time and requires exhausting effort, yet it never can be 100% successful, despite what you've read in spy novels. It will give you great satisfaction, but it shall change forever your ability to be an interesting visitor everyone wants to help.

Get out and see the world while cruising, and don't erect your own language barriers. Wiggle your eyebrows, wave your arms, point to things and words and have fun, but don't ever say to me, "It's *easy* for you, you speak the language." That's precisely why it's not easy many times.

PROVISIONING AND REPAIRS

Do major provisioning in the Walmart, Pueblo and Cash and Carry stores on Route 3 just north of the town of Fajardo. Anchor or take a slip at Isleta and shuttle with the Isleta Ferry to Puerto Real where *publicos* run frequently to Fajardo. *Publicos* also run frequently between Fajardo and the major malls outside on the highway. A more convenient and, in the long run, perhaps a more economic alternative is to put up at Puerto del Rey Marina and hire a car for a day.

In Fajardo bolt ends and reject lengths of Sunbrella can be had at *Cien Almecenes* at the northwest corner of the square.

While shopping on Route 3 do lunch or dinner at *Lolita's*, the best (and most reasonable) Mexican restaurant in Puerto Rico. Across from *Lolita's* is the best deal on Imron paint at a store whose sign reads "*pintula*". Paint in Spanish is *pintura*, but Puerto Ricans often slur their r's into l's, thus the spelling *pintula*.

Sail repair and several good marine and fishing stores are at Villa Marina. You can reach Villa Marina by gofast dinghy from Isleta, or bring the big boat in and lay alongside for the visit.

Puerto Rico's east coast has good haul-out facilities, and good marine stores. For major work, however, you shall eventually travel to hunt things down in San Juan, launching epic travails and travels. St. Thomas may beckon if the job seems beyond the resources of Fajardo. Not a bit! The U.S.V.I.s don't have Puerto Rico's industrial economy, something necessary to support a tough boat job. Industrial strength support is on the south coast, however.

Serious jobs which don't require haulout, such as installing a water maker or auto pilot, are best attacked by taking the boat around to Salinas on the South coast. Salinas is a safe and commodious harbor in which to decommission the boat for extended work, or for wet storage.

Larry's Playa Marine on the Salinas anchorage has the best stainless stock in Puerto Rico, and just about anything else you can think of.

In nearby Ponce is the most amazing warehouse you'll ever visit: Rubber and Gasket of Puerto Rico (843-8450), which has sheet rubber, Teflon, Lexan, and any kind of hose you want, including stainless flex. And they fabricate. Everything can be had in Ponce. Stainless fabrication is at Accurate Tooling (AT Metal) on Hostos in Playa Ponce. Owner Luis Ojeda is also Commodore of the Ponce Yacht Club. Near the yacht club is Benitez Carrillo, a dealer that has vee belts, bearings, gears, seals, motor controls and every ball bearing known to man, even your roller furling's.

Cash

Cash is available in most major tourist centers with American Express cards at any American Express office, and VISA and Master Charge at most commercial banks, including automatic teller machines.

If you carry a lot of cash, don't flash a roll. Keep it in separate pockets. Purses and "belly bags" have been known to get ripped off in some areas of the Caribbean.

Hauling Out

Puerto Rico is dotted with boatyards. You will have no trouble finding one for a quick haul and paint. For more extensive work, as always, shop around before committing.

If leaving your boat for the summer, consider hauling out and leaving it at Ponce Yacht Club (expensive), or Palmas del Mar, near Humacao, or Puerto del Rey, in Fajardo. Puerto del Rey is the largest marina in the Caribbean and very well equipped, though it can be dear, depending.

Croabas, Puerto Real and Isleta have little or no facility for long term storage but are good and fast haulouts. At Palmas del Mar, your boat can be laid up either ashore or afloat and the yard has a marine store with yard owner Hans Grossen as helpful as he can be. Las Croabas is do-it-yourself and usually cheapest.

NAVIGATION AIDS

Most cruisers are consumed with getting to a certain place at a certain time. For this they heavily invest in all sorts of navigational equipment. The real art of navigation, however, is to not be in the wrong place at the wrong time. This should be your criterion for choosing navigational aids.

Charts

NOAA charts 25650, 25653, 25668, 25677 and 25687. These are available in yachting versions in most marine stores as Waterproof Charts from International Marine Supply, or in Imray charts which offer the scale a yachtsman is interested in, showing landmarks of interest to the small boat skipper making for small harbors. Bluewater Books & Charts of Ft. Lauderdale also has one of the country's most comprehensive inventories of charts and guides for all of the Caribbean and other regions.

Both these charts have formats which better fit small boat nav tables than do DMA or NOAA charts, and they have color contrasts.

Tide Tables

In the English Channel I was never without my tide tables and current guides. The tides were, after all, 34 feet at my moorings, and the currents reached 9 knots! In the Caribbean there's nothing to know outside the information on the Pilot Charts which doesn't vary year to year.

None of this is really necessary, however, since most places you can assume high tide *is at 8 o'clock* local time everywhere near open sea *on the day of a* full moon. So you can add 52 minutes a day thereafter and do without tide tables.

NOTE: The south side of the Greater Antilles and the Virgin Islands have diurnal tides with a higher high and a lower low instead of two lows and two highs.

DIVING IN THE SPANISH VIRGINS

These lovely keys and island provide cruising and diving opportunities as good as or better than their Anglophone cousins to the east, but they have the added spice of "going foreign".

As a diving destination, Puerto Rico is still virgin territory. The Puerto Rico Tourism Company estimates that less than 20 per cent of the snorkeling and scuba opportunities in these islands have been exploited to date. For decades, Puerto Rico has been a Mecca for the sportfising enthusiasts. Tourist dive boat operations are a relatively recent development, and significant charter sail operations have only begun.

The islands are edged with narrow shelves of white sand beaches by rocky cliffs over coral outcroppings, where snorkelers wander and wonder. For the scuba divers, most keys and islands are surrounded by precipitous drop-offs of 12 to 14 fathoms, where the windward walls are brilliantly illuminated in the morning, and those off the leeward anchorages are displayed by the afternoon sun.

One doesn't have to go to the South Pacific to explore extensive coral reefs such as the mile-long formations southeast of Culebrita. The Spanish Virgins are also a submarine photographer's dream.

Lobster season in Puerto Rico, thanks to the crustecean's continuous mating season, is year round. Catches are restricted to male adults, or females without eggs, have a carapace (antennae base to beginning of tail) of 3.5 inches or more.

For the more adventurous, there is La Cordillera, the 12-mile long string of islets, keys, reefs and sea mounts which stretch from Cayo Icacos, near Cabo San Juan on the mainland, to Arecife Barriles west of Culebra. Many spectacular snorkeling and diving sites here, and elsewhere in the Spanish Virgins, are available from day anchorages only.

When planning each day's activity, you should cast a cautious eye at the strengths and directions of wind, wave and swell. At many of the recommended day anchorages, and depending on conditions, you should keep an anchor watch aboard while the diving party is out. It is of course always best to snorkel or dive upwind and upcurrent of the boat in exposed areas.

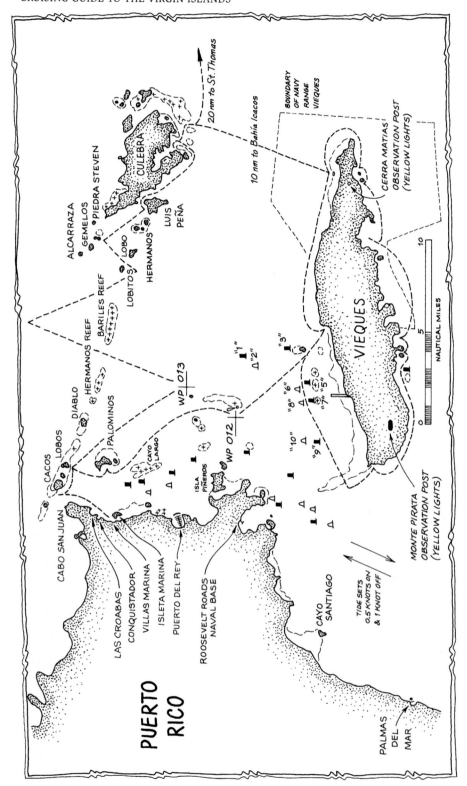

NAVIGATING THE SPANISH VIRGINS

The Spanish Virgin Islands embrace 400 square miles to the west of the U.S. Virgin Islands. Unlike the U.S.V.I.s, Puerto Rico has an extensively developed industrial and agricultural infrastructure. But like the U.S.V.I., the Spanish Virgins are entirely dependent on tourism, yet they are many years behind in the development of tourism infrastructure. Bad for the typical resort tourist, good for the cruiser. It means unaffected townspeople, undisturbed anchorages, pristine beaches and productive fishing (with a year-round lobster season). Ashore, the Spanish Virgins offer immersion in the Spanish Caribbean with the escape clause of bilingualism and the convenience of U.S. institutions. There are three cruising areas in the Spanish Virgins: La Cordillera, Culebra and Vieques. Be sure to schedule ample time to enjoy each. Review Sailing Directions for Vieques Sound.

December through March, distant gales often create swell in exposed northern anchorages, and some day anchorages might be untenable. Fortunately, the lovely harbors of the south coast of Vieques and the reef anchorages of Culebra, Icacos and Palominos are unaffected. Cold fronts that make it this far south are often stalled or have dissipated into troughs which persist for several days. While not good for the avid sailor, these conditions make for fluky winds which in turn create diving and snorkeling opportunities across La Cordillera, in Culebra's outlying keys, and on Vieques' north coast.

GPS Waypoints

Using GPS

All GPS coordinates in this section of the guide are given to the nearest tenth of a mile. This should satisfy either WGS 84 and WGS 72 map datum. These waypoints were taken on site and confirmed several times each on different occasions. All bearings given have intentionally been made as simple and mnemonic as possible, given the marks they refer to. Every attempt was made to make GPS waypoints with safe searoom, and which coincide with critical compass bearings. However, do not rely solely on these GPS waypoints for your navigation. Use them in conjunction with your charts, visual sightings and depth readings. The prudent skipper should never rely solely on one instrument reading when navigating.

The following list of GPS waypoints corresponds to the waypoint readings on the sketch charts in this section.

GPS Waypoint	Location	Latitude (north)	Longitude (west)
#001	Entrance Palmas del Mar	18°04.7 north	65°47.5 west
#002	Cayo Santiago	18°09.0 north	65°44.0 west
#003	Roosevelt Roads R "2" entrance buoy	18°12.4 north	65°36.6 west
#004	North entrance Media Mundo Pass	18°15.6 north	65°36.1 west
#005	South exit Medio Mundo Pass	18°14.3 north	65°35.7 west
#006	Puerto del Rey	18°18.0 north	65°36.7 west
#007	Reef Channel NW of Ramos	18°19.3 north	65°37.2 west
#008	Reef Channel South of Isleta	18°20.0 north	65°37.3 west
#009	Off of Villa Marina	18°20.8 north	65°37.5 west
#010	Off Palominos	18°21.0 north	65°34.7 west
#011	Off Icacos	18°23.2 north	65°35.7 west
#012	Fl "4" west of foul ground Vieques Sound	18°14.0 north	65°32.0 west
#013	NE of East Rock Vieques Sound	18°17.0 north	65°30.0 west
#014	Anchorage Cayo Luis Peña	18°18.9 north	65°20.0 west

GPS Waypoint	Location	Latitude (north)	Longitude (west)
#015	Between Cayos Lobito and Lobo	18°18.0 north	65°23.1 west
#016	Off Punta Soldado	18°16.5 north	65°17.2 west
#017	Grampus Banks Buoy R "2"	18°14.3 north	65°12.4 west
#018	Enter Flemenco Beach	18°20.5 north	65°19.0 west
#019	Enter Bahía Sardinas	18°17.8 north	65°18.5 west
#020	Entrance Bahía de Almodovar	18°17.9 north	65°14.7 west
#021	North of Isla Culebrita	18°20.0 north	65°14.0 west
#022	Off Bahía Salinas del Sur	18°07.1 north	65°18.2 west
#023	Entrance Bahía Icacos, Vieques	18°09.4 north	65°18.5 west
#024	Off Isla Chiva	18°06.1 north	65°23.0 west
#025	Off Ensenada Honda Vieques	18°06.0 north	65°21.8 west
#026	Enter Ensenada Honda	18°06.8 north	65°22.2 west
#027	Heading waypoint Ensenada Honda	18°07.4 north	65°21.6 west
#028	Off Puerto Ferro	18°05.5 north	65°25.0 west
#029	Off Puerto Mosquito	18°05.0 north	65°26.5 west
#030	G "1" buoy west of Esperanza	18°04.7 north	65°29.0 west
#031	Enter Esperanza	18°05.0 north	65°28.2 west
#032	Off Green Beach	18°06.8 north	65°34.9 west
#033	Two Fathom Bridge to Isabel Segunda	18°09.0 north	65°36.0 west
#034	Northwest of Isabel Segunda	18°10.0 north	65°28.0 west
#035	To Bahía Icacos from Isabel Segunda	18°10.0 north	65°27.0 west

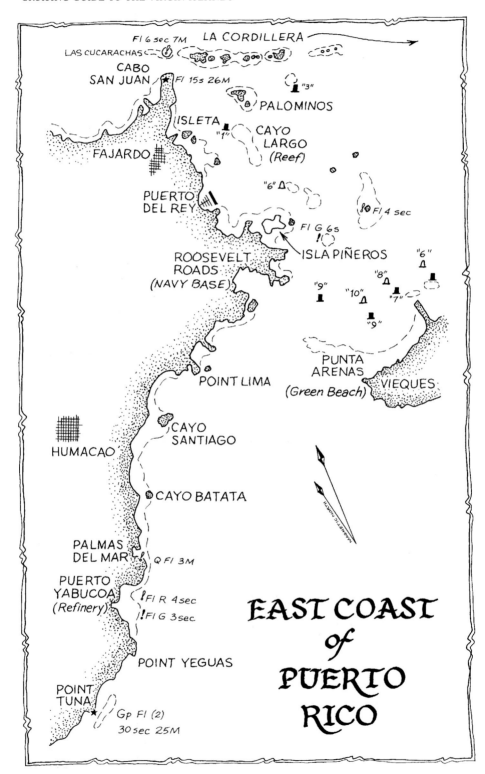

Fl 6 sec 7M   LA CORDILLERA →

LAS CUCARACHAS

CABO
SAN JUAN   Fl 15s 26M

"3"

PALOMINOS

ISLETA
"1"   CAYO
LARGO
(Reef)

FAJARDO

"6" Δ

PUERTO
DEL REY   Fl 4 sec

Fl G 6s

ISLA PIÑEROS   "6"
Δ

ROOSEVELT
ROADS
(NAVY BASE)   "8"
Δ

"9"   "10"   "7"
Δ

"9"

PUNTA
ARENAS   VIEQUES
(Green Beach)

POINT LIMA

CAYO
SANTIAGO

HUMACAO

CAYO BATATA

Magnetic North

PALMAS
DEL MAR   Q Fl 3M

PUERTO
YABUCOA   Fl R 4sec
(Refinery)   Fl G 3sec

EAST COAST
of
PUERTO
RICO

POINT YEGUAS

POINT
TUNA   Gp Fl (2)
30 sec 25M

PUERTO RICO'S EAST COAST

The Spanish Virgin's western boundary is home to six major marinas and five haul out yards. In the shelter of Puerto Rico's highest peak and America's only tropical rain forest, this coast hosts offshore a wealth of cruise-worthy islands.

Palmas del Mar

Enter in good water directly from the east. The anchorage may be temporarily used, some guides notwithstanding. There is good holding in 10-12 feet everywhere except the northeast corner which has silted to a depth of 5-6 feet near the seawall, but that's where you want to be to avoid rolling in swell which can sometimes penetrate the harbor.

Palmas is a resort and condominium project along the lines of Puerto Cervo in Sardinia and José Banús in Spain. Golf, tennis, scuba, sport fishing and sail charters are available to owners or guests of the hotel, marina or shipyard. At a condo slip, in the marina, or laid up ashore at the yard, this harbor affords reasonable hurricane protection. Boats fared well here as hurricane Hugo passed by. If you lay up ashore, ensure for yourself that the jackstands are lashed securely together with nylon warp, and using Spanish windlasses to maintain tension. During Hugo, boats on the hard blew over due to inadequate lashings.

Chez Daniel is an excellent authentic French restaurant. A fisherman's restaurant and seafood store is in the southeast corner of the anchoring basin.

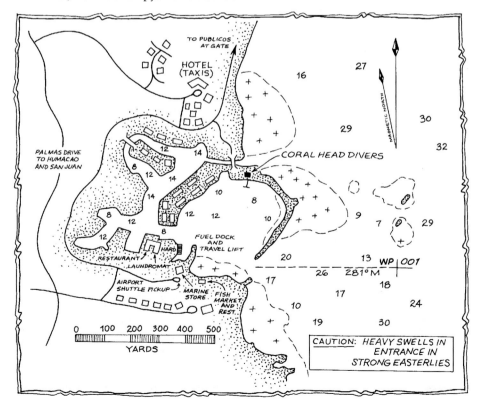

253

Cayo Santiago

Also called "Monkey Island", Cayo Santiago is a free range for the Caribbean Primate Research Center. It is inhabited by well over 1000 monkeys, whose crazy antics include biting persistent tourists. Best to stay on the sand beach and enjoy the cerulean water and the abundant snorkeling behind the island. It is not permitted to go ashore other than on the beach. Do not molest nor feed the monkeys. Enter from the south and east.

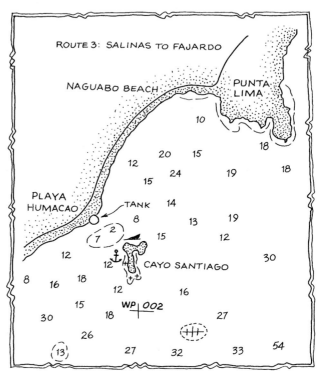

Day charterers and snorkelers from Palmas del Mar may join you, but this anchorage is normally deserted late afternoons and nights.

Rumors are that a resort marina is planned for Punta Lima to the north to compete with Puerto del Rey and Palmas del Mar.

Roosevelt Roads Naval Station

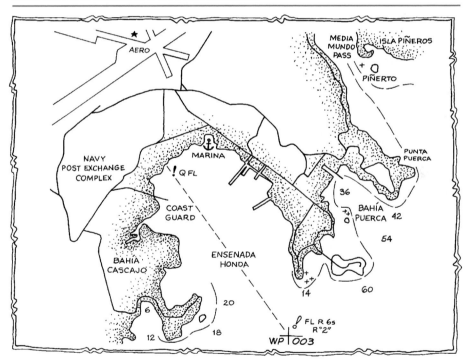

An emergency refuge for all but retired career military and their guests, Roosevelt Roads has a small marina with marine store, limited dockage, med-moorings at the seawall and some moorings. The marina stands by on VHF Ch.16. Telephone (787) 865-3297.

Turn to the chapter about Navy Range Vieques for more on the mission of Roosevelt Roads and how it affects, and helps, the cruising community.

Isla Piñeros

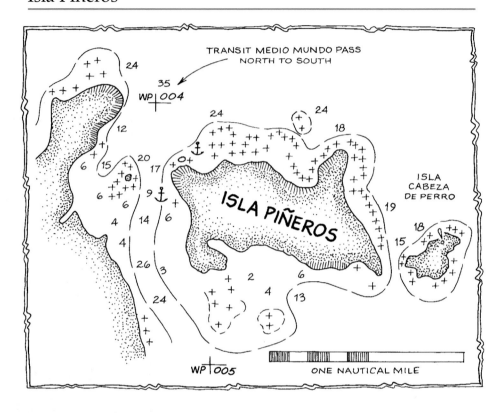

A well protected anchorage which is quite secluded during the week, yet it is only 3 miles south of the largest marina in the Caribbean. This island is part of the Roosevelt Roads Navy Base and the Navy does not allow going ashore. Nonetheless one can anchor overnight for excellent swimming and snorkeling. The cove in the northern reef is a nice lunch anchorage in summer months when the wind is south of east. Enter Pasaje Medio Mundo from the north where the rocks west of the pass are clearly visible. The shoal on the island's southwest corner extends quite far and is less visible. It is not recommended to pass between Isla Piñeros and Cabeza de Perro. Call Puerto del Rey's harbormaster at 860-1000 or on VHF Channel 71 for information regarding Navy maneuvers.

Puerto Del Rey

If visiting San Juan or picking up crew, Puerto del Rey is the port of convenience. With 750 slips and long term land storage it is the largest and most modern marina in the Caribbean. Atlantic Canvas and Sails is here as well as any yacht service desired. Puerto del Rey's 80-ton Travelift is available for emergencies seven days a week, 24 hours a day. Call the harbormaster on VHF channel 71 or 16 for a slip or a transient dock, or anchor temporarily in the turning basin inside the breakwater north of the docks. A rental car agency is on site.

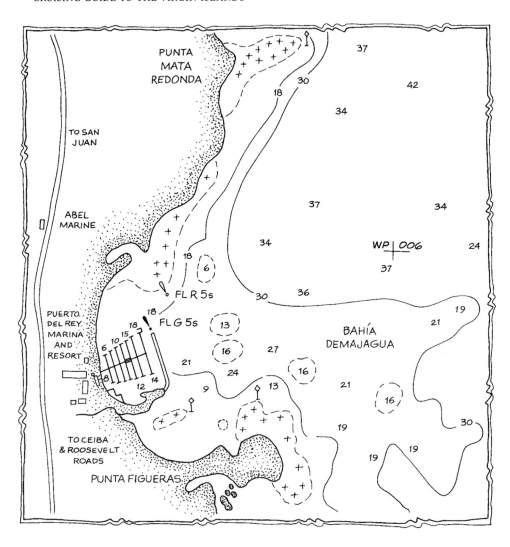

Fajardo

The district of Fajardo caters to yachting enthusiasts from around the world. Major sailing events such as the Heineken International Cup and CORT regattas, as well as the Club Nautico de Puerto Rico's Round Puerto Rico Race are hosted from Fajardo.

Fajardo lies at the foot of the only tropical rain forest in U.S. jurisdiction, the 28,000 acre El Yunque national forest, where annually 100 billion gallons of rain nurture 240 species of trees. The forest's 3,532 foot peak, El Toro, is visible throughout the Spanish Virgins. Excepting Chez Daniel in Palmas del Mar, Restaurant du Port at Puerto del Rey and Rosas Seafood Restaurant in Puerto Real, sailors ashore seeking fine dining need a car.

Ports on the mainland can be approached via the ship channel or via the "inside route", behind the keys and the reefs using a careful eyeball method. If taking the inside route, watch for a cross set at the GPS waypoint shown on the chartlet just south of Isleta.

When approaching downwind from the east, be careful to avoid Cayo Largo. The ground swells to windward of this dangerous reef are not always visible from their backs.

Ramos is a private island. You may anchor outside the string of floats off the beach with which the owner has marked his territory, but you may not go ashore.

Isleta

Anchor at Isleta west of the marked shoal in the bight of the two islands; close to the marina you will suffer from the ferry wakes. There are two ferry services to Puerto Real, one for residents of the con-

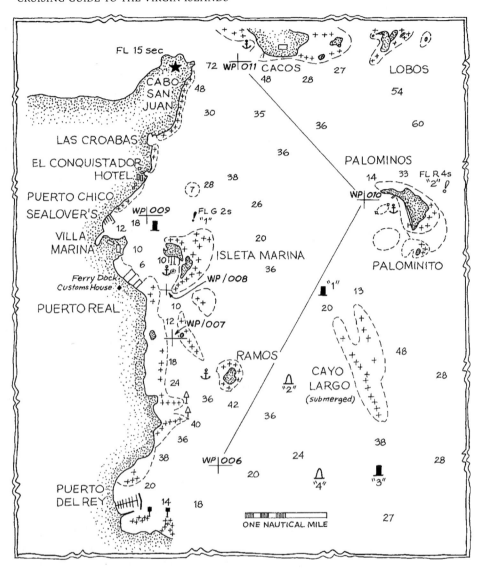

dominium and marina, the other for visitors at a cost. The ferries run from 6:30 to 21:30, quarter after and quarter of the hour.

Puerto Real
Except for dredged ferry channels, Puerto Real is shoal and windward. It is best approached by dinghy or by the ferries from Isleta Marina. Ferries to and from Culebra and Vieques can be had here. Some provisions are at Big Johns across from the Isleta ferry dock. Dine at Rosas Seafood, a short walk inland from there.

Villa Marina
Villa Marina, with 250 slips and a 60 ton Travelift, caters mostly to power craft. Marine stores Skipper Shop and El Pescador behind Villa Marina are the most extensively stocked in the area. On the same street are Fajardo Canvas and Sails, East Side Marine Yacht Sales, and Re-Power Marine Services for engine, prop and machine shop needs.

Puerto Chico / Sea Lovers
Immediately northeast of Villa Marina are the marinas of Sea Lovers, near the beach, and Puerto Chico, larger and to the east behind the seawall. Puerto Chico has a fuel dock and handles drafts to seven feet. Sea Lovers is for smaller craft.

Las Croabas
Las Croabas is a cheap and fun place to haul with lots of nearby tipico restaurants and bars. There are no hardware stores nearby.

Isla Palominos

A jewel of a tropical island from which to watch the sun set over El Yunque on a last night's return to Fajardo. If headed east, Palominos is a must to break up what can be a bear of a windward close-hauled leg.

Facilities ashore are leased by El Conquistador resort on the mainland. Anchor between the harbor's central shoal and the island, or close to Palominitos, to avoid the wash of the hotel ferries.

Whether running west from the U.S.V.I.s, or beating eastward on the start of a cruise, Palominos is a fine farewell or introduction to the Spanish Virgins.

Having overnighted in Palominos, take a morning sail down to Isabel Segunda for lunch and a look at the fort. To continue on to Culebra, tack up to Diablo from behind Palominos, continue tacking east along the Cordillera, making successively shorter tacks as you gain lee from Culebra. Let anchors-down at Luis Peña. (See sketch).

SAILING DIRECTIONS, VIEQUES SOUND

From Vieques Sound (pronounced vee-AYE-case) until the end of the British Virgin Islands, the islands are within sight of each other. Nonetheless, you should not try to cross this stretch in one bound.

For many years I have experimented with sailing to windward across Vieques Sound. I find that I save a couple of hours by tacking in the area south of the Cordillera, where the current and chop is less adverse, into the lee of Culebra. However, a strong motorsailor can barrel down the middle in heavy chop and contrary current with more stress in less time. The south coast of Vieques can be tough going to windward in onshore easterlies against the equatorial current. It's best to sail the south coast of Vieques downwind and with several stops as it has beautiful beaches and anchorages. In short, if you circumnavigate the Spanish Virgins, do so clockwise.

Cross the shoaly Sound with pleasantly short and easy trips. Notice from the chart that to avoid a visit to Isla Palominos, one would have to go out of one's way and bash 9-12 hours to windward across Vieques Sound. From Palominos one can use the lee of Culebra and the keys west of it to pleasantly sneak-tack one's way to Dewey in only six to eight hours.

Currents and Tides

Cruisers in the Spanish Virgins should take special note of set in Vieques Sound. Yachties from the Virgins on their first trek to Puerto Rico and back are surprised to find it sometimes takes twice the time to sail east as it took to sail west, something to bear in mind when setting out late in the day from Fajardo. You don't want to be caught out among the reefs in bad light! The Equatorial Current flows west northwest in this area at a clip of 0.4 to 0.7 knots. When it mounts the shallow plateau of the Sound, sheering forces increase its velocity in chaotic ways. The tide floods west and ebbs east, but on the Sound's north and south borders tidal flow is more north-south as it pours onto or spills off the Sound's shal-

263

Simon Scott

low plateau. These currents approach one knot on flood, a half-knot on ebb. While these effects are not extreme, when taken together, they can lead to unpredictable landfalls and arrival times. Since you want to arrive at reef entrances in favorable light, conservative course planning is essential.

The shallow Sound can whip up a vicious chop above 15 knots, impeding windward progress. If motor-sailing, sheet in hard and tack the chop in comfort. With sail up, you'll make better time over ground as well.

Staging

Start at Punta Arenas and take whatever route you wish to get to Culebra, just not direct. Stop first at Roosevelt Roads for retired militaries, the Fajardo boat yards for those not hauling in Palmas del Mar, or Isla Palominos for those wanting to scrub their bottoms and enjoy a Bahamas-

like respite before going eastward over the Sound.

A stop at Culebra, is required before pressing on to the hurly burly of the commercial U.S. Virgins. Anchor at the little beach behind Luis Peña. Carry on to Dewey or Ensenada Honda the next day. Culebra is also a place to wait out summer storms. Some cruisers make a pattern of summer in Culebra, winter in the Virgins, never moving their yachts more than a few miles in an east or west direction all year. They put down a hurricane mooring in a select spot before the seasonal rush begins and summer there in security, watching the fire drills when the exodus from the Virgins begins with each hurricane warning.

Wait favorable conditions in Dakity Harbor or Bahía Almodûvar before moving on to St.Thomas or Puerto Rico. If bound for a circumnavigation of Vieques, set sail from there for Bahía del Sur after ensuring a cold Navy test range.

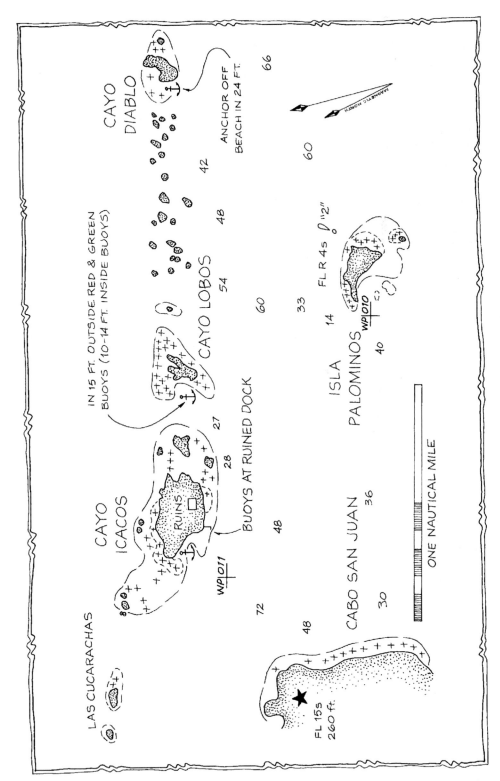

LAS CUCARACHAS

CAYO DIABLO

ANCHOR OFF
BEACH IN 24 FT.

66

60

MAGNETIC NORTH

42

48

IN 15 FT. OUTSIDE RED & GREEN
BUOYS (10-14 FT. INSIDE BUOYS)

CAYO LOBOS

54

60

33

FL R 4s "2"

ISLA
PALOMINOS

14

WPI010

40

CAYO
ICACOS

RUINS

27

28

BUOYS AT RUINED DOCK

36

48

WPI011

72

48

CABO SAN JUAN

30

FL 15s
260 ft.

ONE NAUTICAL MILE

La Cordillera

This 12-mile chain of islets and reefs is Puerto Rico's East Coast Marine Reserve. The larger keys can be used to day-anchor the mother boat in the lee of the easterly trades and in shelter of northerly swell in the winter.

Diving expeditions can then be run by dinghy to the surrounding reefs and walls. Diving opportunities on the Cordillera are constrained in the winter months by wind and swell. Northerly swell and anything but mild easterlies are unusual in the summer months. In general, look for minimum swell days with a favorable wind of 15 knots or less before choosing your day anchorage and dive sites.

Cayo Icacos

Arrive at the waypoint shown on the chart and then proceed into the cove of deeper water by eyeball, snuggling up to the white sand beach in seven feet of glass clear water. Under prevailing trades this can be a good night anchorage and provides endless diving, snorkeling and shelling on the surrounding reefs and secluded beaches. It might be a little rolly in winter, however.

Cayo Lobos

This is a privately owned resort island with a protected harbor marked by red and green floats. Make a day anchorage just inside or outside the buoys and well off the channel, respecting the access and privacy of the owners.

Cayo Diablo

Shoal draft vessels can work close in to the beach, while deeper drafts must avoid the coral formations and anchor in three-to-four fathoms of clear sand farther out.

The rocks and islets downwind can be dived with a reliable motorized tender. Be sure there is enough anchor rode and that it includes chain. This is a day anchorage only, and only in settled conditions of less than 15 knots east. There is a diveboat mooring on the east shore.

Los Hermanos and Barriles

To the east of Cayo Diablo are two long reefs called Hermanos and Barriles which, though in open sea, can provide quite productive diving during calm conditions. These reefs and the many islets strung out to the east, which belong to the Culebra group, are for experienced divers.

CULEBRA AND ITS OUT ISLANDS

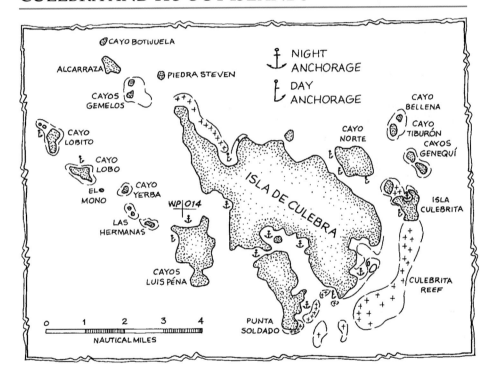

Unspoiled Isla de Culebra is a winter retreat for some and a permanent expatriate refuge for others. Most people are attracted by its seclusion, its spectacular beaches and the quaint and insular town of Dewey.

Unexploited diving opportunities abound in the rocks, islets and full boarded islands centered on Culebra. Dive any number of day anchorages, though swell can affect them in the winter months. Culebra and its outlying islands can absorb the serious cruiser or diver for weeks. Arriving from Puerto Rico, make your landfall at Luis Peña. Arriving from the Virgin Islands or overseas, anchor overnight at Dakity Harbor behind the reef entrance to Ensenada Honda. Proceed next morning to the top of Ensenada Honda to clear in at Dewey.

Cayos Lobo and Lobito

Unless you have a large launch, these keys are too far downwind to safely visit by dinghy from Luis Peña. However, under settled east southeasterlies with no northern swell, it is possible to use day anchorages at either key. There are both reefs and walls to satisfy snorkelers and scuba buffs. As with most day anchorages, the skipper might want to post an anchor watch aboard while the diving party is out. Dive upwind and current of the dinghy.

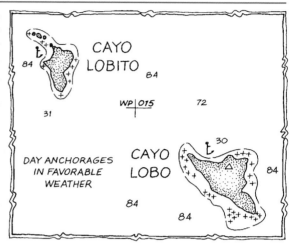

Cayo Luis Peña

In settled easterlies, the beach on the north shore of Luis Peña provides anchoring in clear white sand roads between patches of coral rock. Stay in one-to-two fathoms, since the water shoals quickly.

The anchorage inside the reef is available to drafts of five feet and less. In winter the northwestern point of Culebra shields the anchorage from the worst of the northeast swell. Luis Peña is an uninhabited wildlife refuge with hiking paths and secluded beaches. Except on weekends, you are likely to be alone here, where you will toast the sun disappearing spectacularly over the rocky skerries of Las Hermanas, backed by the majestic peaks of the El Yunque rain forest.

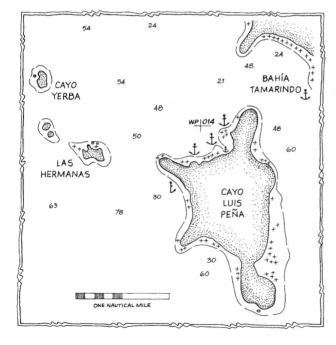

In light conditions, this is a great place from which to launch diving expeditions in gofast dinghies. To the north are the reefs of Culebra's Punta del Noroeste and the offshore keys of Alcarraza, Los Gemelos and Piedra Steven. Closer yet to the west are Las Hermanas rocks and Cayo Yerba.

Culebra

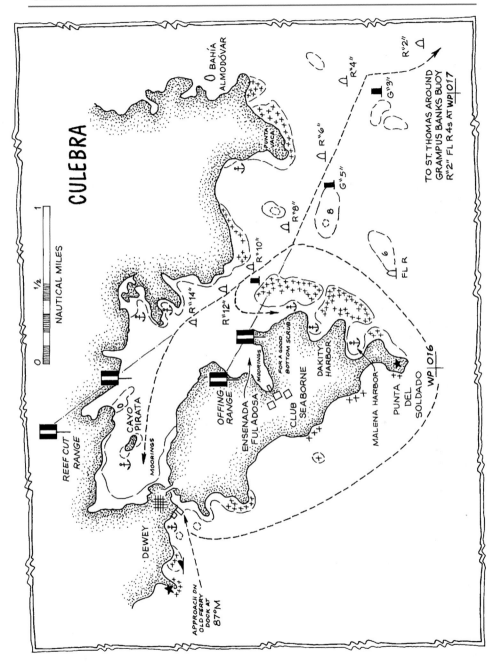

Culebra National Wildlife Refuge

Large seabird colonies are protected by this sea park which consists of 23 keys and islands and four large tracts of land on Culebra itself. Luis Peña and Culebrita are open for exploration ashore from sunrise to sunset.

Ensenada Honda

The narrow reef entrance is clearly marked by green can No. 9 and red buoy No. 10. Enter between the buoys. The holding is poor right off the town. The boats there look like they are at anchor but most are on moorings. To be near town, anchor in 16 feet on a bottom of sand and mud west of Cayo Pirata. The finest anchorage to be had within Ensenada Honda is behind the reef at Dakity Harbor in two-to-three fathoms over white sand. Malena Harbor to the southwest can be tricky; it is best left to local powerboats. Dinghy to the happy hour at the Club Seabourne pool at the foot of Fulladosa Bay.

Flamenco Beach

This is a spectacularly beautiful beach whose anchorage is untenable in northerly wind or swell which often occurs in the winter months. Under those conditions you can visit by road with your camera. It's over the hill from the air-port. Under favorable conditions it is a great sand anchorage until ebb tide when you might find it starts to roll. Plan your trip to go in for lunch on a rise of tide and exit on the ebb in the afternoon. You won't regret it.

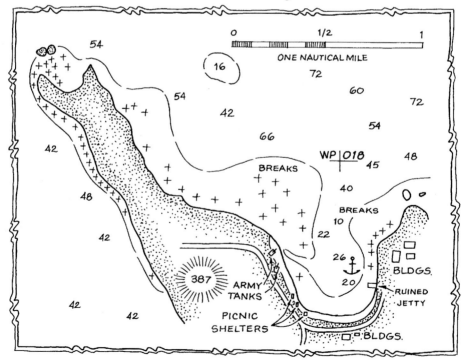

Bahía Sardinas

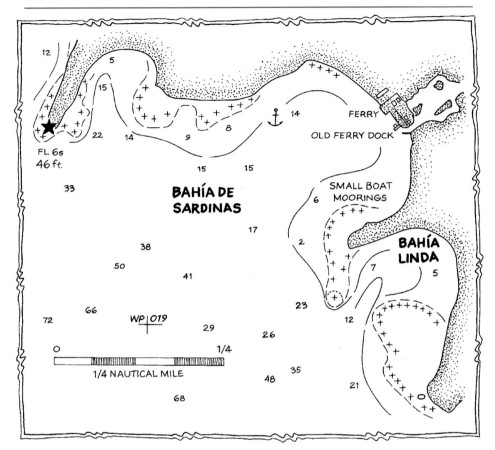

Dewey can be entered at night by Bahía Sardinas. Position yourself one half mile south of the flashing seven second light marking the reefs west and north of the harbor entrance. From there take up a heading of 87° Magnetic on the brightly lit old ferry dock on the south edge of town. Anchor in 12 feet of clear water over white sand to the northwest of the new ferry dock. The ferries stop running after 6pm, so your night should be a comfortable one. You shall be conveniently waked by the 7am ferry, however, should you oversleep. The above advice notwithstanding, it is not advisable to be sailing these waters at night.

If coming from the east you shall need to clear customs and immigration in Dewey from the Ensenada Honda side. Customs is at the airport, a five minute walk from El Batey restaurant whose dinghy dock is a long ell pier northwest of the anchorage, just north of the high school stadium which is visible from the water. See the chartlet of Ensenada Honda.

El Batey has the best sandwiches on the island.

Dewey

See Bruce and Kathy at La Loma art shop, above the town dock, for the latest skinny on what's happening in Culebra. The town offers a variety of restaurants, bars and boutiques with conveniently staggered, if not randomly chosen, opening hours.

Ferries to Fajardo run frequently from Dewey, if you bypassed Fajardo but want to visit it from Culebra. Fresh vegetables are available by truck from the mainland twice a week. The truck parks in front of the Post Office.

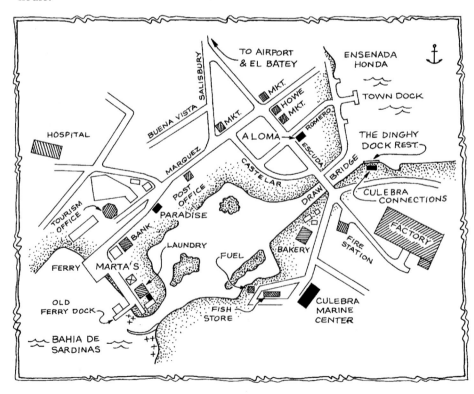

Bahía de Almodóvar

Bahía de Almodóvar and Dakity Harbor are the most tranquil anchorages of Culebra. Round Culebra at Punta Vaca into Canal del Sur. Enter Puerto Manglar heading 325°M on a large wedding cake of a house overlooking the bay. Pass between small red and green markers in three fathoms. Round the double mangrove islet of Pelaita through a 10-foot deep channel and between another set of markers. You are now in Bahía Almodóvar's deep, still waters. Anchor west of the reef in two-to-four fathoms of white sand and gin clear water. The cooling trades blow over the reef out of a clear horizon, where the lights of St. Thomas come on at night. This harbor is locally called La Pelá or Manglar.

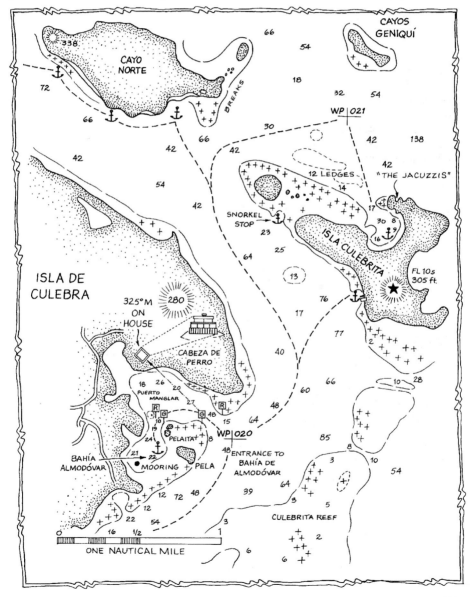

Isla Culebrita

Within the northern arms of Culebrita is a 400 yard diameter basin with 7 to 25 feet of clear water bordered by white beaches. If you missed Flamenco, be sure to do Culebrita. Hike to the seaward pools known locally as "the Jacuzzis". Snorkel the nearby reefs and ledges, or dive the Cayos Ballena, Tiburón and Geniqu' a mile to the north. In 20 knots of wind or more there can be heavy seas between Cayos Geniqu' and Culebrita. Once inside, easterly seas disappear, but occasional heavy northerly swell may penetrate the bay in winter. Overnight here only in settled weather with no north swell forecast.

If conditions don't permit a visit to the northern anchorage, stop on the southwest coast of Culebrita. Visit the northern beach afoot by mounting the hill to the old lighthouse. Take a camera. Anchor by the small piers north of Punta Arenisca in 16 feet of sand surrounded by 4 to 6 foot coral heads and to the east of a 72 foot drop-off for snorkeling and diving. Culebrita Reef stretches almost two miles from here to the south southwest.

Carol Lee

Cayo Norte

Depending on swell, two-day anchorages are available on the southwest shore for diving expeditions by dinghy. Anchor on the shelf in 25 feet of sand off rocky ledges with a 72-foot wall to the west. In settled light easterlies such as in the summer months, one can anchor overnight on the east end of the southern shore in 18 feet of sand, west southwest of the red fisherman's cottage, sheltered by the breaking reef to the east.

VIEQUES — NAVY RANGE

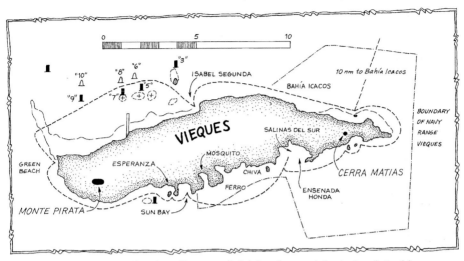

NOTE: *Navigating these reefed islands at night is inadvisable.*

Many consider these anchorages and beaches the best of all Virgin Island anchorages. They have been left untouched by developers. They have been off limits most of this century, and they have been little used as anchorages since they were formed.

For most of the 20th century the U.S. Navy has used much of Culebra and Vieques for weapons training. U.S. and NATO navies still use the east end of Vieques for land, air and sea based war games. However, the anchorages and beaches are available for use by yachts when the test range is not *hot*, as they say.

Weekends are *normally* available, but these anchorages may be visited at any time with Navy permission, which is easy to get. Call VIEQUES RANGE CONTROL on VHF channel 16 and inquire if the range is *hot*. If no response after repeated tries within VHF range of the observation posts on Cerro Matías (see chartlet for Salinas de Sur) or Monte Pirata on the island's west end, consider the range available for your use. If, after diligent

but fruitless attempts to contact the Navy, you wander into a closed zone, not to worry, the Navy will graciously let you know in good time. Keep VHF channel 16 on.

It is unrealistic to depend on constant harmony between the Navy's use of its test range, your cruising schedule and your draw of wind and wave on that coast. A good plan is to launch a cruise of Vieques from Culebra. While enjoying superb *culebrense* cruising, you can watch for a window of favorable weather and no operations in the Vieques Navy ranges. When that happens, which it shall, you'll be off for a memorable cruise.

When visiting the beaches, do not go inshore. Do not molest any devices found on the beach — certainly not shells made by man! As a service to the yachting community, Puerto del Rey Marina in Fajardo will provide the Navy's weekly Vieques hot exercise schedule. Call Puerto del Rey HARBORMASTER on VHF 16 or 71, or dial 860-1000 by land line.

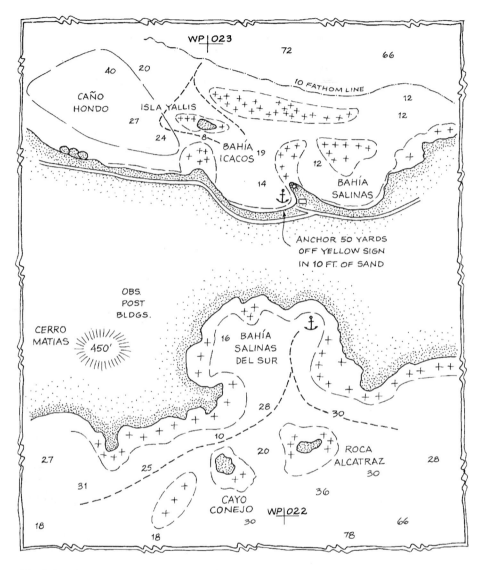

Bahía Icacos

Bahía Icacos is a beautifully protected azure bay surrounded by ranks of reefs for both protection and snorkeling. Approach from the west with high afternoon light over your shoulder. The narrow gap between the mainland shoals and Isla Yallis has eight feet of water and is sheltered from swell. Because there is no clear sand road in this channel, it may be comfortable for only shallow draft vessels. Deeper drafts may take the 17-foot minimum depth of the channel between the breakers on the seaward reef and Isla Yallis. Bahía Salinas, to the east, is a secluded beach exposed to northerly swells through a gap in the reefs. Leave the bay the way you entered by Isla Yallis, in the morning and with light over your shoulder.

Salinas del Sur

Under east to north winds this is a calm, beach lined anchorage. Tuck up into the northeast corner behind the reef and select a patch of bare sand to anchor in 10 feet of water. If you use the beach, don't go further inland nor pick up man-made objects.

Bahía Chiva

Bahía Chiva is a U.S. Navy beach area with many picnic shelters, the anchorage can nonetheless be quiet and private. Holding is good in fern and fan covered sand. The calmest anchorage is in 10 feet of water in front of the southernmost picnic shelter, close to the beach and covered from swell by the reef west of the point. On the west side of Isla Chiva is a fine anchorage tight up against its northern end, or, for a lunch stop with snorkeling, off the rock crevice at the island's midpoint.

Ensenada Honda

Ensenada Honda is a wonderfully tranquil and secluded mangrove anchorage and a fine hurricane hole for hurricanes that cooperate and don't blow from the west. Enter northwest by north on the first point of land inside the bay. Turn northeast at three fathoms toward a baby mangrove off the tip of the third point. When north of a set of rocks called Los Galafatos ("The Thieves"), turn east southeast for the anchorage. See the chartlet for waypoints.

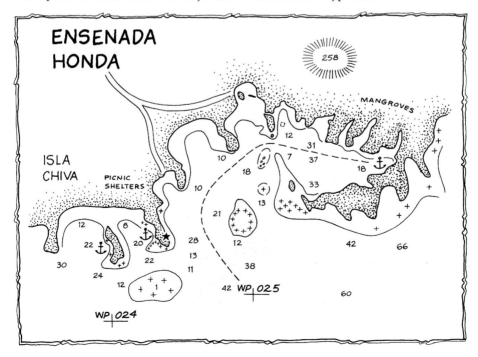

Bioluminescent Bays of Vieques

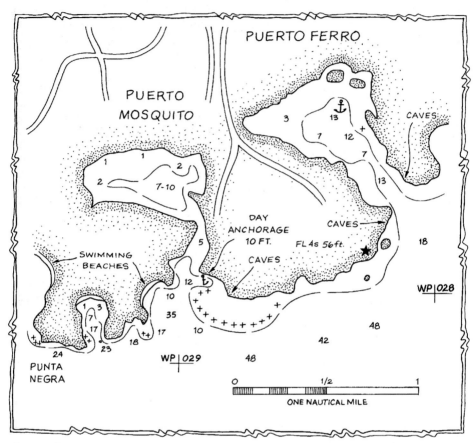

Both Puerto Ferro and Puerto Mosquito are strongly phosphorescent. If you don't overnight at them, you can visit by dinghy from Sun Bay or Esperanza, or you can take night tours from Esperanza arranged through several local dive and tour operators.

Puerto Ferro

Puerto Ferro is a mangrove anchorage with a narrow entrance and only a seven foot controlling depth on the bar. A day anchorage is feasible outside the bar when the wind is north of east or less than 15 knots south of east.

Puerto Mosquito

Puerto Mosquito is accessible only to drafts under five feet, or slightly more at high tide (with infinite patience). A day anchorage is available which, under settled conditions, can be used for snorkel trips to the rocks and caves about the harbor's mouth. To the west of the entrance is perhaps the loveliest palm lined, white sand, azure water swimming beach in the Caribbean.

TURTLE WATCH PROGRAM

Playa Resaca and Playa Brava on the north coast of Culebra, east of Flamenco Beach are turtle nesting beaches. The Culebra Leatherback Project conducts nightly beach surveys from April 1 to August 30th. Interested cruisers may participate by previous arrangement with project management. To participate, call 787-742-0115.

VIEQUES — CIVILIAN

Initially a redoubt of Taino and Caribe Indians from which they could maraud the Spaniards, Vieques became a refuge for all stripes, from army deserters and runaway slaves to the renegade "portugee", as were called the whites of any extraction who were on their own in the Caribbean. Today the island hosts a fiercely independent and proud population dotted by (sometimes dotty) expatriates.

Sun Bay

This southern anchorage is outside the Navy zone and next to the fishing village of Esperanza. Enter the middle of the bay headed north, steering clear of the shoal off its southeast arm. Anchor in grassy sand tight against the east southeast shore to avoid roll in strong wind east or south of east. This is a public beach more than a mile in length. A bath house is in the northwest corner of the bay.

Punta Arenas

Punta Arenas, on the northern end of the western shore of Vieques, is a good stopover either entering or leaving Vieques Sound. Depending on conditions and wind direction on leaving Palmas del Mar, Punta Arenas may be a better first tack than Isla Palominos. A good anchorage is 40 yards off a flat crescent beach, which the Navy calls Green Beach, and which is one half mile south of Punta Arenas. Another is just south of a ruined dock backed by a couple of large rusty tanks. Head east to the point and turn to the anchorage when in 30 feet of water. Pick a grassy sand spot to avoid the patches of sand colored coral ledges here.

The anchorage is isolated on weekdays and the water is clear. Great for bottom scrubbing and skinny dipping. Conch and an occasional lobster are available on the rocky shores to the south. The Escollo de Arenas is the name of extensive sandbores with rock stretching north northwest from the northwest tip of Vieques with only 8-10 feet covering them. Be warned: escollo means trouble. This permanent rocky ridge collects storm detritus for the entire Sound. Though it can be crossed without inci-

dent, each season some foolish yachtie brags to me that he's gone across the Escollo in a high chop and never saw less than 10 feet. Let him try it ten times in a row! Don't be fooled by these one time experts. Play it safe. Debris on the bottom can combine with 3 foot troughs to give you a nasty bump on some old wreck or steel tank. I usually go around the Escollo except in a calm. It is a pleasant, reaching sail compared to motoring across it.

Esperanza and Puerto Real

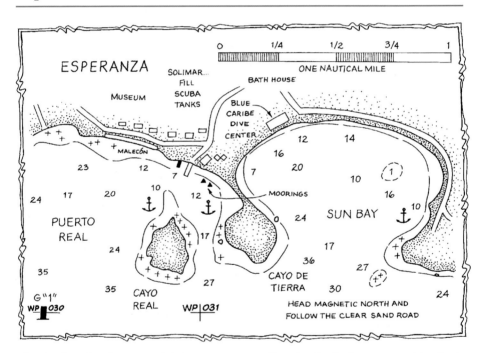

Blue Caribe Dive Center maintains moorings at the north end of the anchorage. They are worth the fee to use them, if you wish to use this anchorage. The bottom is Teflon coated grass in fluffy sand. Puerto Real, the anchorage northwest of Cayo Real, can be rolly, but once dug in, the holding is fair in sand and coral. Lunch ashore after a pleasant stroll on the balustraded malecón and visit the

small archeological museum. For fresh seafood, see the fishermen when they bring in their catches in the morning, or when they gather at the town pier to pack them off on the ferries later on. West of Esperanza, there is a two fathom shoal where seas can build up in strong easterlies or southeasterlies. Official charts notwithstanding, it is marked only by a green can, No. 1, on its eastern edge.

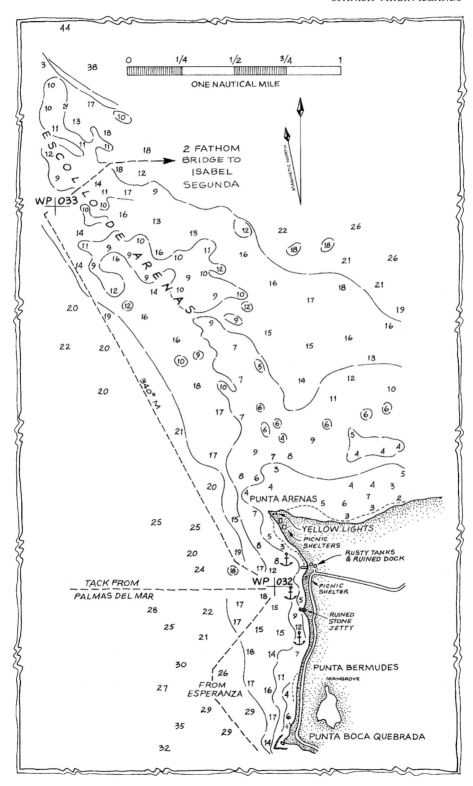

44

3

38

0   1/4   1/2   3/4   1

ONE NAUTICAL MILE

10

10   12

17

10

13

18

11

11

18

12

9

14

11   17   9

WP 033

10 10

16

13

10

13

18   12

2 FATHOM
BRIDGE TO
ISABEL
SEGUNDA

MAGNETIC NORTH

26

22

18

18

21

26

14

11

9

16

16

10

11

16

12

16

18

21

9

9

10

17

21

14

12

10

12

19

20

19

16

9

10

12

16

19

22

20

16

15

15

16

16

20

18

10

9

7

15

13

20

10

9

5

14

12

10

18

10

7

6

11

6

6

17

7

6

6

6

4

9

5

6

4

4

4

17

9

7

8

5

20

8

6

4

3

5

4

Punta Arenas

5

6

7

3

2

25

25

15

7

Yellow Lights

3

3

Picnic
Shelters

20

19

8

5

3

Rusty Tanks
& Ruined Dock

24

(18)

17 12

8

Picnic
Shelter

TACK FROM
PALMAS DEL MAR

WP 032

5

28

22

17

18

15

Ruined
Stone
Jetty

25

21

17

15

15

9

12

30

18

14

7

Punta Bermudes

26

11

Mangrove

27

FROM
ESPERANZA

17

16

4

29

29

17

6

35

29

Punta Boca Quebrada

32

14

Isabel Segunda

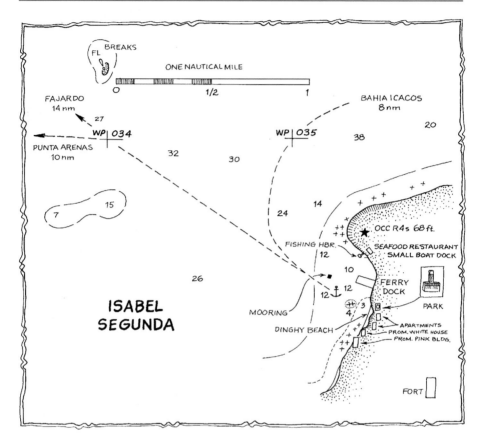

Arrive at Isabel Segunda in mid morning in time for a walk up the hill and a visit to the museum and gallery in El Fortín, the Conde de Mirasol fort protecting the harbor. This was the last fort constructed by Spain in the new world. A $20 million resort is in the works on the beach west of here. Visit Isabel Segunda now before the tourist boom.

This anchorage can roll viciously. After a seafood lunch in a harborside restaurant, up anchor in time to make Punta Arenas or Fajardo to the west, or Bahía Icacos to the east, both calm anchorages in prevailing winds and easy to make while the light is still high and westing.

West Indian Grub & Grog

Few recipes have actually survived from the days of the Arawaks, although we know they hunted agouti and iguana, made cassava bread and seasoned their foods with salt and pepper. Arawak hunters reputedly caught wild duck and fowl by covering their heads with gourds (cutting tiny eye slits) and standing neck-deep in the swamps or lagoons until an unwary bird passed near enough to grab it by the legs and drown it!

The Caribs' favourite recipes are unlikely to prove popular today, but the pirates provided us with a still-popular cooking technique: The word *boucan* means to cure meat by smoking strips over a slow fire, which is what the early Brethren did with the wild pigs and cattle which escaped or were "liberated" from the farms of Spanish settlers. Hence these men came to be called *boucaniers*. Eventually they returned to the sea as *buccaneers*, where, of course, they drank rum, still the basis for many West Indian drinks. Made by the fermentation of molasses or cane juice, rum was defined in 1909 as "the spirit of sugar" and was originally called *kill-devil* or *rumbullion*.

Generally, West Indian foods represent the cosmopolitan visitors who have passed through the islands over the centuries — South Americans, East Indians, Chinese, Europeans and Africans — so there is no single "West Indian" style of cooking. What has evolved, however, is a fascinating hodgepodge of customs and cuisines reflecting their diverse origins.

While the Caribs and the buccaneers enjoyed their own style of cooking, in modern times, the chefs aboard many charter yachts have developed their recipes. Jan Robinson is captain and chef aboard her 60-foot motorsailer "Vanity." Over the past several years she has developed a series of cookbooks that detail the favorite recipes of charter yacht chefs. Among these books is "Sea To Shore, A Cook's Guide To Fish Cookery." On the following pages are a sampling of recipes from this popular book.

GOOMBAY CONCH CHOWDER

Preparation Time: 30 minutes
Cooking time: 2 hours
Marinating time: 1 hour
Serves 6
Chef: Mardy Array
Yacht: *Emerald Lady*

1 lb. conch, tenderized, chopped or
  (processor ground)
4 Tblsp. lime juice
6 strips bacon
2 large onions, chopped
3 stalks celery (with tops), chopped
3 (14-1/2 oz.) cans chicken broth
1 bottle clam juice
2 bay leaves
1 tsp. Worcestershire sauce
2 shakes Tabasco
1/3 cup sherry
2 cups new potatoes
1 (1 lb.) can chopped tomatoes
1/4 tsp. paprika
2 tsp. chopped parsley
1/4 tsp. oregano
1/4 tsp. basil
1/4 tsp. thyme
1/8 tsp. turmeric

Marinate chopped conch in lime juice for 1 hour. Strain off juice, reserving 2 tablespoons. In a large kettle cook bacon until almost crisp. Remove, drain and chop into 1 inch pieces. In the bacon drippings, saute onion, garlic and celery until tender. Add broth, clam juice, bay leaves, Worcestershire sauce, Tabasco, sherry. Peel and cube potatoes and add. Stir to blend and simmer briefly. Add tomatoes, conch and seasonings. Simmer 1-1/2 hours. Remember to adjust the seasonings to your taste. Serve with a shake of hot pepper sauce on top of each serving.

CRAYFISH WITH GARLIC

Preparation time: 15 minutes
Cooking time: 35 minutes
Serves: 4
Chef: Jan Robinson
Yacht: *Vanity*

3 lbs. crayfish meat
1/4 lb. butter
1 large onion, chopped
2 shallots, chopped
4 cloves garlic, chopped
1/2 tsp. black pepper
pinch of cayenne
1 Tblsp. freshly chopped parsley

Melt the butter in a heavy skillet and add onion, shallots, cayenne and garlic. Cook over medium heat, stirring constantly, for 15 minutes. Season, remove from heat and add the parsley. Serve with rice.

FISH FONDUE

Preparation time: 20 minutes
Cooking time: varies
Serves 4
Chef: Mary Usmar
Yacht: *Voyager*

2 lbs. tuna, or any red-fleshed fish
oil

Cut fish into bite-size pieces and proceed as with meat fondue. Invent dips. Chutney — Seafood Cocktail Sauce — tartar sauce — curry in yogurt — lemon butter — chili sauce — sweet mustard sauce. Serve with fluffy rice and a tossed green salad. Note: a shrimp fondue is also good.

B.B.Q. MACKEREL

Preparation time: 10 minutes
Marinating time: 2 hours
Cooking time: 20-25 minutes on BBQ grill
Serves: 6
Chefs: Sylvia & Stanley Dabney
Yacht: *Native Sun*

> 3 lbs. mackerel fillets, or tuna, wahoo,
>   bonito
> 1 stick (4 oz.) butter
> 1 (8 oz.) bottle lime juice
> Worcestershire sauce

Melt butter, add lime juice and Worcestershire to make a dark sauce. Marinate fish 2 or more hours. Remove fillets, reserve marinade. Wrap fillets (skin side down) in aluminum foil, make holes every 3 inches. Lay over grill (medium-to-low heat) to cook slowly. Baste with reserved marinade during the 20-25 minutes of cooking. Do not turn.
Alternatives: Tuna, Dolphin

STUFFED SNAPPER FILLETS

Preparation time: 20 minutes
Cooking time: 20 minutes
Serves: 6
Chef: Kate Hinrichs
Yacht: *Mystique*

> 1 (7-1/2 oz.) can crab, drained
> 6 snapper fillets
> mayonnaise
> 1/4 cup chives
> 1/2 cup white wine
> Hollandaise sauce

Preheat oven to 350 degrees F. Prepare crab with mayonnaise and chives. Spread over one side of fillets. Roll jelly roll fashion, securing with toothpick. Stand in pan and pour 1/2 cup wine around. Cover with foil. Bake at 325 degrees F. for 20 minutes until fish is firm to the touch.
Serve on a bed of fresh steamed spinach with Hollandaise sauce. Serve with rice.

DELICIOUS DOLPHIN DISH

Preparation time: 10 minutes
Cooking time: 20 minutes
Serves: 4
Chef: Jennifer Dudley
Yacht: *Chaparral*

> 2 Tblsp. melted butter
> 1/4 cup water
> 1/4 cup olive oil
> 3 Tblsp. dijon mustard
> 2 Tblsp. fresh herbs, basil, thyme
>   (or 1 tsp. dried)
> 1/2 cup breadcrumbs
> 4 fresh dolphin fillets
> Garnish: fresh basil and lemon wedge

Preheat oven to 400 degrees F. Place fillets in buttered baking dish. Sprinkle with lemon juice, olive oil, and herbs. Spread mustard over each fillet. Add breadcrumbs. Pour water around fillets. Bake in 400 degree F. oven for 15-20 minutes until flakes easily. Garnish.

SQUID SLICES

Preparation time: 15 minutes
Cooking time: 30 minutes
Serves: 4
Chef: Gilhian Bethell
Yacht: SS PAJ

8 squid (defrosted or fresh cleaned)
4 rashers bacon
1 cup breadcrumbs
mixed herbs
salt and pepper
2 medium onions
sesame seeds
1 egg
sherry (optional)

Cut the tentacles from the squid and chop finely. Chop bacon and onions finely. Fry bacon and onions until soft, add tentacles and fry quickly together. Remove from heat and mix all other ingredients together and add the fried mixture after draining off all excess fat.

Stuff the squid and bake for 20 minutes or until squid are white and tender on a lightly buttered tray. Remove when cooked. Slice into round or serve whole with a wine or sherry sauce.

WEST INDIAN WHALE

Preparation time: 4 weeks
Cooking time: 5 weeks
Serves: 3,500
Chef: Jan Robinson
Yacht: Vanity

1 whale, large
1 truckload potatoes, chopped
1 truckload carrots, chopped
2 wheel barrow loads of onions,
   thinly sliced
Sea salt and pepper
Garnish with Sea grape leaves

Peel whale and cut into 1-inch squares, this should take about 4 weeks. Place in a 500 gallon pot. Add potatoes, carrots and onions. Salt and pepper to taste. Cook 5 weeks over a kerosene stove at 650 degrees F. Garnish. Drain oil and blubber!!!

● ● ●

NOTE: This may be cooked in a microwave oven, if there is one available. Cooking time can then be cut to two weeks if cooked on HIGH.

THE ORIGIN OF GROG

True "grog" had its beginning in the Royal Navy in the 18th century — specifically on August 21, 1740. It is the most traditional of all sea drinks.

Prior to 1740, Pusser's Rum was issued to the men "neat" — that is without water. But Admiral Vernon, the hero of Porto Bello and Commander-in-Chief West Indies was to change all this by the issuance of his infamous **Order to Captains No. 349**, given on board his flagship HMS Burford on August 21, 1740.

His order refers to the

"...unanimous opinion of both Captains and Surgeons that the pernicious allowance of rum in drams, and often at once, is attended with many fatal effects to their morals as well as their health besides the ill consequences of stupefying their rational qualities.

...You are hereby required and directed...that the respective daily allowance...be every day mixed with the proportion of a quart of water to a half pint of rum, to be mixed in a scuttled butt kept for that purpose, and to be done upon the deck, and in the presence of the Lieutenant of the Watch, who is to take particular care to see that the men are not defrauded in having their full allowance of rum."

The tars had already nicknamed Vernon "Old Grog" from the grosgrain cloak he often wore when on the quarterdeck. The watered rum gave great offense to the men, and soon they began referring to it contemptuously as "grog: from the name they'd already provided Vernon.

Vernon's order provided that every man's half-pint Pusser's Rum allowance be diluted with one quart water. This was later changed to two parts water and one rum. In 1756, the daily ration was increased to one pint per man! Just before the end in 1970, it was reduced to one-eighth pint.

On board another ship of Vernon's squadron, the HMS Berwick, and just after the issuance of Vernon's order, one of the men wrote this poem that became famous throughout England:

"A mighty bowl on deck he drew
And filled it to the brink.
Such drank the Burford's gallant crew
And such the Gods shall drink.
The sacred robe which Vernon wore
Was drenched within the same,
And Hence its virtues guard our shore
And Grog derives its name."

LIMEY

Tall glass or old-fashioned glass
  filled with ice cubes
2 ozs. Pussers Rum
Soda water

Squeeze the juice from one half lime. Add sugar to taste (optional, but not traditional). Top off with soda water, stir, and float the expended lime peel on top.

ROYAL NAVY FOG CUTTER

Ice cubes to fill shaker
2 ozs. Pusser's Rum
1/2 ounce gin
1/4 cup lemon juice
2 tbsps. orange juice
1 tbsp. orgeat syrup
1 tsp. dry sherry
Fruit slices for garnish

THE BIG DIPPER

Ice cubes to fill shaker
1 oz. Pusser's Rum
1 oz. brandy
1 tbsp. lime juice
1/2 tsp. sugar
dash of Cointreau
Club soda

Shake well rum, brandy, lime juice, sugar and Cointreau. Strain into an old-fashioned glass with several ice cubes, fill with club soda and stir slightly. This is a popular drink on Atlantic crossings just before star time.

EMPIRE TOP

2 parts Pusser's Rum
1 part French Vermouth
1 part Grand Marnier
1 dash Angostura bitters
Crushed ice

Shake all the ingredients well and serve.

DIFFERENT DRUMMER

3 cups orange juice
3/4 cup coffee liqueur
6 orange or lemon slices (garnish)
3/4 cup Jamaican or dark rum
2 dozen ice cubes

Combine ingredients and shake well. Garnish with orange or lemon slices and serve immediately. Serves 6.

PLANTER'S PUNCH

1 cup cracked ice
3 ozs. Pusser's Rum
1 oz. lime juice
1 oz. sugar syrup
3 -5 dashes Angostura bitters
soda water

Shake all ingredients together well and pour unstrained into tall glass with several ice cubes. Top off with soda water, stir, garnish with lime slice and serve with a straw.

THE DEEP SIX

Tall glass filled with crushed ice
2 ozs. Pusser's Rum
1 tbsp. lime juice
1'2 ounce sugar syrup
Champagne

Combine rum, lime juice and sugar, and stir well. Fill glass with champagne and stir gently. Garnish with a slice of lime. This is an unusual drink — smooth, flavorful & powerful.

FORCE 12

Ice cubes to fill shaker
1/4 cup Pusser's Rum
1 oz. vodka
1 tbsp. lime juice
1 tbsp. grenadine
1/4 cup pineapple juice

Shake well and pour into tall glass. Garnish with fruit slices. This drink is a good test for sea legs.

"The Origin of Grog" and the above recipies are provided courtesy of Pussers Ltd., Road Town, Tortola, B.V.I.

Fabulous Island Fruits & Vegetables

A collection of some of the most delicious tropical produce to be found in the Virgin Islands.

Sugar Apple

A favourite throughout the islands, the sugar apple looks like it wears a coat of armour! Actually when ripe, it breaks open easily and the delicious, custard-like interior can be scooped out by the spoonful or by eating it by the mouthful, taking care to spit out the shiny seeds inside. It is well worth the effort, as the inside is sweet, with a wonderful sort of soft texture.

Illustrations by Joan Potter

289

Guava

This colourful fruit is used for making jams, jellies, and is scrumptious in pies and tarts. The guava is a small, usually round fruit that grows on a tree. The skin is green to yellow-green, and pulp inside is pink or peach to an almost red colour, with lines of seeds. Guava ice cream is a delicacy not to be missed.

Passion Fruit

Despite the connotation of the name, this fruit may be rather baffling to the first time taster. It is actually quite unattractive with a tough, wrinkly, brownish skin and is about the size of a lemon. The interior has a yellow green jellyish pulp with edible brown seeds. When the seeds are removed, the passion fruit essence is used to flavour exotic drinks, ices, tarts and pies, becoming an interesting, perfumey addition to many recipes.

Genip

Looking like a bunch of green grapes, these small, round fruits are a bit more challenging to eat! First the somewhat tough skin encasing the pulp must be pulled off (usually with your teeth). Once the skin is gone, the inside is yours to tug the sweet, sometimes tart pulp from the rather large pit. Although not easy fruits to eat, genips can keep you busy for quite awhile!

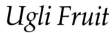

Ugli Fruit

Resembling an ugly version of a grapefruit the ugli fruit is light green to a yellowy orange colour, and can be the size of an orange to the size of a large grapefruit. Succulent and dripping with juice it is best eaten the same way as a grapefruit or an orange (the skin is easily peeled). If you have an opportunity to try this wondrous fruit, be sure to enjoy its blessings.

Tamarind

Growing from large, lovely shade trees are the pods of the tamarind tree. Used in many sauces such as Worcestershire, chutney, and piccalilli, tamarind is also used for sweet candies, and jams. One has to develop a taste for this often tart fruit, but, once acquired, it is hard to stop the attachment. To eat you must first crack open the pod, remove the threads and then consume the sticky paste attached to the large seeds.

Papaya

Growing from a tall, slender umbrella-shaped tree, the fabulous "paw-paw" varies from an eggplant shape to an oval or round shape. The colours vary from a green to orange or yellow, but the fruits must be tested by squeezing to ascertain whether it is ripe or not. The texture of the lovely orange, melon like interior of the fruit is almost as heavenly as the taste, especially when sprinkled with a bit of fresh lime. Green papaya still hard to the squeeze, is used as a cooked vegetable in many delectable recipes.

Sapodilla

About the size of a medium apple, the sapodilla should be eaten only when very ripe and almost mushy like a plum. The skin is a pale tan or beige colour with shiny black seeds inside that should not be eaten. This fruit is used in making many dessert dishes, and is delicious when eaten with other fruits in a fruit salad.

Soursop

A very unlikely looking delicacy this fruit is large (often weighing several pounds), with a green, spiny exterior. The shape is like that of a large pine cone irregularly formed. Only very few are eaten fresh, as most are used in flavouring other dishes with it's sweet fragrance, like soursop ice cream, or in tropical fruit drinks with a healthy measure of rum!

Mango

The mango grows from a large, leafy tree that during mango season becomes heavily laden with its scented fruit. Mangos come in many varieties, but are usually best eaten at the beach, where one can jump into the sea to clean off the delicious stickiness. Grafted mangos are less fibrous, and when peeled are a delight. One may see children and adults sucking on mangos to extract the juicy, orange flesh from the fibers and bulky seed in the middle.

Breadfruit

The breadfruit tree is a
common sight on many
Caribbean islands. Mature
fruits have dimpled green
skins and grow to 6 inches or
larger in clusters on magnificent
trees of up to 60 feet in height
with huge, long-fingered leaves.
Inside, the soft, fleshy fruits are
yellowish-brown to white in color and
rich in carbohydrates and vitamins A, B and C.
Breadfruit can be cooked as a starchy vegetable
side dish or in breadfruit breads, puddings and
pies. Try it baked with salt, pepper and butter.

Dasheen

This versatile plant grows to a height of four to six feet. The large, handsome, arrow-shaped leaves, sometimes called elephant ears, are similar to spinach. The young, tender leaves are used in callaloo soup, while the tubers, shown here, are generally stubby and similar in size to potatoes. Also called *cocoyam, taro, eddo* and *kalo*, the dasheen tubers are usually boiled, roasted or baked and eaten like potatoes.

Christophene

The pear-shaped christophene originated in Mexico where it is known as *chayote*, and is a member of the gourd family. It can be eaten raw or cooked and is crisp, juicy and nutty flavored, with a taste like fresh, young squash. Large christophenes may be stuffed with a mixture of bread crumbs, meat, cheese, onions, herbs and seasonings and broiled or baked.

Aubergine

This egg-shaped member of the potato family is a common plant throughout the Caribbean, as it relies on the warm climate and plentiful rain supply to support its growth. The large, glossy fruits are known by various other names, including *Chinese eggplant, Jew's apple, egg fruit, melongene, garden egg and mad apple*. The skin colors range from dark purple to mottled purple-and-white. Served as a vegetable, the ripe aubergines may be cubed and boiled or cut into strips or slices, battered and fried. Comprised of over 90 percent water, aubergines are low in both calories and nutritional value.

Medical Information

> **British VI: Ambulance/Fire/Police 999**
> **USVI: Ambulance 922 / Fire 921 / Police 915**

The sailing area comprising the Virgin Islands stretches from St. Thomas in the U.S. Virgin Islands to Anegada in the British Virgin Islands. Therefore, it is reassuring to know that good medical help is never far away. Both St. Thomas and Tortola have well-equipped hospitals should a serious injury occur, but the majority of minor boating mishaps require only the attention of a physician; hospitalization is seldom required. Accidents do happen, however, and when they do, it is good to know what facilities are available and where they are located.

When you are cruising or vacationing in the Virgin Islands, the last thing which you anticipate is sickness or injury. These notes are based on years of experience in practice in these Islands treating the visitor who unexpectedly becomes sick. They are not intended to replace any good first aid book issued by the Red Cross or St. John's Ambulance Brigade.

If you have a medical condition that requires ongoing medication, check with your physician before leaving home to ensure that you have enough medication to last during your vacation. *Please* carry the medication with you in your hand luggage, as checked baggage can be temporarily mislaid during flight changes and may not arrive until the next day. While most commonly used medications are available at Peebles Hospital (494-3497), pharmacies, or any of the six health centers in the islands, there may be a delay before these can be dispensed and valuable time may be lost.

Peebles Hospital in Roadtown, Tortola, is a small, modern 60-bed hospital with an operating room, x-ray department, pharmacy and laboratory, and can handle most routine emergencies. The hospital is staffed with a general surgeon, gynecologist, internist, anaesthetist and two general physicians. These physicians, as well as several others, are in private practice. There is also a private clinic specializing in plastic and reconstructive surgery. In the event of a more serious illness or accident requiring more specialized care, the hospital is only 15 minutes by air from St. Thomas, U.S.V.I., and 35 minutes by air from Puerto Rico; air evacuation can be arranged if necessary.

Should you require emergency medical treatment, a doctor is on call at Peebles Hospital 24 hours a day; there is also a resident doctor in Virgin Gorda.

Radio Tortola can patch a ship's radio through the telephone system to any of these physicians in an emergency; sometimes advice on the radio may suffice without the necessity of returning to home port.

The water around the islands gives you some of the best sailing, swimming, snorkeling, and scuba diving in the world. Enjoy it — but cultivate a deep respect for it.

Sunburn

Probably the commonest ailment. This area is classified as subtropical, and the sun can be very harmful if taken in large doses at the beginning of vacation. On a boat there is a lot of reflected sunlight from the surface of the water.

Wear a long-sleeved shirt and light, long pants part of the day for the first few days. Socks will protect the tops of your feet and wearing a T-shirt while swimming will protect your back. Use plenty of sunscreen lotion — the higher the SPF factor, the better the protection.

If, in spite of these precautions, you suffer a severe burn, cover up and use an anti-allergic cream such as Benadryl or Phenergan. Solarcaine or other burn lotion, liberally applied, and a couple of aspirin or acetaminophen every four hours or so will diminish the pain.

If the burn develops blisters, leave them intact as long as possible to protect the sensitive tissues beneath. Once the blisters have burst, apply an antibiotic ointment to prevent infection.

Eye
Conjunctivitis

Wind, dust, overchlorinated water in pools, aerosol sprays, etc., can cause mild to moderate discomfort. Symptoms include constant watering of the eye(s) with redness due to vascular congestion. Wash the eyes with clear water and use decongestant eye drops every four hours. Wear sunglasses as a preventative measure.

Foreign Body In The Eye

When examining the eye for a foreign body, a good source of light is necessary.

Lay the patient on his back and have an assistant hold a flashlight from the side of the eye. Check the lower lid first by pulling the lid down with the thumb. The upper eyelid can be examined by having the patient look down towards his feet. Hold the upper eyelashes with the thumb and forefinger and roll the lid back over the shaft of a Q-tip.

Gently remove the foreign body with a *moist* Q-tip and instill eye drops afterwards. Do not use a dry Q-tip as it can damage the surface of the eye.

Bowel Upset
Constipation

Constipation is rarely a problem in the tropics but may be worrisome during the first few days while acclimatizing to a new diet and the crowded quarters on a boat. Eat plenty of fruit and drink fruit juices, prune juice, and plenty of other fluids. If these remedies are unsuccessful, try some Milk of Magnesia or a mild laxative of your choice. If the condition persists, call a physician.

Diarrhea

Diarrhea is a common ailment on a tropical vacation, probably due to a change in diet and the availability of many exotic fruits. If you suspect the drinking water, boil it before drinking. If the diarrhea lasts more than a day, rehydrate using a glucose/salt solution like Gatorade or a solution of 1 pint water with 1/4 teaspoon salt and 1 tablespoon sugar, and stick to clear liquids only for 24-36 hours. If the diarrhea is accompanied by fever, contact a physician, who will probably prescribe an intestinal antibiotic.

Hemorrhoids

A frequent complication of the above conditions. Treat with long soaks in warm water and use glycerine suppositories twice a day and after each bowel movement. Suppositories should be kept refrigerated.

Burns

Minor burns can be treated with a simple antibiotic ointment and covered with vaseline gauze and then gauze dressings held in place by a bandage. If blisters appear, leave them intact as long as possible; puncturing them may lead to infection. If the burn appears to have penetrated through the skin layer, consult a physician.

Fish Hooks

The best way to remove a fish hook is to cut the shaft of the book with wire cutters and pull the hook, point first, through the skin with a pair of pliers. Treat afterwards as a puncture wound with antibiotic ointment and gauze dressing.

Fractures

The immediate first aid treatment is to immobilize the limb and use an analgesic or painkiller to relieve pain. Splints can be improvised from everyday items such as pillows, magazines, broom handles, or paddles, padded and tied firmly around the limb. In suspected fractures of the neck or back, lay the patient flat and prevent any movement, rolling or otherwise, by the use of pillows or other supports. Seek medical attention as soon as possible.

Headaches

May be due to too much to drink the night before, eyestrain (wear sunglasses), sinusitis from swimming and diving (take aspirin, acetaminophen or sinus tablets every four hours), or from too much direct sun (wear a hat). Bed rest and icepacks will relieve the ache. If the symptoms do not resolve in 24 hours, seek the advice of a physician.

Sprains

The early application of icepacks to the affected area during the first 8 hours will greatly reduce the amount of swelling. Elevate the limb on a pillow and apply an ace bandage from the affected area to above it.

Stings from Sea Urchins, Jellyfish or other Aquatic Creatures

First and foremost, watch where you are going. A weedy or stony approach to a beach means you may find sea urchins — don't step on them.

If you do get stung, do not attempt to dig the stinger out, as this can cause a secondary infection. Dab tincture of iodine on the stingers, and take antihistamines to reduce the reaction.

There are no lethal creatures in these waters, but there are a few with self- protection devices that can give you a nasty painful sting.

Cystitis & Urinary Tract Infections

Urinary infections are most frequently caused by sitting around in wet bathing suits. Drink plenty of fluids — cranberry juice is a favourite home remedy. A doctor will likely prescribe a urinary tract antibiotic.

Insect Bites

For bites of mosquitoes, sandflies, no-see-ums or blister bugs, apply an anti-allergic cream, such as Phenergan or Benadryl, to the area.

For prevention, there are a wide variety of insect repellent sprays, lotions and creams which are very effective when applied to exposed skin, especially in the late afternoons or early evenings, when the cooler temperatures lure these insects from their hiding places.

Allergic Dermatitis

The leaves of several tropical plants such as manchioneel or oleander, especially after rain, can produce a severe skin reaction. Apply antihistamine cream and

Suggestions for a Marine Medical Kit

If you will be cruising out of sight of land for any length of time, a first aid kit is essential. The following items will meet most of your medical requirements:

- Ace bandages
- Antacid tablets
- Antibiotics (ampicillin, erythromycin, tetracycline, etc.)
- Antibiotic ear drops
- Antibiotic eye drops & ointment
- Antihistamines (Benadryl 25 mg., Phenergan 25 mg., etc.)
- Anti-seasickness medication (Dramamine, patches, etc.)
- Antiseptic powder or cream
- Aspirin, acetaminophen (Tylenol, etc.), ibuprofen (Nuprin, Advil, etc.)
- Assorted dressings: Rolled gauze, gauze squares, bandage strips, roll bandages, cotton, adhesive tape, triangular bandage, butterfly strips, safety pins, etc.
- Azo gantrisin or Septrin
- Insect repellant sprays
- Laxatives (Milk of Magnesia, etc.)
- Lomotil tablets 2.5 mg.
- Oil of cloves
- Paregoric
- Rubbing alcohol
- Solarcaine
- Sunburn relief cream
- Sunscreen lotions
- Thermometer

take Phenergan or Benadryl 25 mg., 4 times a day.

The manchioneel tree produces a fruit resembling a small green apple, which is highly poisonous. *Do not eat it.*

Earache

Ear discomfort is frequently due to wax buildup after swimming, snorkeling and diving. The mixture of salt water and wax can create swelling which may cause temporary deafness.

If you are subject to wax formation in the ear canal, visit your physician and have him or her syringe your ears before vacation. Frequently a few drops of warm olive oil in the ear will soften the wax and alleviate the symptoms.

Earache associated with a runny discharge may denote an infection in the canal and will usually respond to antibiotic ear drops with hydrocortisone used 4 times a day. There are numerous preparations on the market containing isopropyl alcohol and boric acid crystals, which are helpful for drying the ear canals after swimming.

Fishing in the Virgin Waters

The vast numbers of sailors who cruise the Virgin Islands waters each year attest to the fact that there is a seldom quelled sense of adventure lurking in all of us; but few who come to these islands in search of excitement ever really delve below the sparkling surface of the turquoise and indigo waters to meet the equally cosmopolitan inhabitants below.

The colourful underwater residents come in every size, shape and character from mean-toothed barracuda to genially smiling grouper, and the annual pelagic visitors are just as varied; sleek, powerful marlin, graceful sailfish and vivid, rainbow-hued dolphin.

The range of gamefishing is therefore broad enough to please every type of angler, whether their inclination is towards a peaceful, reflective stroll along a quiet beach to cast for bonefish or the lusty adventure, so glamourized by Hemingway, tossing about on the high seas to battle with solitary billfish or giant tuna.

Fishing can be a very enjoyable supplement to a sailing vacation and one of the beauties of the sport is that a lucky novice has as much chance as an expert of landing a good sized fish. As the saying goes, "gamefishing is the only sport in which a complete novice has a realistic chance at a world record."

The modes of fishing in the Virgin Islands can vary from jetty fishing (guaranteed to keep the kids occupied for hours to the dedicated pursuit of the Atlantic blue marlin, requiring boat, tackle and a skilled crew. Generally, however, the fishing available can be categorized into three main areas: shoreline angling, inshore fishing and blue water trolling.

Marlin are the quarry of offshore anglers. •

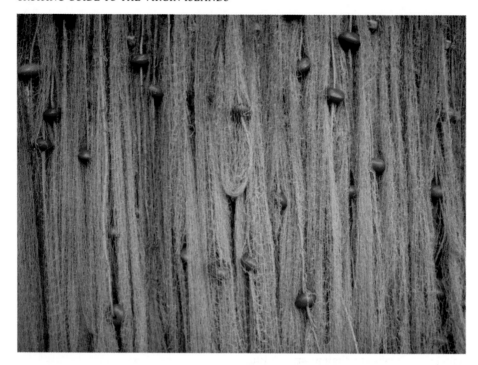

SHORE FISHING

Shore fishing and the variety of sport this provides is probably the least documented and the least utilized of all the types of fishing in the Virgin Islands, and yet for zealots of this king of sport, the area really has it all. The quarry includes bonefish, tarpon and permit, fish that in other parts of the world have as many ardent followers as the blue marlin, yet the potential in these waters is largely untapped and relies mainly on the reports of a few who, without the availability of a guide, still manage to locate enough of these wary demons of the shallows to return year after year.

Fresh water casting gear, fly rod or spinning tackle can be put to good use along the shoreline. In the lagoons and shallow banks a variety of smaller fish can be found, and the meandering channels that wind sluggishly through walls of mangroves are a have for jacks, parrot fish, schools of snappers, lady fish and the occasional barracuda or grouper.

Live shrimp are excellent bait for fishing off these banks, but good results can also be obtained with strips of fish, flies, small spoons, feathers or spinners.

Off rocky ledges snapper can be enticed with feathers or bucktailed jigs, and with spinning tackle and light test line the battle must be won quickly before the fish dives for cover to cut the line on a sharp-edged cranny.

Off the beach, the shallows are sometimes frequented by jacks, mackerel and runners for which ordinary fresh water casting tackle with surface lures and six to eight pound test line is ideal.

The same type of tackle can be used to hunt bonefish, permit and tarpon in the surf or on banks and flats where the angler can wade out into the warm shallows to peer eagerly into the weed for the flash of silver.

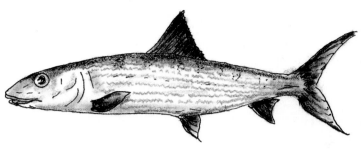

Bonefish

The bonefish can be found in shallow flats or off quiet beaches, feeding like a grey ghost along the bottom. A narrow, streamlined fish with a pointed snout, it ranges from 3-16 pounds, with an average size of about 5 pounds. It is a fussy eater with a highly suspicious nature, fickle and difficult to persuade; however, it can be tempted with conch, crab or shrimp and artificial lures such as streamer flies. Small feathers or bucktails can be successfully used with spinning tackle, but accurate casting and skillful working of the lure helps considerably. Because of its nervous disposition better results can be achieved by stealthy wading rather than poling out into the shallows in a dinghy.

The scientific name for bonefish, Abula vulpa means white fox, an accurate name for this wily, fast-moving fish which, when hooked, produces an astonishing turn of speed, zig-zagging with sizzling fury in one of the most exciting battles to be found in angling.

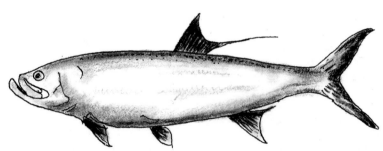

Tarpon

These bulky, energetic fish, largest member of the herring family, can be found in a variety of feeding grounds including harbours, reefs, shallow flats and creeks. They are a good-sized fish ranging from 20 to 280 pounds, but are more commonly found at less than 80 pounds. They tend to snooze through the day in holes and deep creeks and feed at night, when they can be heard splashing and leaping in pursuit of their prey — small fish, crabs and grass shrimps. Fly rod plugs and spinning gear are sure to produce some good sport with these hefty adversaries who are very willing to plunge after a variety of baits, tackle and fishing modes. The larger specimens require a considerable weightier test line, yet still give excellent sport. Local fishermen should be consulted for advice on the best areas and tackle for tarpon.

Permit

Largest of the pompanos, the permit ranges in size between 5 and 50 pounds, though is more common between 12 and 25 pounds. It is a flat-sided fish with an angry frown which warns that, for its size, it possesses surprising strength. It can be found bottom feeding, looking for crabs, sea urchins, clams, starfish and shrimp in the surf, the creek estuaries or on the reefs. Permit are fast feeders, flit-ting from one spot to another with flashing birdlike movements, always alert and on the go.

Permit can be taken on artificial lures, live bait or, if conditions are right, a skillfully used fly. Besides frequenting the shallows they like to feed in waves crashing over a reef or in curling breakers on sandy beaches.

INSHORE FISHING

Inshore fishing covers a multitude of species and equally diverse methods of capture. By far the most popular method is trolling around shallow reefs and headlands with the principal quarry being the kingfish or mackerel. At a slower speed, trolling with a 59-pound test line and strip bait, whole baits or spoons, large grouper of up to 75 pounds or snapper between 10 and 20 pounds can be caught.

Most practical for the yachtsman is bottom or still fishing which can be done more easily from a sailboat. This can produce fine catches of snapper and grouper, hogfish, grunts, hinds and many other bottom dwellers. For the still fishing enthusiast one just needs to anchor over any of the deeper reef areas — say 16 to 20 fathoms — and drop over a handline or two, or maybe a leadhead jig and the fish will do the rest. In calm weather drifting rather than anchoring will always produce better results. Strips of cut fish are commonly used as bait, but small live bait is by far the best and easily obtained by swiping the results of the kids' jetty fishing.

Chumming conch or tiny bits of any fish will often get the action going as the smaller fish will start to feed, stimulating the larger ones into striking at the bait.

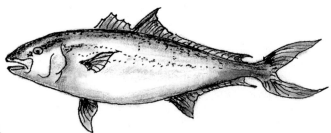

Amberjack

The amberjack is a long fish with heavy shoulders and tapered body. Like the bone-fish it has crushers instead of teeth. When hungry or excited it displays feeding stripes — a black band across each side of the head. They range in size from

20 to 150 pounds, more usually between 30 and 40.

Known for its dogged stubbornness and line-cutting tactics, amberjack provides first class sport on any tackle. Live bait is best,although the amberjack can readily be persuaded to gulp a properly worked bucktail or feather jig, and can also be tempted towards the surface with popping plugs or spinning lures. These fearless fish are often found around wrecks, travelling in small groups or schools at a fair depth. When hooked they rush for the bottom, but if one can be brought up, often the rest of the school will follow, allowing other anglers an excellent chance for a good battle.

Barracuda

This sleek, wolfish, sharp-toothed fish is one of the most easily captured in the area. Found everywhere from deep ocean to shallow flats, the barracuda is a voracious and impulsive feeder, happy to pounce on practically any bait offered. The usual specimen is about 12 pounds, but often goes over 50 and occasionally up to 80 pounds.

Barracuda are most often caught when anglers troll the reefs and "drop offs" for other gamefish. Despite the ease with which it can be caught, "cuda" is not a popular prey in the Virgin Islands, where it not only is considered inedible but also has a stench which can make the entire boat smell like a garbage tip. Nevertheless, if an angler is prepared to throw it back promptly, barracuda gives some good sport on light tackle.

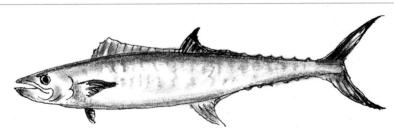

Kingfish

The kingfish is actually a member of the mackerel family and a fine food fish, sought by commercial fishermen as well as sportsmen. Ranging from 4 to 80 pounds it is more often found between 7 and 20. Like the amberjack, the kingfish prefers the depths but will race upward in pursuit of a trolled lure often clearing the surface of the water in its enthusiasm. When drifting or still fishing, plug casting gear or spinning tackle can tempt the kingfish, as can a carefully worked feather or bucktail jig. Having a similar shape to the speedy wahoo, kingfish can be tremendous sport on light tackle.

BLUE WATER TROLLING

Made famous the world over by the likes of Hemingway and Zane Grey, and more recently in the Virgin Islands by a string of world records, blue water trolling is by far the most popular method of angling in the area and also the most advanced as far as providing services for the would-be angler. The technique is to trail behind the boat a variety of baits and artificial lures at speeds usually ranging from four to eight knots and occasionally faster, working a pattern back and forth across the edge of the continental shelf.

This edge, or "drop-off" as it is usually known, plunges from an average depth of 25 fathoms to in excess of 300 fathoms, and in places is within two miles of the Virgin Islands group. Ocean currents striking this formidable cliff create a huge upswelling of microscopic food from the depths and, in turn, a food chain of small fish and larger predators. It is for the sepredators that the offshore angler is looking and the results of his search depend on such things as weather, moon and tide and of course, most importantly, the skill of the captain and crew. To go after the bigger pelagic (ocean roaming) species it is necessary to use a fishing boat, equipment and skilled crew. These can be chartered with ease throughout the Virgin Islands.

The various types of pelagic fish one normally encounters here include blue marlin, white marlin, sailfish, dolphin fish or dorado, wahoo, tuna and bonito.

Blue Marlin

Found in the Virgin Islands from July to September, the Atlantic blue marlin, grandaddy of the fleet, probably the most difficult of the pelagic fish to locate, to tempt into striking, to hook successfully and then to land. A marlin can get really mad at a bait, so mad that it keeps coming back over and over again to "kill" it or swallow it, smashing at it with its powerful bill. Anyone observing this fury will surely be hooked themselves. The challenge of this extraordinary fish matches its size which ranges from 90 to over 1,000 pounds. Up to 500 pounds is most common.

To tempt these solitary billfish that roam where there is plenty of space in the deep, a whole 2-5 pound mackerel, bonefish or mullet is used as bait. These, or large artificial lures, are trolled from outriggers to skip enticingly across the surface of the waves. Often a "teaser" is dragged behind the boat to create additional commotion.

Some anglers use light tackle — 30 to 50-lb. test line — or a medium 80-lb., but the majority prefer a heavier 130-lb. line. A hooked marlin is perhaps the most exciting fish in the world, leaping out of the water in enormous bounds, "tail-walking" on the surface, shimmering with rushes of bright colour in its fury. A "green" fish (one brought in so quickly that it isn't even tired) has been known to wreck a boat without much difficulty and the fight can be long and arduous, sometimes lasting for several exhausting hours that require grim determination and constancy from the angler.

However, the satisfaction of catching and tagging one of these monsters is well worth all the tossing around on high swells, the empty hours of no fish and the hard physical work involved.

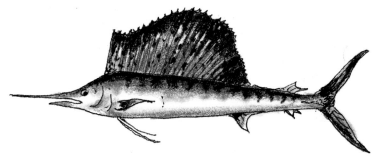

Sailfish

Easily recognised and distinguished from other billfish by the enormous dorsal fin, the sailfish ranges from 20-140 pounds in size. It first arrives in the Virgin Islands in December, peaks in January and early February and generally leaves by March.

Its habits are somewhat different from the other pelagic fish in that it prefers to feed in shallow waters of 20 fathoms or so. Small ballyhoo or strips of fish trolled at 5-7 knots are a very effective enticement and, for the expert, a live bait worked in the right manner can produce good results.

With an average weight in these waters of 30-40 pounds, sailfish are not normally eaten and are usually released.

Like the blue marlin, when the sailfish becomes excited, as when going for the trolled bait, it frequently "lights up," as waves and waves of irridescent blue ripple up and down its body. When hooked, the sailfish puts on a magnificent acrobatic display, its slender body leaping out of the water with extraordinary grace and beauty.

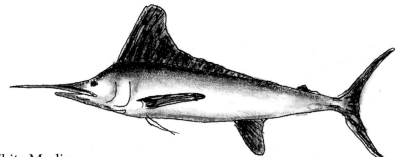

White Marlin

The smaller cousin of the big blue, the white marlin ranges between 40 and 60 pounds. The methods of capture are the same as for the bigger marlin, although, of course, the tackle is lighter (20-50 pound test), and the bait smaller.

Like sailfish, white marlin readily strike a variety of artificial lures or even a simple yellow-feathered lure trolled in the wake.

Dolphin

Although also named dolphin, this fish bears no resemblance to the porpoise. The dolphin start to arrive in numbers in late March, and depart in late May, though they are caught occasionally year-round. For the light tackle enthusiast few fish can give such a good account of themselves leaping and somersaulting repeatedly into the air, their brilliant blue and golden bodies flashing in the sunlight. They also jump in long leaps to catch their prey which, due to their sharp eyes, they can spot from quite a distance.

Dolphin are always greedily on the move and will savage almost any offering trolled at a good clip. They range in size from 5-85 pounds, most commonly from 10-20. On 8 or 12-lb. test line and spinning tackle the dolphin can give a spectacular battle, the aerial display being followed by a dogged broadside fight. It is quite common to have every rod on the boat bending when these fish are around, for they like to school, particularly around floating flotsam or driftwood. Dolphin also provide some of the best table fare in the islands.

Tuna

There are several types of tuna around the Virgin Islands, the black fin being the most common. Usually weighing from 5-15 pounds, they tend to school in large numbers. Their compact bodies are powerful and speedy, always providing some hard action, with the angler only too aware that, if it is not boated quickly, the tuna will fall prey to a marauding shark; and sharks just love tuna!

Growing considerably larger than the blackfin tuna, the Allison or yellowfin tuna reaches weights in excess of 300 pounds, and, pound for pound, can match any other fish in the sea for brute strength and pigheadedness. Around the Virgin Islands the Allison is seldom found over 100 pounds and more usually around 40 pounds. They can be caught all year round, although the larger specimens seem to show up around June. The Allison will feed on almost any trolled offering, from the favourite ballyhoo through a whole range of strip baits and artificial plastics and feathers.

Tuna are steady, stubborn opponents which, once hooked, will usually sound several hundred feet and there engage the angler in a tiring and dogged fight. On the right test, the tuna will provide some of the best sport in gamefishing.

Bonj

The usual size of the oceanic bonito is between 10 and 20 pounds, though they range between 3 and 40 pounds. The smaller fish are popular as live bait for marlin, but the bonito can be a worthwhile catch in itself, the large schools often providing plenty of action for a boatful of fishermen.

Like the blackfin tuna, the bonito feeds on bait fish, which can be found in clusters of thousands. The feeding frenzy leaves scraps floating in the churning water which are promptly dived on by quarreling seabirds. It is these birds, hovering over the feeding schools, which will give away the presence of tuna or bonito. If the boat can get there before the birds finish feeding, feathers, or lures trolled rapidly around the roiling mass will almost certainly be snatched.

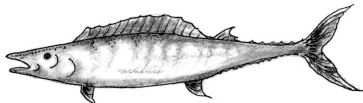

Wahoo

One of the most elegant fish to be found in the islands, the wahoo is sleek and torpedo-shaped, its upper body tiger-striped in shades of blue, its pointed mouth lined with razor-sharp teeth. This long, lean body slashing through the water has the appearance of a marine projectile. It ranges in size between 10 and 150 pounds, but is more often found between 30 and 50.

The wahoo is world famous for its immensely powerful strike and fantastic speed. Light tackle, 12 to 30 pound test, will guarantee the best sport, but 50 to 80 pound test is often used as 60 or 80-pound wahoo are not unusual.

They can usually be found singly or in small groups, prowling along the edge of a drop off, and will readily attack any trolled offering be it real or artificial. Wahoo have also been known to go after the teaser itself. Although present all year round they do predominate from late October through December.

For the competitive angler, the various gamefishing clubs of the Virgin Islands and Puerto Rico offer numerous tournaments throughout the year. The majority of these are run during July, August and September, when the blue marlin season is at its peak.

B.V.I.:
BVI Yacht and Anglers Club
284-494-3286

U.S.V.I.:
Virgin Islands Game Fishing Club
St. Thomas, USVI 00801
340-775-9144

Real Estate in the Virgin Islands

BRITISH VIRGIN ISLANDS

For many a property investor in the B.V.I. the love affair begins on the first day of the first charter when, upon clearing the harbour, the decision to go to port is as difficult as the decision to go to star-board, because in every direction there is Virginal splendour to be explored.

For some, a whirlwind romance en-sues, with the decision to purchase prop-erty transpiring within a week or two; for others it is a long and pleasurable en-gagement, the visitor returning year af-ter year, each time promising himself that next year he will purchase property.

Why this enduring love affair with the B.V.I. for so many people?

Certainly there are a number of obvi-ous reasons, such as a perfect climate, miles and miles of pristine sailing wa-ters and an underwater habitat to rival that of almost any resort area. Add to these an extremely stable and self-deter-

mining government, numerous tax ad-vantages and proximity to both the U.S.V.I. and Puerto Rico. The U.S. dollar economy is the biggest selling point in the British Virgin Islands.

The reasons go beyond the obvious, however — they also include a proud and friendly people and an environment that, as one of nature's finest achievements, is jealously guarded against outside in-trusion or influence unless these are for the common good of the people of the B.V.I.

Around us is the land and the sea, and the use or abuse to which we subject these elements has a far-reaching and permanent effect on the environment. It doesn't take long for the potential inves-tor, looking for his home in the sun, to realize that it is the local government's program of directed and controlled de-velopment that has maintained the re-laxing and unhurried atmosphere that prevails in the B.V.I.

Having made the decision to buy, the question of just where to purchase prop-

erty is relatively simple, as properties are available the whole length and breadth of the B.V.I. on over a dozen different islands. Making contact with a local real estate agent at this point will considerably cut the search time needed and will also provide the investor with up-to-date information on the laws and Government requirements pertaining to property purchase. Though many of the local agents market the same properties, by "shopping around" one may find a property that no one else has.

In short, the purchase of property in the B.V.I. revolves around a "Non-Belonger's Land Holding License" which is issued by the Government after consideration of certain factors, including how much property is involved. The purchaser, if a non-belonger, is required to develop the property within three years.

Apart from a careful scrutiny of potential buyers, the Government's main concern is the sale of previously undeveloped land; its chief concerns are how many acres are involved, what does the intended development consist of, and how much money will be spent in the Territory on the project.

The licensing procedure is relatively straightforward with a developed property such as an existing residence. With larger projects that will bring money into the territory, the government is amenable to expediant approval.

Throughout the B.V.I. there is a wide range of existing houses and condominiums for sale. Prices range from $200,000 and well up. For those intent on building there is a limitless variety of sites to choose from, either on the waterfront or on one of the many hillsides that make up the islands. Most investors opt for the hillsides, to take advantage of the spectacular views and also benefit from year-round trade winds — a definite advantage in the summer.

Building a house in the B.V.I. is not the trial it used to be. With increased shipping from both England and the U.S. mainland, together with the advent of container service in recent years, the variety of building materials, fixtures and fittings now available has eased the burden on local architects and contractors, who can now purchase locally everything that is required for the average residence. Building is still expensive, however, with concrete blocks being the only material locally produced.

Although far less demanding than Stateside or British authorities, the local Building Department and Planning Authority do have guidelines and regulations which must be followed. It is recommended that a local architect be consulted during the planning stages, preferably before the land is purchased. Generally, the guidelines control building setbacks, sewage disposal, cistern requirements and hurricane proof construction, together with special applications such as for jetties and land reclamation.

Most of the banks in the B.V.I. are active in the home mortgage market, although their individual policies do vary from time to time, often in relation to the prime lending rate. Represented in the B.V.I. are Barclays Bank International, Chase Manhattan Bank, Bank of Nova Scotia and the Banco Popular of the B.V.I. At time of writing, one could still obtain 50% on land and 75% on development of property. Interest rates vary, but the average is 2.5% over the New York prime lending rate at the time of the loan agreement.

In any case, the investor's main concern is normally capital appreciation, and in that department the B.V.I. has always been and should continue to be a good investment.

The British Virgin Islands may not be for everyone and the area is certainly an expensive place to live; but the people of the B.V.I. do live well and enjoy not only the magnificent environment but also many other advantages.

The B.V.I. is a close-knit, friendly society, and there is no lack of facilities. Considering the combined activities of the Sports Club with its squash and tennis division, the Yacht Club with its sailing, angling and rugby division, both Lions and Rotary clubs, soccer, baseball, golf and cricket clubs, plus a ladies' club, botanic society and drama group, the only problem can be having enough time left to relax and take a vacation!

There's always something happening in the B.V.I., but it's also a perfect place to relax and do absolutely nothing — so if the pressures of the big smoke have been getting you down, the B.V.I. just may be for you.

UNITED STATES VIRGIN ISLANDS

When the United States bought St. Thomas, St. Croix and St. John from Denmark in 1917, it cost them less than $300 an acre. Inflation has taken its toll since then, and today the average price for a home in the Virgin Islands is over $200,000. By modern real estate standards, however, buying property here is still an excellent investment.

With some of the finest weather and scenery to be found under the protection of the U.S. flag, the U.S.V.I. has a great deal to offer the prospective buyer. Stunning views are complemented by beautiful beaches, fascinating historical buildings, good restaurants and a leisurely approach to life.

Because the tourist industry is so vital to the island economy, there are plenty of facilities for sports, entertainment and the arts. Both St. Thomas and St. Croix have top quality golf courses, and sailing is, of course, an integral part of the lifestyle throughout the Virgins.

The U.S. Virgin Islands differ enormously in their character. St. Thomas is the busiest of the three; it contains the headquarters of most of the major businesses in the U.S.V.I., most of the government agencies and most of the people.

Charlotte Amalie is the commercial heart of the U.S. Virgins; the town bustles with tourists and traffic, and the harbour teems with yachts, cruise ships and visiting naval vessels. In consequence, St. Thomas offers the broadest range of facilities and events and the choice of shops, restaurants, hotels and entertainment is pleasingly varied.

St. Croix is somewhat quieter. Set apart from the rest of the Virgin Islands it is, in fact, the largest of the group and was once the main agricultural producer. The miles of gently rolling hills are liberally dotted with ancient sugar mills and gracious colonial homesteads like Whim Great House and Sprat Hall.

The historic buildings of Christiansted and Frederiksted still look out over a slower pace of life, and the attractions of this island have persuaded many talented artists and musicians to make it their home.

St. John, the quietest of them all, once belonged to Laurence Rockefeller, who donated it to the United States under the proviso that most of it be designated as a National Park. Consequently the island is very unspoiled and, with its uncluttered beaches and untouched hills, it truly lives up to its name as a Virgin Island. In terms of property investment, this pristine quality means that the available real estate is often the most expensive, the most highly restricted and the most exclusive in the U.S. Virgins — and often the most spectacular, too.

Visitors considering the purchase of property in the U.S.V.I. must first choose which island most suits their taste, then examine the alternative types of property. Whether to buy land and build, whether to renovate an old building or invest in a new, whether a self-contained residence or a condominium is best, are some initial questions. The choices are considerable and an experienced realtor can give invaluable advice at this stage.

In some ways an undeveloped homesite may be the easiest way to start. There is no time limit for

how long land can be held before development must begin, and so the new owner can take his time in deciding on the kind of home he wants and financing.

Depending on the view and the location, a half-acre homesite can vary in price to over $800,000 for waterfront property. In general, building costs run to roughly over $150 per square foot. There are plenty of competent architects and, though slower than on the mainland U.S., construction has become a good deal easier over the last few years.

Buying a finished home, of course, saves time. Condominiums are a popular choice; they can generate a healthy income if rented as vacation units and usually have excellent amenities, such as swimming pools, beaches, tennis courts, golf courses, restaurants, etc.

Most condominiums offer an on-site management team whose function is to advertise the apartments as resort hotel rooms, book reservations on a rotating or pool basis, provide maid service, do the accounting and disburse income to the owners. Management fees vary from 35% to 60% of the gross income, however, and there is generally a monthly maintenance charge, depending on the size of the unit. Typically this covers upkeep of the exterior of the building and the grounds, pool service, cleaning, gardening and insurance.

The major advantage of having a condominium is the relatively worry-free ownership. There is always adequate security, and all the details of rental and maintenance are taken care of by the management.

An alternative to purchasing a condominium outright is time-sharing, which provides a refinement of the traditional condominium ownership. Instead of holding the unit year-round, the buyer can own it for as little as two months per year.

Perhaps better suited to those who want to spend a greater proportion of their time in the islands, an individual residence offers more privacy and space. Most sites are at least half an acre and keen gardeners can take advantage of the profusion of fast-growing tropical plants to create colourful and imaginative surroundings.

Single-family homes are as varied in type as they are in price, which ranges from about $225,000 to $1.5 million. Maintenance on a home is generally less expensive than on a condominium and mortgage interest, maintenance and property taxes are all tax-deductible items.

The government maintains an efficient system of surveys and titles, and title insurance can also be arranged though local attorneys.

Anyone can buy real estate in the U.S.V.I. There are no restrictions on nationality or on speculation purely for investment purposes. Land can be held for any length of time and no development plan is required by the government.

Land use, however, is another matter. It is dictated by zoning laws, deed restrictions and building permit requirements, including approval by the Coastal

Zone Management Committee. The ease with which this approval is obtained is largely dependent on the location of the property and the type of development proposed.

The Coastal Zone Management is the organization responsible for keeping the U.S.V.I. looking good enough to be described as the "American paradise." They have a scale of restrictions designed to preserve the beauty of the island by limiting such things as density, height of building, type of construction and so on. The severity of the limits varies according to the area.

For example, the majority of St. John's land belongs to the National Park Service. The remaining land available for development is R1 density, which mean no more than two dwelling units per quarter acre. These are mostly concentrated around Cruz Bay and Coral Bay areas.

Other restrictions may include details like clothesline placement and other visual features. Fortunately, St. John has excellent architects and builders, making building a home remarkably hassle-free.

St. Thomas and St. Croix have more medium and high density residences available, as well as extensive business and commercial areas. The choices for potential real estate buyers are wide. Many begin by trying out something from the range of rental and leasing arrangements which, like cohabitation before marriage, allow the participants to try the lifestyle before making a heavier commitment.

The advantages of V.I. living are less tangible — the islands are obviously sunny, pretty and cosmopolitan, but for many people the fascination runs deeper. They find themselves returning again and again, spending longer periods of time and scraping their savings together to buy a foothold. Down here, the islanders call it "getting sand in your shoes," and a sailing vacation is often just the beginning.

People go on to buy real estate in the Virgin Islands because they want to make an investment and because they like the lifestyle and the environment. From an investment point of view, the chances of a worthwhile return are good.

So if you get home and unpack to find half the beach in your docksiders, it could be that your next visit to the Virgin Islands will include "just checking it out" at the nearest real estate office.

Restaurants & Bars

Arriving at a restaurant by dinghy is a unique and special experience for most. This is one area where it is not at all unusual to see people arriving for dinner with wet bottoms from the dinghy ride in to shore! The Virgin Islands offer many restaurants and bars that cater to sailors. The food ranges from casual, served on the beach; to sophisticated and elegant, but almost all have unforgettable views of these exquisite islands. Credit cards are taken in most establishments, but some of the more casual restaurants do not have credit card capabilities. Reservations are also important at many restaurants, again wise to check first.

We have tried to include most of the restaurants that are accessible by dinghy and a few others that you wouldn't want to miss. For a more complete listing pick up some of the free tourist literature available in the airports, most marinas and hotels.

*Asterisk denotes restaurants accessible by dinghy, or within easy walking distance of a dinghy dock. The others may require the services of a taxi or rental car.

BRITISH VIRGIN ISLANDS

Jost Van Dyke

*Sandcastle   White Bay, 495-9888, VHF 16. Serves breakfast, lunch and a four course dinner by candle light. Reservations for dinner requested by 4pm. Visit the Soggy Dollar Bar for a Painkiller. *(see our ad on page 80)*

*Rudy's Mariner   Great Harbour, 495-9282, VHF 16. Serves dinner specializing in seafood. Located on the western end of the beach.

*Ali Baba's   Great Harbour, 495-9280, VHF 16, Baba serves breakfast, lunch and dinner West Indian style. Reservations for dinner requested.

*Club Paradise   Great Harbour, 495-9267, Hard to miss, this restaurant is painted bright pink and purple. Open daily from 7am until serving lunch and dinner.

*Happy Laury's   Great Harbour, 495-9259, Open daily from 8am until late, Happy Laury's serves sandwiches, chicken, burgers and snacks. On the beach.

*Foxy's Tamarind Beach Bar   Great Harbour, 495-9258, The famous Foxy's on the beach at the eastern end serves lunch, and dinner with reservations by 5pm. Catch Foxy himself entertaining with his Calypso ballads. Foxy's has it's own dinghy dock. *(see our ad on page 81)*

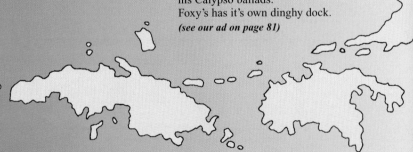

*Abe's Little Harbour, VHF 16, On the eastern end of the bay, Abe's serves West Indian fare for lunch and dinner. Check for their pig roasts. Reservations for dinner requested.

*Harris' Place Little Harbour, 495-9302, Serves breakfast, lunch and dinner. Good place for lobster and fish.

*Sidney's Peace and Love Little Harbour, 495-9271, West Indian dishes and seafood served. Open for breakfast, lunch and dinner.

Tortola, *Cane Garden Bay*

*De Wedding 495-4236, On the western end of the beach, their specialty is fresh seafood caught in their own boat. Open daily from 11am for lunch and dinner. Reservations requested.

*Myett's Garden & Grill 495-9543, Amongst the sea grape trees on the beach this newly remodeled grill offers fish, lobster, steak, chicken and vegetarian meals. Breakfast, lunch and dinner are available daily.
(see our ad on page 87)

*Stanley's Welcome Bar 495-9424, On the beach by the tire swing. Open for happy hour and dinner. Casual.

*Rhymer's 495-4639, VHF 16, the pink building on the beach serving breakfast, lunch and dinner.

*Big Banana Paradise Club 495-4606, Open daily from 7am, on the beach, breezy atmosphere, breakfast, lunch and dinner.

*Quito's Gazebo 495-4837, On the beach next to the dinghy dock, Tuesday through Sunday, lunch and dinner. Quito entertains several nights in the week.

Tortola, *West End*

*Pusser's Landing West End, 495-4559, Two restaurants on the water at Soper's Hole. Downstairs serves lunch and snacks until close. Dinner upstairs is more elegant dining. Reservations requested.
(see our ad on inside covers)

*Jolly Roger West End, 495-4559, Next to the ferry dock serves breakfast, lunch, and dinner from 7:30am until. Casual fare.

Frenchman's Cay Hotel 495-4844, On Sir Francis Drake channel serving breakfast, lunch and dinner. A short walk from Soper's Hole. Pool and tennis priviledges for diners. Reservations requested for dinner.

Other restaurants near West End

Long Bay Hotel & Resort Long Bay, 495-4252, The Beach Cafe serves breakfast, lunch and dinner from 7:30am until 9:30pm. The more elegant Garden Restaurant dinner from 6:30 to 9:30pm with reservations.

The Apple Little Apple Bay, 495-4437, Serves dinner (West Indian specialties) with reservations and has a great Happy Hour from 5pm to 7pm.

Bomba's Shack Capoons Bay, 495-4148, Famous for his full moon parties on the beach the building is comprised of flotsam and jetsam accumulated over the years. Very casual, casual fare.

Sebastian's On the Beach Little Apple Bay, 495-4212, Beachside dining on the north shore. Serves breakfast, lunch, happy hour and dinner. Reservations requested.

Clem's by the Sea Carrot Bay, 495-4350, Real local food served. Open all day, reservations for dinner requested.

Mrs. Scatliffe's Restaurant Carrot Bay, 495-4556, Mrs. Scatliffe offers real home cooked West Indian specialities for lunch and dinner. Reservations required.

Sugar Mill Hotel Apple Bay, 495-4355, Gourmet meals served in an old sugar mill. Reservations required.

Nanny Cay

*Marina Plaza Cafe Nanny Cay, 494-4895, In the marina plaza this casual restaurant serves breakfast, lunch and dinner from 7am to 9pm.

*Peg Leg Landing Nanny Cay, 495-4895, Overlooks Sir Francis Drake Channel, this whimsical restaurant serves happy hour and dinner.

Struggling Man's Place 494-4163, A local restaurant on Sea Cow's Bay a short walk from the marina serves West Indian fare for lunch and dinner.

Road Town

*Callaloo Prospect Reef, 494-3311, Upstairs overlooking the harbour serves breakfast, lunch and gourmet dinner with reservations.

*Scuttlebutt Bar & Grill Prospect, 494-3311, Downstairs, serves casual food for breakfast, lunch and dinner.

*Fort Burt 494-2587, Views of Road Harbour, serving breakfast, lunch and dinner with reservations.

*The Pub 494-2608, At Fort Burt Marina with dinghy dock, serves burgers and sandwiches for lunch and steak fish etc. for dinner. Open Monday through Saturday from 7am until and on Sunday from 5pm. *(see our ad on page 98)*

*Seaview Hotel 494-2483, Serves breakfast, lunch and dinner. Just up the hill from the Fort Burt Marina. Reservations requested.

*Capriccio di Mare 494-5369, Across from the ferry dock on the waterfront, serves breakfast, lunch and dinner Italian style. Good cappuccino and pastries for breakfast and pasta and salads. From 8am to 9pm Monday through Saturday. *(see our ad on page 113)*

*Le Cabanon / Cell 5 494-1409, Across from the ferry dock on the waterfront, serving breakfast, lunch and dinner.

*Pusser's Pub 494-3897, On the waterfront serves traditional pub food, pizza and deli sandwiches. Air conditioned. Open from 11am to 10pm daily. *(see our ads on the inside covers)*

*Tavern in the Town 494-2790, On the waterfront, pub fare serving lunch and dinner. Casual atmosphere.

*Maria's By the Sea 494-2595, On the harbour serving breakfast, lunch and dinner from 7am until. Dinner reservations requested.

*Cafe Sito 494-7412, in the Romasco building near the administration building. Serves Spanish & Mediterranean style food. Lunch and dinner from 11am to 11pm. Dinner reservations requested.

*Captain's Table 494-3885, At Inner Harbour Marina serving lunch Monday through Friday, dinner nightly with reservations.

*Fish Trap 494-3626, At Columbus Centre. Varied menu for lunch and dinner. Lunch and dinner from Monday through Saturday and dinner only on Sunday.

*Village Cay Dockside 494-2771, overlooking the docks and harbour, casual fare for breakfast, lunch & dinner.

*Spaghetti Junction 494-4880, A short walk from Village Cay serving fine Italian cuisine nightly from 6 to 11pm. Reservations suggested. *(see our ad on page 106)*

*Virgin Queen 494-2310, Not far from Village Cay serving West Indian, pizza, and continental food. open from 11am to midnight, and from 6pm until late on Saturday night.

*Oliver's Restaurant 494-2177, Next to the roundabout on Wickham' Cay, Chef Oliver Clifton serves breakfast, lunch and dinner from 7:30am to 11pm. Dinner reservations suggested.

*Lime 'n Mango 494-2501, Across the street from the Footloose Dock, in the Treasure Isle Hotel. Serves breakfast, lunch and dinner with Caribbean and Mexican fare. Cool and breezy location.

*Mariner Inn 494-2332, At the Moorings Marina this airy restaurant serves breakfast, lunch and dinner daily. Reservations suggested for dinner.

Brandywine Bay

*Brandywine Bay Restaurant 495-2307, VHF 16, Elegant dining on the terrace overlooking the Sir Francis Drake Channel. Moorings available for dinner guests. Reservations requested. *(see our ad on page 114)*

Maya Cove

*Pelican Roost 495-1515, On the water at Tropic Island Yacht Management, Maya Cove. Breakfast, lunch and dinner in a casual atmosphere.

*Calamaya 495-2126, Features Mediterranean and Caribbean menu on the dock at Hodges Creek Marina. Serves breakfast, lunch, happy hour with tapas, and dinner. *(see our ad on page 113)*

East End

*The Bistro 494-1132, At the Seabreeze Marina serving casual food. Lunch and dinner from 10am until.

*Penn's Landing 495-1646, Seafood specialties, as well as steak and pasta. Open for dinner daily except Tuesday. *(see our ad on page 121)*

*Virgin Queen Harbour View 495-2797, Casual meals for lunch and dinner across from Wheatley's Harbourview Marina.

Beef Island

*Conch Shell Point 495-2285, VHF 16, On the point overlooking Trellis Bay, specializes in gourmet foods with an Asian influence. Serving dinner with reservations. Moorings available in Trellis Bay.

*De Loose Mongoose 495-2303, VHF 16, on the beach at Trellis Bay at the Beef Island Guest House. Serving breakfast, lunch and dinner. Hearty food, casual surroundings. Moorings available. *(see our ad on page 124)*

*The Last Resort 495-2520, VHF 16, Bellamy Cay, Lunch and sumptuous buffet dinner followed by hilarious cabaret entertainment by Tony Snell. Fun gift shop open during lunch and dinner. Reservations requested. Moorings available. *(see our ad on page 123)*

Marina Cay

*Pusser's Marina Cay 494-2174, VHF 16, Free ferry service to this tiny island. Moorings available. A great island setting, with an delicious array of choices. Lunch and dinner daily. Also check out the Company Store. *(see our ad on page 127)*

Norman Island

*Billy Bones Beach Bar & Grill 494-4090, VHF 16, In the Bight, Open at 9:30am until the last person leaves in their dinghy. Casual surroundings for lunch and dinner. Great spot. Reservations suggested. *(see our ad on page 133)*

*William Thornton 494-0183, VHF 16, Floating bar / restaurant anchored in the Bight. Serves lunch and dinner daily from 11am until. Casual food — fun location.

Peter Island

*Peter Island Yacht Club 495-2000, Elegant dining in the Tradewinds Restaurant. Check on dress code. Serving lunch and dinner with reservations. Lunch and dinner served on the beach at Deadman's Bay Bar & Grill (casual). Moorings and dockage available.

Cooper Island

*Cooper Island Beach Club VHF 16, Lunch and dinner served in Manchioneel Bay daily. Fantastic sunset view. Moorings available. *(see our ad on page 140)*

Virgin Gorda
The Valley (Spanish Town)

*Bath & Turtle 495-5839, Located at the Virgin Gorda Yacht Harbour, casual surroundings serving lunch and dinner. A fun and convenient location. Free lending library and liquor store on the premises. *(see our ad on page 148)*

*Chez Bamboo 495-5963, Refined dining Creole style. Next to the Yacht Harbour. Serving dinner with reservations. *(see our ad on page 148)*

*Fischer's Cove 495-5252, on the beach in the Valley. West Indian cuisine. Good spot for sunsets.

Flying Iguana 495-5277, Near the airport overlooking the sea in an airy setting serving breakfast, lunch and dinner daily. Interesting array of menu choices. *(see our ad on page 144)*

*Giorgio's Table 495-5684, Great location in beautiful Savannah Bay. Italian and Mediterranean cuisine served daily. Open from 9am to 10pm. Reservations requested for dinner. *(see our ad on page 148)*

*Lobster Pot 495-5252, West Indian fare for lunch and dinner, check out their pig roast and seafood buffet on certain nights of the week.

Little Dix Bay Hotel 495-5555, Refined dining at this world renowned resort. Lunch and dinner with reservations. Casually elegant dress requested.

Mad Dog 495-5830, Near the Baths this airy bar is a great place for drinks and sandwiches. Open from 10am to 7pm.

*Top of the Baths 435-5497, VHF 16, At the top of the famous Baths with a spectacular view to the west of Drake Channel. Serving breakfast, lunch and dinner.

North Sound

*Drake's Anchorage 494-8854, VHF 16, Gourmet French style cuisine. Open for breakfast, lunch and dinner. Private island, lovely setting. Moorings available. Reservations essential.

*Pusser's Leverick Bay 495-7369, Upstairs with a view of North Sound, good menu in nice surroundings, reasonably priced, some evenings live music. Lunch is also available downstairs at the beach bar. Moorings and dockage available *(see our ad on inside covers)*

*Sand Box Seafood Grille and Bar 496-0982, VHF 16, Open for lunch and dinner. Free boat pick up from Gun Creek or Leverick Bay by request, moorings available. Beach bar and grill, casual atmosphere. *(see our ad on page 156)*

*Saba Rock Resort 495-7711, VHF 16, Opening in 1998 with two bars, a restaurant, long dinghy dock, check them out. *(see our ad on page 159)*

*Bitter End 494-2746, VHF 16, Welcomes yachtsmen, serves breakfast, lunch and dinner in The Clubhouse, snacks in the Emporium. Frequent entertainment. Moorings available. *(see our ad on page 157)*

*Biras Creek 494-3555, View of North Sound from their renowned restaurant. Serves breakfast, lunch and dinner (dress code at night). Moorings & dockage available.

*Fat Virgins Cafe 495-7045, Located on the service dock on the west side of Biras Creek. Open for breakfast & lunch. *(see our ad on page 160)*

Anegada

*Anegada Grill House 495-8002, VHF 16, At the Anegada Reef Hotel specializing in grilled lobster and fish, serving breakfast, lunch and dinner. Reservations recommended. *(see our ad on page 165)*

*Anegada Beach Club 495-9466, VHF 16, On the beach at Setting Point, featuring grilled seafood serving breakfast, lunch and dinner. Reservations by 4pm please.

*Neptune's Treasure   495-9439, VHF 16, On the beach, open for breakfast, lunch and dinner specializing in fresh fish caught in their own boat. Bakery items also for sale. *(see our ad on page 166)*

*Pomato Point   495-9466, VHF 16, Open for lunch and dinner on a fantastic beach near Setting Point. West Indian food and seafood. Call for reservations.

Cow Wreck Beach Bar and Grill 495-9461, VHF 16, Offering local fare, burgers, chicken, fish and lobster. A taxi ride away at lower Cow Wreck Beach.

Big Bamboo   495-2019, VHF 16, A great place to lunch on Loblolly Bay at the western end of the beach. Grilled seafood and burgers available.

Flash of Beauty   495-8014, VHF 16, On the eastern end of lovely Loblolly Bay open for lunch and dinner with burgers, seafood daily.

U.S. VIRGIN ISLANDS

Cruz Bay

*Pusser's Wharfside   693-8489, Three floors of Pussers. Overlooks Cruz Bay with a beach bar and upstairs restaurant. Open from 11am until midnight. Another great Pusser's location. *(see our ad on inside covers)*

*Sting Ray Deli & Cafe   779-4140, Enjoy breakfast and lunch on the beach or in the A/C. Full deli and wine shop. At Wharfside Village. *(see our ad on page 205)*

*Ellington's   693-8490, At Gallows Point with exquisite view of Pillsbury Sound. Open for dinner and drinks from 4:30pm. Reservations recommended. *(see our ad on page 203)*

*Fish Trap Restaurant   693-9994, A short walk from the ferry dock in a tropical setting in the Raintree Inn. Inspired cuisine *(see our ad on page 201)*

*La Tapa   639-7755, Sidewalk cafe full of charm features tapas, main dishes for lunch and dinner.

*The Lime Inn   776-6425, In the Lemontree Mall for lunch and dinner in an airy spot in the middle of Cruz Bay.

*Morgan's Mango   693-8141, Across from the Nat'l Park Dock. Dinner served from 5:30pm. Caribbean cuisine. Reservations recommended.

*Paradiso   693-8677, Located in the Mongoose Junction shopping center a short walk from Cruz Bay. Lunch and dinner serving steak and seafood. A/C. *(see our ad on page 202)*

*Mongoose Restaurant Deli & Bistro 693-8677, Breakfast, lunch and dinner and take out for picnics. *(see our ad on page 202)*

Coral Bay

*Serafina Seaside Bistro   693-5630, Fine seaside dining in Coral Bay, open Tuesday through Sunday for dinner and drinks. *(see our ad on page 213)*

*Shipwreck Landing Restaurant 693-5640, Open for lunch and dinner daily on the bay in a breezy locale. *(see our ad on page 213)*

St. Thomas, *Red Hook*

*Cafe Wahoo   775-6350, On the water at the Picola Marina next to the ferry dock. Open for dinner. *(see our ad on page 191)*

*Latitude 18   779-2495, At the Fanfare dock across from the ferry dock. Casual ambience, check for entertainment. *(see our ad on page 191)*

*Mackenzie's Restaurant & Tap Room
779-2261, Upstairs in the American
Yacht Harbor building. Serves lunch
and dinner daily.

The Lagoon

*Finn McCools 775-6194, Open Tuesday
through Sunday for lunch and dinner in
the Compass Point Marina.

Raffles International 775-6004, Compass
Point Marina, serving dinner from
6:30pm.

*Windjammer 775-6194, In the Compass
Point Marina, German-American fare
open for dinner Monday through
Saturday from 6:00pm.

*Bottoms Up 775-4817, Light fare and
drinks at Independent Boatyard and
Marina for breakfast, lunch, dinner and
drinks.

Secret Harbor

*Blue Moon Cafe 779-2262, On the water
at Secret Harbor, dinghy over for good
wine and a great dinner. Reservations
requested. *(see our ad on page 190)*

Charlotte Amalie

There are so many restaurants in Charlotte
Amalie to discover, and many more restaurants than we could possibly list. We suggest
you start with the many free tourist publications that list the dining establishments and
details. Bon Apetite!

Christiansted

*Baggy's Marina Bar 713-9636, At St.
Croix Marina in Gallows Bay, a casual,
breezy spot serving breakfast, lunch and
dinner from Monday through Saturday
and Sunday for brunch.

*Commanche 773-2665, On Strand Street,
a Christiansted favorite for thirty years.
Harbor view, second floor, serving lunch
and dinner Monday through Saturday.

*Indies 692-9440, Charming downtown
historic courtyard open for lunch week
days, and dinner nightly. Reservations
suggested. Creative cuisine.

*Kendricks 773-9199, Located in a historic
West Indian cottage serving inspired array
of dinner selections and wine. Open for
dinner Monday through Saturday.
Reservations requested.

*Stixx On the Waterfront 773-5157,
Downtown Christiansted with a
fabulous harbor view from the deck.
Serving breakfast, lunch and dinner
daily. Moderately price, good selection.
(see our ad on page 223)

Salt River

*Columbus Cove 778-5771, In the Salt
River National Park overlooking the Salt
River Marina. Open for breakfast, lunch,
happy hour and dinner. Saturday and
Sunday try their brunch.

*Green Cay 773-9949, Overlooking
the Green Cay Marina, serving drinks
at the piano bar and dinner with a
good selection of wine. Reservations
suggested.

CRUISING GUIDE PUBLICATION'S
VIRGIN ISLANDS DIRECTORY

This directory is arranged in three sections: BVI and USVI. The two largest British Virgin Islands are listed first, followed by the other, smaller islands, in alphabetical order, followed by the U.S. Virgin Islands in alphabetical order. Also, Puerto Rico. F = Fax; VHF = VHF Radio Channel

To call from outside the BVI, dial 1-284 plus 7 digits.

BRITISH VIRGIN ISLANDS
GENERAL INFORMATION

AIRLINES
Air Ambulance Network, 518-993-4153, 800-631-6565.
Air Anguilla Inc., 495-1616.
American Eagle, 495-2559, F: 495-1784.
British Airways, 494-2215.
Eastern Caribbean Airways, 495-2396.
Fly BVI, 495-1747, F: 495-1973.
Four-Star Air Cargo, 495-2256,
  F: 495-1438.
Gorda Aero, 495-2271, after hours
  495-2261 F:495-2838.
Liat, 495-1187/8/9, F: 494-3317.
National Air Ambulance Ft. Lauderdale, 954-359-9900, F: 359-0039.
Caribbean Wings, 495-6000, F: 495-2032

FERRIES
Beef Island to Virgin Gorda Service,
  495-5240, 495-5235. Speedy's Fantasy
Inter-Island Boat Services, 495-4166.
Jost Van Dyke, 494-2997
Marina Cay, 494-2174
Native Son, Inc., 495-4617.
North Sound Express, 495-2271.
Peter Island Ferry, 495-2000.
Smith's Ferry Services, 494-2355,
  495-4495.
Speedy's, 495-5240

MISCELLANEOUS
Ambulance/Fire/Police, 999/911

Bluewater Books & Charts, (305)
  763-6533.

BVI Customs & Immigration, 494-3701,
  F:494-6906.
BVI Dept. Conservation & Fisheries,
  494-5681.
BVI Port & Marine, 494-3435.
BVI Post Office, 494-3701.
BVI Tourist Board, 494-3134.
Cable & Wireless (WI) Ltd., 494-4444.
Tortola Radio Marine Operator,
  494-4116,
Virgin Islands Search & Rescue (VISAR),
  494-6613, 494-4357, VHF 16.

TORTOLA
Auto/Bicycle/Moped Rentals
Airways Car Rental, 494-4502; Airport
  495-2161, F: 494-4676.
Anytime Car Rental, 494-2875.
Avis Rent-a-Car, 494-3322, 494-2193,
  F: 494-4218.
Budget Rent-a-Car, 494-2639,
  F: 494-4975.
Del's Jeep & Car Rentals, 495-9356.
Denully's, 494-6819.
Dollar, 494-6093
Hertz Rent-a-Car, 495-4405, F: 494-6060.
Honda Scooter Rentals, 495-5212.
International Car Rental, 494-2516,
  494-6351.
Island Suzuki, 494-3666.
National Car Rental, 494-3197.
Rancal Rent-a-Car, 494-4535.
Tola Rentals, 494-8652

BANKS
Banco Popular, 494-2117/8/9,
  F: 494-5294.
Bank of Nova Scotia, 494-2526,
  F: 494-4657.

Barclays, 494-2171, F: 494-4315.
Chase Manhattan, 494-2662,
  F: 494-5106.
Development Bank of the VI, 494-3737.
DISA Bank BVI Ltd., 494-6036.
VP Bank, 494-1100

CHANDLERIES
Cay Marine Chandlery, 494-2992.
Golden Hind, 494-2756, F: 494-4707.
Island Marine Supply, 494-2251,
  F: 494-2290.
Nanny Cay Chandlery, 494-0329.
Richardson's Rigging, 494-5169,
  494-2739.

CHARTERS
BVI Bareboats & Yacht Charters,
  494-4289, 800-648-7240.
Catamaran Charters Sales, LTD,
  800-262-0309, 494-6661, 494-6706.
Conch Charters, 494-4868, F: 494-5793
Downwind Sailing Vacations,
  800-677-0804
Ed Hamilton & Co., 207-549-7855, 800-
  621-7855
Footloose Sailing, 494-0528,
  800-814-7245.
Misty Isle, 495-5643.
The Moorings, 494-2331; F: 494-2226,
  800-535-7289.
North South, 800-387-4964.
Regency Yacht Vacations, 495-1970
Seabreeze Yacht Charters, 495-1560,
  800-668-2807.
Stardust Charters, 800-634-8822,
  494-1000.
Sun Yacht Charters, 800-772-3500,
  494-5538.
Sunsail, 495-4740, F: 495-4301,
  800-327-2276.
Swift Yacht Charters, 1-800-866-8340.
Tortola Marine Mgmt., 494-2751, 800-
  633-0155
Tropic Island Yacht Mgmt., 494-2450,
  800-356-8938, Canada, 800-463-3933.
Virgin Islands Sailing, 494-3658,
  494-2774, F: 494-6774.
Yacht Connections, 1-800-386-8125.

DIVING, SNORKELING
Baskin In The Sun, 494-2858, 495-4582,
  800-233-7938.
Blue Water Divers, 494-2847.
Caribbean Images Tours Ltd., 494-1147.
Dive BVI, 495-5513, 800-848-7078
Kilbrides Sunchaser Scuba, 495-9638
Offshore Sail & Motor, 494-4726
Rainbow Visions, 494-2749
Tradewinds Yacht Charters, 494-3154
Underwater Safaris, 494-3235;
  (800) 537-7032.

ELECTRONICS
Al's Marine Ltd., 494-4529.
Big Leo Video Productions, Ltd.,
  494-3983.
BVI Electronics, 494-2723.
Cay Electronics Ltd., 494-2400,
  F: 494-5389
CCT Boatphone, 494-3825, F: 494-4933.
Clarence M. Christian Ltd., 494-2492,
  F: 494-5807.
Island Care Electronics, 494-6183,
  494-3998.

EMERGENCY/MEDICAL
Ambulance/Fire/Police, 999.
Bouganvillea Clinic, 494-2181,
  F: 494-6609.
K.P. Adamson, Dentist, 494-3274.
N. Joyce Brewley, M.D., 494-2196,
  494-3882.
BVI Red Cross, 494-6349.
Jana Downing, M.D., 494-4477.
Marvin E. Flax, Dentist, 494-3474.
Health Department, 494-3701.
*Medicure Health Center, 494-6189,
  494-6469.*
Q.W. Osborne, M.D., 494-1198.
Peebles Hospital, 494-3497, 494-6836.
J.E. Rhymer, Dentist, 494-5303,
  494-6865.
D. Orlando Smith, M.D., 494-3330.
Robin E. Tattersall, M.D., 494-2482.
Heskith A. Vanterpool, M.D., 494-2346.
Virgin Islands Search & Rescue
  (VISAR), 494-4357.

HAUL-OUT

Nanny Cay Marine, 494-2512, 494-4895.
Tortola Yacht Services, 494-2124.
Frenchman's Cay Slipway, 495-4353, F:
495-4678.

LAUNDRY/DRY CLEANERS

A & M Coin Laundry, 494-5656.
Brackwell's Laundromat, 495-2369.
Freeman's Laundromat, 494-2285.
Sylvia's Dry Cleaners, 494-2230.
West End Laundromat, 495-4463.

LIQUOR, BEER, WINE

A.H. Riise Ltd., 494-4483, 494-6615.
Ample Hamper, 494-2494.
Bubblin' Barrel, 494-5564.
Esme's Shoppe, 494-3961.
Fort Wines & Spirits, 494-2388.
Rite Way Food Market, 494-2263,
494-2266.
Santo's, 494-3799.
TICO, 494-2211.

LODGING

A & L Inn House, 494-6343.
Beef Island Guest House, 495-2303.
BVI Aquatic Hotel, 495-4541.
Fort Burt Hotel, 494-2587.
Fort Recovery, 495-4354, 1-800-367-
8455.
Frenchman's Cay Hotel, 495-4844,
800-235-4099.
Hall Guest House, 494-3946.
Last Resort, 495-2520.
Long Bay Beach Resort, 495-4252,
495-4306.
Maria's Hotel by The Sea, 284-494-2595
Moorings Mariner Inn, 494-2332,
494-3776, 494-3876, 800-535-7289.
Nanny Cay Resort, 494-2512, 494-4895.
Prospect Reef Resort, 494-3311,
800-356-8937.
Rhymer's Cane Garden Beach Hotel,
495-4639.
Sebastian's On The Beach, 495-4212,
495-4272, 800-336-4870.
Smuggler's Cove Hotel, 495-4234.

Steele Point, 494-2983.
Sugar Mill Hotel, 495-4355,
800-462-8834.
Treasure Isle Hotel, 494-2501,
800-437-7880.
Village Cay Marina/Hotel, 494-2771,
495-2849.
Way Side Inn Guest House, 494-3606.

MARINAS

Frenchmans Cay Marina & Shop
494-2595, F:495-4686
Fort Burt Marina, 494-4200.
Hodges Creek Marina, 494-5538.
Inner Harbour Marina, 494-4502,
VHF 16.
Leverick Bay Hotel & Marina,
495-5450/7365.
Moorings/Mariner Inn, 494-2331,
494-3776, 494-2331/2/3.
Nanny Cay Resort & Marina,
494-2512/4895.
Penn's Landing 495-1134, F: 495-1352.
Prospect Reef Resort, 494-3311.
Road Reef Marina, 494-2751.
Soper's Hole Marina, 495-4740.
Sunsail Yachts, 495-4553, 495-4740.
Tortola Yacht Services, 494-2124.
Tropic Island Yacht Mgmt., 494-2450,
494-4150, 495-2655, 800-356-8938.
Village Cay Resort Marina, 494-2771.
Wheatley's Harbourview Marina,
495-1775

MARINE REPAIR & SUPPLIES

Air Devices, 494-2314.
Al's Marine Ltd., 494-4529.
BVI Diesel Sales & Service, 494-2298.
BVI Marine Management, 494-2938,
494-3382; F: 494-5006.
BVI Marine Services, 494-2393,
494-3870, 494-0047.
Caribbean Battery, 494-2938.
Clarence Thomas Ltd. Plumbing
Supplies, 494-2359.
Frenchmans Cay Slipway, VI Ship-
wrights, 495-4353, F: 495-4678
Golden Hind at Tortola Yacht Services,
494-2756.

Moor Seacure, 494-4488.
Nanny Cay Marine Center, 494-2512.
Napa Auto Parts, 494-2193, 494-2122.
Nautool Machine Ltd., 494-3187.
Parts & Power Ltd., 494-2830/6974.
Richardson's Rigging Services, 494-2739.
T&W Machine Shop, 494-3342.
Tortola Marine Mgmt. Ltd., 494-2751.
Tortola Yacht Services Ltd., 494-2124.
Tradewind Yachting Services Ltd., 494-3154.
Triton Marine Services, 494-4252.
Underwater Boat Services, 494-0024
Wickham's Cay II Rigging, 494-3979.
Wood's Marine T&F 494-0002.

MISCELLANEOUS

Alcoholics Anonymous, 494-3125.
American Express, 494-2872.
BVI Port Authority, 494-3435.
BVI Tourist Board, 494-3134, 494-3489, 495-5181.
Conservation & Fisheries, 494-5681, 494-5682.
Customs, 494-3475, 494-3701.
DHL Worldwide Express, 494-4659.
East End Public Library, 495-2472.
Federal Express, 494-2297.
Happy Heart Barber Shop 494-7196, 494-2260.
Happy Heart Snack Bar, 494-2260.
Immigration, 494-3701.
Inland Messenger Service, 494-6440.
Miracles Unisex Beauty Salon, 494-3525.
Monelle's Beauty Salon, 494-2546.
Narcotics Anonymous, 494-3125.
National Parks Trust, 494-2069, 494-3904.
New Image Beauty Salon, 495-5135.
Public Library, 494-3428.
Rhymer's Beauty Salon, 495-4847.
Rush-It Inc., 494-4421.
Tortola Humane Society, 494-2284.
Tortola Travel, 494-2215/2672.
Tortola Vision Center, 494-2020/4497.
Veterinarian, C.W. George, 494-4498.
Vision Cinema, 494-2098.
Waves Hair Salon, 495-4208.

PHARMACIES

Lagoon Plaza Drug & Hardware Stores, 494-2498.
J.R. O'Neal Ltd. Drug Store, 494-2292.
Medicure Ltd., 494-6189, F: 494-6284.
Ruth's Drug Store, 495-1173.
Vanterpool Enterprises Ltd., 494-2702.

PROVISIONS

Ample Hamper, 494-2494, 494-2784.
Bobby's Supermarket, 494-2189.
Bon Appetit Delicatessen, 494-5199.
Brewley's Superette, 494-3839.
C & F Grocery, 494-4941.
Central Bakery, 494-6854.
Dorothy's Superette, 494-3757.
Fine Foods Supermarket, 495-2362.
Franklyn's General Market, 494-3905, F: 494-4126.
Frett Butcher Shop, 495-2253.
K-Mark's Supermarket, 494-4649, VHF 16.
La Baquette, French bakery, 494-5717.
Little Circle Provisioners, 494-3779.
M & S Pastry Shop, 494-6364.4634/4528.
Port Purcell Market, 494-2727, 494-2724.
Rite Way Breeze 495-1682.
Rite Way Food Markets, 494-2263.
Santo's, 494-3799.
Sunbeam Grocery, 494-2307.
Sunrise Bakery, 494-2425.
Sunshine Grocery & Restaurant, 494-2520.
Tortola Ice, 494-3333.
Trellis Bay Market, 495-1421.
TICO Deli, 494-2211

REAL ESTATE

Caribbean Realty, 494-3566, F: 494-5127.
Island Real Estate, 494-3186, 494-4386.
Romney Associates, 494-3352, F: 494-4877.
Smiths Gore Overseas Ltd., 494-2446, F: 494-2141.
Trude Real Estate, 494-5115; 494-4546, F: 494-6969.

SAILING, WATER SPORTS

Boardsailing BVI, 495-2447.
Capricorn Charters, 494-3174.
HIHO, 494-8304.
Club Mariner, 494-2501; F: 494-2507.
Encore, 494-3623.
Endless Summer II, 494-3656,
  800-368-9905.
Johnny's Maritime Services, 494-3661.
King Charters Ltd., 494-5820.
Kuralu Charters, 495-4381.
The Last Resort, 495-2520.
Marine Enterprises, 494-2786, 494-6300.
Patouche II, 494-6300.
Prospect Reef Resort, 494-3311.
Sail Vacations, 494-3656, 800-368-9905.
Sea Escape Daysails, 496-0044.
Smith's Ferry Services, 494-2355.
Trimarine Boat Co. Ltd., 495-5643,
  800-648-3393.
White Squall II, 494-2564.
Yacht Promenade, 494-3853,
  800-526-5503.

SAILMAKERS

Doyle Sailmakers, 494-2569.
Elm. Sailmakers Ltd., 494-6455.
Nanny Cay Sailmakers, 494-6455.

SHOPPING, GIFTS

Babyland, 494-3121.
Bolo's Department Store, 494-2867.
Bonker's Gallery Boutique, 494-2535.
Bounty Boatique, 494-3615.
BVI Apparel, 494-5511: F: 494-3867.
Caribbean Handprints, 494-3717.
Carousel Gift Shop, 494-4542.
Castaways Ltd., 494-5240.
Clovers Department Store, 494-3724,
  494-4110. Sewing Services.
Cockle Shop, 494-2555.
E. A. Creque, footwear, 494-3368.
Crown Jewellers Ltd., 494-3399.
Esme's Shoppe, 494-3961.
Family Fashion, 494-4232.
Fluke's Designs, 495-1421.
Hodge's Department Store, 494-3943.
Hollywood Discount Store, 494-3554.

Island Treasures, 495-4787.
J & C Department Store, 494-3121.
Jehmary's Gift & Souvenir Centre,
  494-4512.
Jennings Fashion Store, 495-2144.
Kids In De Sun, 494-3343.
Learn 'N' Fun Shop, 494-3856.
Little Circle, 494-3779.
Malone Sporting Goods, 494-4591.
Naucraft Galleries Ltd., 494-4790.
Ooh La La Gift Shop, 494-2433.
Pace Setter Store, 494-2162.
Pasea Stationery & Book Store,
  494-2556.
Pusser's Co. Store & Pub, 494-2467.
Pusser's Landing, 495-4554.
Roadtown Wholesale, 494-2263.
Royal Shop, 494-3209.
Samarkand Jewelers, 494-6415.
Sea Urchin Shop, T&F, 494-6234,
  494-4108.
Shirt Shack, 494-4851.
Smith's Boutique, 495-2204.
Sunny Caribbee Spice Co., 494-2178,
  494-5481.
Tortola Department Store, 494-3109.
Tropical Touch, 495-9358, 494-6982.
Turtle Dove Boutique, 494-3611.
Unique Fashion, 494-6471.
Violet's, 494-6398.
Zenaida, Dress Shop, 495-4867.

TAXIS/TRANSPORTATION

BVI Taxi, 494-3942, 494-3456, 494-2322.
Scato's Bus Service, 26 Seats,
  Public 494-2365.
Style's Taxi, 494-2260 (day),
  494-3341 (night).
Turtle Dove Taxi, 494-6274, 494-3942.

VIRGIN GORDA

Auto/Bicycle/Moped Rentals
Andy's Taxi & Jeep Rental, 495-5511.
L & S Jeep Rental, 495-5297.
Mahogany Car Rental, 495-5469,
  495-5212.
Potter's Car Rental, 495-5329, 495-5960.
Speedy's Car Rental, 495-5235.

CHANDLERIES
Virgin Gorda Yacht Harbour
  Ship's Store, 495-5513, F: 495-5685.

CHARTERS
Misty Isle Yacht Charters, 495-5643.

DIVING, SNORKELING
Baskin In The Sun, 494-2858, 495-4582,
  800-233-7938.
Dive BVI Ltd., 495-5513, 800-848-7078.
Kilbride's Sunchaser Scuba, 495-9638.
Mahogany Watersports, 495-5469,
  F: 495-5072, 800-932-4286.

LAUNDRY/DRY CLEANERS
Stevens Laundry & Dry Cleaners,
  495-5525.

LODGING
Biras Creek Hotel, 494-3555/6.
Bitter End Yacht Club Hotel, 494-2745,
  800-872-2392.
Drake's Anchorage, 494-2254, 494-5871.
Fischer's Cove Beach Hotel, 495-5252,
  800-621-1270.
Leverick Bay Hotel, 495-7421,
  800-848-7081.
Little Dix Bay Hotel, 495-5555,
  800-928-3000.
Mango Bay Resort, 495-5672.
Necker Island, 494-2757, 800-557-4255.
Olde Yard Inn, 495-5544.
Paradise Beach Resort, 495-5871.
Virgin Gorda Villa Rentals, 495-7421,
  495-7365.

MARINAS
Biras Creek Estate, 494-3555/6.
Bitter End Yacht Club, 494-2746,
  800-872-2392.
Leverick Bay Resort, 495-7365,
Virgin Gorda Yacht Harbour,
  495-5500/5555.

MISCELLANEOUS
American Express, 494-2872, 494-6239.

BVI Tourist Board, 495-5181.
Hair Creation, 495-5670.
Massage Parlour, 495-7375.
New Image Beauty Salon, 495-5135.
Public Library, 495-5518.
Sandra's Exquisite Hair Designs,
  495-7222.
Vivian's Beauty Salon, 495-5641.

PHARMACIES
Medicure Ltd., 495-5479.
O'Neal Marketing, 495-5325.

PROVISIONS
Andy's Ice Chateau, 495-5987.
Bitter End, 494-2745; F: 494-4756.
Buck's Food Market, 495-5423,
  F: 495-5141.
Leroy B. Frett Butcher Shop, 495-2253.
North Sound Superette, 495-7424.
Pool's Economart / Virgin Gorda
  Freight & Trade Co., 495-5465.

REAL ESTATE
Trude Real Estate, 495-5648.

SAILING, WATER SPORTS
Bitter End Yacht Club, 494-2746.
Euphoric Cruises, 495-5542.
Leverick Bay Watersports, 495-7376,
  495-7364.
Misty Isle Yacht Charters, 495-5643.
Power Boat Rentals, 494-5511.
Speedy's Fantasy, 495-5240.

SAILMAKERS
Next Wave Sail & Canvas, 495-5623,
  495-5662.

SHOPPING, GIFTS
Flamboyance Perfume Shoppe,
  495-5946.
Kaunda's KYSY Tropix, 494-6737,
  495-5636.
O'Neal Variety Store, 495-5230.
Roadtown Wholesale of Virgin Gorda,
  495-5228, F: 495-5572.

Virgin Gorda Craft Shop, 495-5137.

ANEGADA
LODGING
Anegada Reef Hotel, 495-8002,
  F: 495-9362.
Neptune's Treasure, 495-9439;
  F: 495-9443.

DIVING
Dive BVI, 495-5513.

SHOPPING
Pat's Pottery (no phone).

COOPER ISLAND
LODGING
Cooper Island Beach Club, 494-3721.

SHOPPING
Underwater Safaris Gift Shop, 494-3235.

JOST VAN DYKE
PROVISIONS
Harris' Place, 495-9295, F: 495-9296.
Nature's Basket, (no phone).

PETER ISLAND
DIVING
Dive BVI Ltd., 495-9705,
  800-848-7078, 495-9705 PI.

LODGING
Peter Island Hotel and Yacht Harbour,
  494-2591, F: 495-2000.

MARINAS
Peter Island Hotel & Yacht Harbour,
  494-2591, VHF 16, 494-2500.

MARINA CAY
DIVING
Dive BVI, 495-9363, 800-848-7078.

LODGING
Marina Cay Hotel, 495-9363.
Pusser's, 494-2174, F: 494-4775.

SHOPS
Marina Cay Boutique, 495-9791.
Pusser's Company Store, 494-2467.

U.S. VIRGIN ISLANDS
GENERAL INFORMATION

To call from outside the VI, dial
1-340 plus 7 digits.

Airlines
Air Anguilla, 776-5789.
American Airlines, 1-800-474-4884.
American Eagle, 1-800-474-4884.
Continental Airlines, 1-800-231-0856.
Delta, 1-800-221-1212.
LIAT, 774-2313.
Virgin Air, 776-2722.

MISCELLANEOUS
Inter-Island Boat Services, 776-6597.
Smith's Ferry, 775-7292.
Transportation Services of St. John,
  776-6282.
USVI Coast Guard, 776-3497, 774-1911.
USVI Customs, 774-6755, 774-1719.
USVI National Parks Service/Visitor
  Information Center, 776-6201.
Virgin Islands Port Authority, 774-2250.
Virgin Island Radio, Marine Operator,
  776-8282.
Western Union, 1-800-325-6000.

ST. JOHN
Auto/Bicycle/Moped Rentals
Avis, 776-6374, 800-331-1084.
Budget Rent-a-Car, 776-7575.
Cool Breeze Car Rental, 776-6588.
Delbert Hills, 776-6637, 776-7947.
Hertz, 693-7580.
O'Connor Car Rental, 776-6343.
Penn's Jeep Rental, 776-6530.
Spencer's Jeep Rentals, 693-8784.
St. John Car Rental, 776-6103.
Varlack Car Rental, 776-6695.

CHARTERS
Ocean Incentives, 775-6406.
Proper Yachts, 776-6256.

DIVING, SNORKELING
Cinnamon Bay Watersports Center,
  776-6330.
Coral Bay Water Sports, 776-6850.
Cruz Bay Watersports, 776-6234.
Low Key Watersports, 693-8999.
National Park Guided Snorkeling Trips,
  776-6201, 776-6330.
Ocean Diver, 776-6201, 776-6922.
Paradise Watersports, 779-4999.
St. John Water Sports, 776-6256.

EMERGENCY/MEDICAL
St. John Clinic, 776-6400, or 911.

HAUL-OUT
Caneel Bay Ship Yard, 693-8771.

LAUNDRY
Paradise Laundromat, 776-8060.

LODGING
Caneel Bay, 776-6111.
Cruz Inn, 693-8688/9991.
Gallows Point Suite Resort, 776-6434.
Hyatt Regency/St. John, 693-8000,
  800-233-1234.
Intimate Inn of St. John, 776-6133.
Raintree Inn, 693-8590.
Serendip Condo Hotel, 776-6646.
Zootenvaal Estate, 776-6321.

MARINE REPAIR & SUPPLIES
Barry's Small Engine Repair, 776-7464.
Caneel Bay Shipyard, 693-8771.
Coral Bay Marine Service, 776-6665.
D. Knight & Co., 776-7958.

MISCELLANEOUS
Decisions Hair Salon, 776-6962.

PROVISIONS
Convenience Market, 776-6193.

Hercules Self-Service Market, 776-6352.
Marcelino's Bakery, 776-6873.
Marina Market, 779-4401.
Neli Mini-Mart, 776-6272.
Supermarket & Deli, 776-7373.
Supernatural Foods, 776-7781.
Starfish Market, 779-4949.

REAL ESTATE
Cruz Bay Realty, 693-8808.
Holiday Homes of St. John Inc.,
  776-6776.
Islandia Real Estate, 776-6666.
St. John/St. Thomas Board of Realtors,
  776-0050.

SAILING, WATER SPORTS
Big Planet Adventure Outfitters,
  776-6638.
Cinnamon Bay Watersports Center,
  776-6330.
Coral Bay Water Sports, 776-6850.
Cruz Bay Watersports, 776-6234.
Low Key Watersports,693-8999.
Paradise Watersports, 779-4999.
Royal Overseas Yachting, Co. Ltd.,
  877-693-9292
St. John Watersports, 776-6256.
St. John Windsurfing, 776-6052.
Windseekers Parasailing, 776-7048.

SAILMAKERS
Canvas Factory & Lee Sails, 776-6196.
Coral Bay Sails, Marine Services,
  776-6665.

SHOPPING, GIFTS
Batik Caribe, 776-6465.
Batik Kitab, 776-7828.
Bamboula Collections, 693-8699.
Bodywear Fashion Jewelry, 776-8363.
Canvas Factory, 776-6196.
Caravan Gallery, 693-8550.
Caribbean Casting Co., jewelers,
  693-8520.
Clothing Studio, 776-6585.
Colombian Emeralds International,
  776-6007.

Donald Schnell Pottery Studio, 776-6420.
Fabric Mill, 776-6194.
I Catchers Sportswear, 776-7749.
Lee Sails, 776-6196.
Little Planet Kids' Stuff, 776-7828.
Mongoose Junction, 776-6267.
Mongoose Trading Co., 776-6993.
Pink Papaya 693-8535
Pusser's Wharfside, 693-8489
R & I Patton Goldsmithing, 776-6548.
Verace, 693-7599
Wicker, Wood & Shells, 776-6909.

ST. THOMAS

ATTRACTIONS
Coral World, 340-774-8687,
  800-467-0488, F: 340-774-7368.

AUTO/BICYCLE/MOPED RENTALS
Airways Rent-a-Car, 776-2877.
American Yacht Harbor, 775-6454.
Avis, 774-1468, 774-4616, 800-331-1084.
Budget Rent-a-Car, 776-5774,
  800-626-4516.
CM Jeep Rental, 776-7100.
Cowpet Auto Rental, 775-7376.
Dependable Car Rental, 774-2253,
  800-522-3076.
Discount Car Rental, 776-4858.
E-Z Car Rental, 775-6255.
Hertz Rent-a-Car, 774-1879.
National Auto Rental, 776-8616,
  776-3616.
Paradise Car Rental, 775-7282, 776-5335,
  774-2203.
Real Deal Rentals, 776-7100.
Sea Breeze Car Rental, 774-7200.
Sun Island Car Rentals, 774-3333.
Tri-Island Car Rental, 775-1200,
  776-2879.
VI Auto Rental & Leasing, 776-3616.
Zenith Rent-a-Car, 776-2095.

BANKS
Banco Popular de Puerto Rico, 693-2777.
Bank of Nova Scotia, 774-0037.
Barclays Bank, 776-5880.
Chase Manhattan Bank, 775-7777.
Citibank, 774-4800.

First Federal Savings, 774-2022.
First Virgin Islands Federal Savings,
  776-9494.

CHARTERS
CYC, 800-225-2520.
CYOA, 774-3677.
Fanfare Yacht Charters, 715-1326
Island Yachts, 775-6666.
Journeys By Sea, 775-3660; F: 775-3070.
Neptune Charters, 800-637-6402.
Regency Yacht Vacations, 776-5950,
  F: 776-7631.
VIP Power Yacht Charters, 776-1510,
  800-524-2015.

DIVING, SNORKELING
Aqua Action, 775-6285.
Caribbean Divers, 775-6384.
Coki Beach Dive Club, 775-4220.
Chris Sawyer Dive Center, 775-7320,
  F: 775-9495.
Dive In, 775-6100.
Sea Trade, LTD., 774-2001, F: 777-3232.
St. Thomas Diving Club, 776-2381.
Underwater Safaris, 774-1350.
Virgin Islands Diving School, 774-8687.

ELECTRONICS
Ace Communications, 775-2750.
Audio-Video Electronics, 774-8476.
Boatphone Inc., 774-7599.
Boatphone USVI Inc., 777-8615.
Boolchand's Electronics, 776-0302,
  776-0794.
Cellular One, 774-0005/7777,
  F: 777-5190.
Cruisephone Ltd., 774-6711.
Electronics Unlimited, 776-4742,
  777-7000.
Topp Electronics, 775-7069.
Virgin Islands Telecom, 776-1716.
Vitel Cellular, 776-8599, 777-8891.
Vitelcom, 776-9900.

EMERGENCY/MEDICAL
Ambulance/Fire/Police, 911.
Doctors-On-Duty, 776-7966.

Thomas E. Drakes, dentist, 776-8018.
Francis J. Farrell, M.D., allergist, 776-0506.
William J. Henderson, dentist, 775-6200.
Island Eye Care, 775-6211.
Richard A. Lloyd, dentist, 774-8155.
Pearle Vision Express, 774-2020.
St. Thomas Hospital, 774-8311.
Stuart M. Wechter, Dentist, 774-1420.

HAUL-OUT
Haulover Marine, 776-2078.
Independent Boat Yard, 776-0466.

LAUNDRY/DRY CLEANING
Island Laundry & Dry Cleaning, 774-4567, 774-2076.
One-Hour Martinizing, 774-5452.
One-Stop Laundry, 776-1111.
Red Hook Laundry & Dry Cleaning, 775-7955
Rodgers Laundromat, 776-9697.
Sea Side Suds, 774-9998.
Solberg Supermart & Laundromat, 776-5121.
Supercat Laundromat, 774-6056.
Washboard Laundry, 774-8276.

LIQUORS
Al Cohen's Discount Liquors, 774-3690.
Colorao's, 774-7910, 776-0950, 776-6162.
Plaza Cellars Fine Wines, 774-2960.
A.H. Riise Gifts & Liquors, 776-2303, 777-4222.
Thrifty Liquors, 776-8000.
Universal Liquor & Gifts, 776-3287.

LODGING
Blackbeard's Castle, 776-1234.
Bluebeard's Castle Hotel, 774-1600.
Bunker's Hill Hotel, 774-8056.
Carib Beach Hotel, 774-2525.
Danish Chalet Inn, 774-5764.
Emerald Beach Resort, 777-8800.
Heritage Manor Guest House, 774-3003.
Island Beachcomber Hotel, 774-5250.
Island View Guest House, 774-4270.

Lime Tree Beach Hotel, 776-4770.
Mafolie Hotel, 774-2790.
Midtown Guest House, 776-9157.
Ramsey's Guest House, 774-6521.
Sapphire Beach Resort, 775-6100.
Secret Harbour Beach Resort, 775-6550, 800-524-2250.
Soto Town Guest House, 774-1124, 776-1107.
Stouffer Grand Beach Resort, 775-1510, 800-768-3571.
West Indies Inn, 774-1376.

MAIL DROP
Beverly's Mailbox Rental, 777-8273.
Executive Mailing Services, 777-8444.
Havensight Boxes, 774-4470.
Nisky Mail Boxes, 774-7055, 777-8910.
Red Hook Mail Services, 775-5262.
St. Thomas Communications 776-4324.

MARINAS
American Yacht Harbor, 775-6454.
Avery's Boathouse, 776-0113.
Compass Point Marina, 775-6144.
Crown Bay Marina, 774-2255, VHF 16.
Fanfare, 715-1326
Fish Hawk Marina, 775-9058.
Haulover Marine Yachting Center, 776-2078.
Independent Boat Yard, 776-0466.
Red Hook Marina, 775-6501.
Saga Haven Marina, 775-0520.
Sapphire Beach Marina, 775-6100.
Vessup Point Marina, 779-2495.
Safe Haven Marina, 774-9700.

MARINE REPAIR & SUPPLIES
Allen Yacht Services, 774-3308.
Avery's Marine, 776-0113.
Caribbean Battery, 776-3780.
Caribbean Inflatable Service, 775-6159; F: 775-2014.
Crown Bay Maritime Center, 774-8780.
Island Marine Supply, 776-0753, 776-0088, 775-6621, 775-6789.
Island Rigging and Hydraulics, 774-6833.
Lighthouse Marine, 774-4379.
MD Marine, 776-0032.

Monty's, 774-4538.
Offshore Marine, 776-1416, 776-5432.
Power Products, 774-6085.
Quartermaster Diesel, 776-4025.
Reefco Marine Refrigeration, 776-0038.
Ruan's Marine Service, 775-6346.
TradeWind Yachting Services Ltd.,
   494-3154, F: 494-5892.
Tropical Marine, 775-6595.
Virgin Islands Canvas, 774-3229.
VI Tecno Services, 776-3080.
Yanmar Diesels Island Yachts, 775-6666.

MISCELLANEOUS
Alcoholics Anonymous, 776-5283.
Animal Hospital/St. Thomas, 775-3240,
   775-1705, 776-1201.
Atlantis Submarines, 776-5650, VHF 18.
Bruno's Le Salon, 774-2086.
CG's Barber & Beauty Salon, 774-1337.
Colon Barber & Beauty Salon, 776-0110.
Frank's Lock & Key Service, 774-1094.
Genesis Hair Care Center, 776-7687.
Helen's Beauty Salon, 774-0977.
Jan Michael's Hair Studio, 776-1151.
Lock-It Please, locksmiths, 775-9790.
Moore Veterinary Clinic, 775-6623,
   775-6446.
Nisky Business Center, 774-7055.
Priscilla Unisex Beauty, 776-4644.
Pure Tropical Water (bottled), 776-4245.
Rush-It, Inc. Courier, 776-9414.
Saunders Veterinary Clinic, 774-7788.
UPS, 776-1700.
Vitel Cellular, 776-8599, 777-8899.
Western Union, 800-325-6000.

PHARMACIES
Doctors' Drug Prescription Center,
   776-4801.
Drug Farm Pharmacy, 776-7098,
   776-1880.
Family Health Center, 776-3805.
Frenchman's Reef Drug Store, 776-8681.
Frenchtown Drug Center, 774-1466.
Havensight Pharmacy, 776-1235.
Nisky Pharmacy, 776-4759.
St. Thomas Apothecary, 774-5432,
   775-5050.

Sunrise Pharmacy
Virgin Islands Apothecary, 774-1341.

PROVISIONS
A & F Bakery, 776-5145.
Bachman's Bakery, 774-4143.
Daylight Bakery, 776-1414, 774-6328.
E & M Grocery, 774-6836.
Vincent Garcia, Grocers, 774-4219.
Joe's Convenience Market, 776-1809.
La Bottega, 775-5175.
Long Path Superette, 774-1090.
Majo Market, 776-5530.
Marina Market, 779-2411.
Natural Food Grocery & Deli, 774-2800.
Nordside Grocery, 774-4852.
Ocean Treasure Seafood, 776-2027.
Pueblo International, 776-0607,
   777-8195.
B&F Market, 775-1949.
Red Ball Grocery, 774-1682.
Shop Rite Grocery, 774-2645.
Solberg Supermart, 776-5121.
Super Foods, 774-4200.
Tri-Mart Convenience Center, 775-1024.

REAL ESTATE
April Newland/Terry Moran R.E.,
   774-8888.
St. Thomas/St. John Board of Realtors,
   776-0050.
Sun Real Estate, 774-0027.

SAILING, WATER SPORTS
Abigail Sport Fishing, 775-6024.
Atlantis Submarines, 776-5650.
Caribbean Boardsailing, 776-3486.
Charter Fishing Fleet, 775-3690.
Cruzan Gold Sport Fishing, 775-3339.
Mad Max Waterskiing, 775-5178.
Nauti Nymph Power Boats, 775-5066.
Ocean Incentives, 775-6406.
Phoenix Sport Fishing, 775-6100.
Tradewinds Parasailing, 776-8500.
West Indies Windsurfing, 775-6530.

SAILMAKERS
Manfred Dittrich Canvas Works, 774-4335.
West Ray Corporation, 774-8354.

SHOPPING, GIFTS
Alstein Dress Shop, 774-1949.
Amsterdam Sauer Jewelry, 774-2222, 776-3828.
Blue Diamond, 776-4340.
Bobby's Jewelers, 776-1748.
Boolchands, 776-0794.
Caribbean Sportswear, 776-4322.
Cardow Jewelers, 776-1140, 774-5905.
Cartier, Les Must, Jewelers, 774-1590.
Chang's Imports, 776-5239.
Coin D'Oro Jewelers, 774-2275
Colombian Emeralds, 774-4401.
Colorao's Perfumes, Inc., 774-7910, 776-0950.
Cosmopolitan, Apparel, 776-2040.
Crystal Shoppe, 776-3282.
Dockside Bookshop, 774-4937.
The English Shop, 776-3776.
Europa Shop, Jewelers, 776-5252, 774-4252.
Gem Palace, 774-6181.
Gold Haven, 776-2049.
Island Fever of St. Thomas, 774-7154.
Jonna White Art Gallery, 774-3098.
J.S. Dress Shop, 776-3478.
Julie's, Toys, 774-3703.
Land of Oz, Toys, 776-7888.
Leather Loft, 776-1347.
Leather Shop, 776-0290.
Little Switzerland, 776-2010.
Mango Tango,777-3995
Name Dropper, 774-0577.
Ninfa's Gift Shop, 774-0460.
Nita's Jewelry & Gift Shop, 776-3042.
Phil's Paradise, 774-5549.
Poor Richard's Tropical Boutique, 776-1344.
A.H. Riise, 776-2303.
Scandinavian Center, 776-5030, 776-0656.
Shopper's Paradise, 776-4588.
Soft Touch Boutique, 776-1760.
Sona International, 774-4202, 774-5204.

H. Stern Jewellers, 776-1939, 800-524-2024.
Tillett Gardens Art & Craft Gallery, 775-1929.
Trident Jewelers, 776-7152.
Tropicana Perfume Shoppes, 800-233-7940.

TAXIS/TRANSPORTATION
Carey Limousine, 775-9035.
Dohm's Water Taxi, 775-6501.
East End Taxi, 775-6974.
Four Winds Taxi, 775-2800.
Independent Taxi, 776-1669, 776-1006.
Islander Taxi, 774-4077.
Reliable Taxi, 774-0888.
24-Hour Taxi, 776-0496.
VI Taxi, 774-4550.
Wheatley Taxi, 775-1959, 776-0496.

ST. CROIX
Auto/Bicycle/Moped Rentals
Berton Car Rental, 773-1516.
Budget Rent-A-Car, 778-9636.
Caribbean Jeep & Car Rental, 773-4399, 778-1000, 1-800-548-4452.
Centerline Car Rental, 778-0450.
Go Around Rent-A-Car, 778-8881, 778-8552.
Hertz Rent-A-Car, 778-1402.
Maurice's Rent-A-Car, 778-9884.
Midwest Auto Rental, 772-0438.
Olympic Rent-A-Car, 773-2208,
St. Croix Jeep & Honda Rental, 773-8370, 773-0161.
Thrifty Car Rental, 773-7200.
Travellers Car Wash & Car Rental, 773-1649.

BANKS
Banco Popular-St. Thomas, 693-2777, 774-2300.
Bank of Nova Scotia, 778-6553, 778-5350.
Barclay's Bank, 773-8500.
Chase Manhattan Bank, 773-1222, 773-1200.
First Federal Savings Bank, 773-0504.

DIVING, SNORKELING

Anchor Dive Center, 778-1522.
Blue Dolphin Divers, 773-8634.
Cane Bay Dive Shop, 773-9913.
Cruzan Divers, 772-3701.
Dive Experience, 773-3307.
Dive St. Croix, 773-3434.
Sea Shadows Scuba, 778-3850.

ELECTRONICS

Glentronics, 778-6505.
Radio Shack, 778-5667, 778-6351.
Roberts Electronics, 778-6640.

Emergency/Medical
Aubrey A. Andukze, Dentist, 773-0085.
Frank T. Bishop, M.D., 778-0069.
Rodney A. Fabio, Jr., Dentist, 778-6900.
Daniel T. Kenses, Dentist, 692-9770.
Med Link, Free Medical Information, 773-1711.
Arakere Prasad, M.D., 778-7788, 773-8173.

LAUNDRY/DRY CLEANING

Classic Cleaners Wash Club, 773-6979.
CT Laundromat, 692-2770.
Fast Dry Cleaners, 773-1101.
Johannes Laundry, 778-7602.
Neighborhood Laundry, 778-6138.
Suds & Duds, 778-6606.
Sunny Isle Laundromat, 778-6606.
Tony's Laundromat, 772-4580.
Town Laundromat, 772-2066.
Tropical Cleaners & Launderers, 773-3635.
Wash-It Laundry, 778-0545.
WFB Laundromat, 773-9755.

LIQUOR, BEER, WINE

Cruzan Rum Distillery, 692-2280, 800-225-3699.
People's Drugstore, 778-5537, 778-7355.

LODGING

Ackie's Guest House, 773-3759.
Breakfast Club, 773-7383.
Buccaneer Hotel, 773-2100.

Caravelle Hotel, 773-0687, 773-2995.
Caribbean Country Club Guest House, 692-2277.
Chenay Bay Beach Resort, 773-2918.
Club St. Croix, 773-4800.
Frederiksted Hotel, 772-0500, 800-524-2025.
Hill View Guest House, 773-1375.
Hilty House, 773-2594.
King Christian Hotel, 773-2285.
King's Alley Hotel, 773-0103.
Prince Street Inn, 772-9550.
St. Croix by the Sea Hotel, 778-8600.

MARINAS

Green Cay Marina, 773-1453.
Salt River Marina, 778-9650.
St. Croix Marine, 773-0289.

MARINE REPAIR & SUPPLIES

Excursion Management Inc., 778-1004.
Holiday Refrigeration & A.C., 773-4710.
Island Marine Supply, 773-0289.
Paint Locker, 773-0105.
Sailboat Supply Co., 778-1992.
St. Croix Marine, 773-0289.

MISCELLANEOUS

Ada's Creative Touch Beauty Salon, 773-6944.
Beautiful Hair, 773-7212.
Blue Mountain Mineral Water, 778-6177.
Caledonia Springs, bottled water, 778-1281.
Class Plus Unisex Beauty Salon, 773-7228.
Crago Animal Clinic, 692-9099.
Dee Dee's Hair Care Center, 772-4091.
Gem's Beauty Salon, 778-7808.
Monique Beauty Studio, 778-5889.
Cruzan Rum Distillery, 692-2203
Security Unlimited, Locksmiths, 773-5000.
Stef's Beauty Place, 773-5277.
The Shop, Barbers, 773-3815.
Veterinarian, Karen Clarke Ashby, 773-7109.

PROVISIONS

Centerline Bakery, 772-1541.
Central Meat Market, 772-0362.
Edcel Bakery, 778-3434.
Estate Mountain Grocery, 772-4660.
Food Basket, 772-4303.
Gallows Bay Food, 773-4200, 773-6640.
Hendrick's Meat Market, 773-2935.
Island Pastries, 773-6965.
Pueblo Supermarket, 778-1272,
  773-0118.
Schooner Bay Market Place
Solitude Country Store, 773-9354.
Stop & Save Food Market, 773-7050.
Town Super Market, 772-3232.
Tradewind Deli Bar & Liquor Store,
  772-0718.

REAL ESTATE

Byrne-Brown Realty Assocs., 773-3401.
Farchette & Hanley, 773-4665, 772-4704.
Landmark Realty, 773-6688.
Pitterson Real Estate, 772-0412.
Pivar Real Estate, 778-8595,
  800-537-6242.

SAILMAKERS

Canvas Loft, 773-3044.
Leading Edge Sailmakers, 773-7414.
Shipshape, 778-5731.
Wesco Awning & Marine Canvas,
  778-9446.

SHOPPING, GIFTS

Avant-Garde, 778-6122.
Calypso Cobbler, 773-0880.
Cardow Jewelers, 800-cardow
Cinderella Dress Shop, 772-0160.
Colombian Emeralds International,
  773-1927.
Cotton Club, men's apparel, 772-4428.
Eagles Fashion, 778-5588, 778-2447.
Eileen's Fashion Boutique, 778-5944.
The Elegant Woman, 773-7194.
Enchantment, 773-2070.
Foot Locker, 778-3585, 778-1990.
Frog Legs & Coconuts, Toys, 773-3376.
The Gold Shop, 773-0365.
Holyland Store, 772-0482.

Janette's Fashions, 772-3240.
Java Wraps, 773-3770, 773-7529,
  778-8147.
La Femme Amore, 772-2019.
La Vancia's Gift Shop, 772-9202.
Land of Oz, 773-4610.
Le Fantasie Ltd., 773-1224.
Little India Gift Shop, 778-6104.
Me Dundo's Place, 772-0774.
Personal Touch Boutique, 772-4100.
Royal English Shop, 772-4886.
Sentimental Gallery & Gift Shop,
  772-1103.
Shoe Palace, 778-5752.
Simply Cotton, 773-6860.
Spindrift Ltd., 778-8833.
Sylvia's Dress Shop, 772-4380.
Violette's Boutique, 773-2148.

TAXIS

Antilles Taxi Service, 773-5020.
Bright Star Taxi, 773-3873.
Caribbean Taxi Service, 773-9799.
Cruzan Taxi, 773-6388.
Frederiksted Taxi, 772-4775.
Gold Dust Taxi, 773-0228.
St. Croix Taxi, 778-1088.
St. Croix Taxicab Assoc., 778-6887.

OUTSIDE THE VIRGIN ISLANDS AREA

Boat Facts (Texas) 713-334-3365,
  F: 713-538-4424.
Budget Marine (Philipsburg, St. Maarten),
  5995-22068.

PUERTO RICO
GENERAL INFORMATION

AIRLINES

Air Calypso, 253-0020.
Air Canada, 800-776-3000.
Air France, 800-237-2747.
Air Guadalupe, 253-0933.
Air Jamaica, 800-253-5585.
Air St. Thomas, 800-522-3084, 791-4898.
American, Amer. Eagle, 800-433-7300,
  749-1747.
British Airways, 800-247-9297.
BWIA, 800-538-2942.

Canadian Airline, 800-426-7000.
Caribbean Air Exp, 800-283-2426,
  721-5345.
Carnival, 800-274-6140, 800-824-7386.
Continental, 800-525-0280.
Delta, 800-221-1212.
Flamenco, 723-8110, 725-7707.
Hill Aviation & Helicopters, 723-3385.
LIAT, 791-3838.
Martinair Holland, 800-627-8426.
Northwest, 800-225-2525, 800-447-4747.
Pan Am, 800-359-7262.
Towers Air, 800-221-2500.
TWA, 800-221-2000, 800-892-8466.
United, 800-241-6522, 800-538-2929.
USAir, 800-842-5374.
Vieques Air-Link, 722-3736.
Ambulance, 911.
Bacardi Rum Plant, 788-1500.

CAR RENTAL
(in San Juan unless noted)
AAA, 791-1465.
Afro, 723-8287.
Avis, 721-4499.
Budget, 791-3685.
Charlie, 728-2418.
Discount, 726-1460.
Hertz, 800-654-3131, 791-0840.
L&M, 725-8307.
Leaseway, 791-5900.
National, 791-1805.
Target, 783-6592.
Thrifty, 253-2525.
Emergencies, 911.

FERRY SERVICE
Fajardo-Vieques-Culebra, 863-0852.
Passenger and car (reservations
  required for cars).
Call for current daily departure times.

Information, 800-223-6530
The Puerto Rico Tourism Company
Maintains an extensive network of
offices worldwide.
Internet, www.discoverpuertorico.com

CITY/TOWN ACTIVITIES
Fajardo
Blackbeard West INdies Charter,
  887-4818.
Captain Jack B's Getaway, 860-0861.
Captain Jack's Spread Eagle, 887-8821.
Chamonix Catamaran, 860-4421.
Club Nautico Powerboats, 860-2400.
Erin Go Bragh Charger, 860-4401.
Fajardo Tours, 863-2821.
Palominco Island Divers, 863-1000.
Tropical Fishing & Tournaments,
  863-1000, ex.1910.

San Juan
Caribbean School of Aquatics,
  728-6606.
Caribe Aquatic Adventures, 729-2929.

Vieques Island
Blue Caribe Dive Center, 741-2522.
Island Adventures, 741-0720.

ABOUT THE AUTHORS

Nancy and Simon Scott are well qualified to write a guide book on the Virgin Islands, as they met while cruising in these fabulous islands in 1974. Managing a major bareboat charter company for the next eight years in the Virgins enabled them to see things through the eyes of both the cruising yachtsman and the charterer.

Now living in Florida, Simon continues his work in the bareboat charter field, while Nancy manages the offices of Cruising Guide Publications. Several trips a year, sailing with their two daughters, keeps the Scotts informed and involved in the happenings above and below the sparkling blue waters of the Virgin Islands.

Advertisers Directory

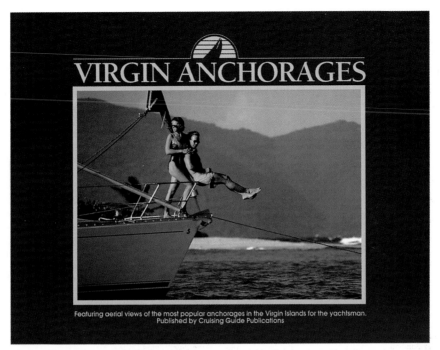

Featuring aerial views of the most popular anchorages in the Virgin Islands for the yachtsman.
Published by Cruising Guide Publications

Sail with a sense of déja vu... and save!

Just fill out the questionnaire on the next page and mail it in or fax it with your order to receive a discount on the purchase of *Virgin Anchorages.*

Let's face it — entering an anchorage for the first time can be a nerve-wracking experience. It doesn't have to be. With *Virgin Anchorages*, you can sail with a sense of having been there before.

This companion cruising tool to the *Cruising Guide to the Virgin Islands* features spectacular aerial views of the most popular island anchorages.

Valuable navigational information is superimposed to clearly delineate safe passages. Reefs, landmarks, and channels are revealed with crystal clarity. Full color photographs and sketch charts are invaluable for navigation.

Now you can receive your copy for only $20.00 plus shipping (see order form on pages 339-340 for details) just by filling out the questionnaire on the next page and forwarding it with your order!

337

QUESTIONNAIRE

All you have to do to receive your copy of VIRGIN ANCHORAGES for $20.00... discounted from the regular price (plus shipping and handling) -- is take a few minutes to fill out this questionnaire (no photocopies accepted), and mail it in with the order form on the next page. It's that easy! Your answers will help Cruising Guide Publications improve our editorial and advertising content throughout our publications. Thank you for your time.

State _____ Age _____ Sex _____

Occupation _____ Marital Status _____

Annual Household Income:　☐ under $50,000　☐ $50,000-$100,000　☐ over $100,000

Do you own a boat? _____

If you chartered a yacht, how many people were in your charter party? _____

If you cruised the Islands, how did you cruise?　☐ On my own boat

　　☐ Bareboat Charter　☐ Bareboat Charter w/Hired Captain　☐ Crewed Charter

How long was your cruise? _____

How often do you cruise?　☐ Less than once a year　☐ Once a year　☐ More than once a year

How did you book your charter?　☐ Through a charter broker　☐ Directly

What activities did you participate in during your cruise?　☐ Fishing　☐ Diving　☐ Snorkeling

　　☐ Windsurfing　☐ Underwater Photography　☐ Other _____

What activities did you participate in ashore?　☐ Dining　☐ Shopping　☐ Tennis　☐ Golf

　　☐ Tours/Sightseeing　☐ Entertainment　☐ Other _____

Did you travel between islands by:　☐ Ferry　☐ Plane

Hotel or rental property use:　☐ Before cruise # of nights _____

　　☐ After cruise, # of nights _____　☐ Did not stay at hotel

Did you rent a car?　☐ No　☐ Yes　(#of days _____)

How many times did your party eat in a restaurant? _____

What type of items did you and your party purchase during your cruise?

　　☐ Perfume　☐ Clothing　☐ Jewelry　☐ Alcoholic Beverages　☐ Real Estate　☐ Souvenirs

　　☐ Art　☐ Tobacco　☐ Dive Equipment　☐ Other _____

Did you visit an advertiser *as a result of seeing their ad in this guide*　☐ No　☐ Yes

What was most useful to you in this guide? _____

What would you like to see more of? _____

_____

What was the most memorable place you visited? _____

_____

COMMENTS: _____

Thank You

CRUISING GUIDE PUBLICATIONS
ORDER FORM
To order, please fill out coupon on back and send check or money order to:
Cruising Guide Publications, P.O. Box 1017, Dunedin, Florida 34697-1017.
For credit card orders only, call 1-800-330-9542 • 727-733-5322
E-mail: cgp@earthlink.net

❏ $19.95   CRUISING GUIDE TO THE VIRGIN ISLANDS
(9th Edition) by Simon and Nancy Scott. Expanded to include Spanish Virgin Islands.

❏ $24.95   VIRGIN ANCHORAGES (New color aerial photos and color graphics)

❏ $24.95   CRUISING GUIDE TO THE LEEWARD ISLANDS — *With GPS Coordinates* (5th Edition) by Chris Doyle.

❏ $19.95   SAILOR'S GUIDE TO THE WINDWARD ISLANDS
(9th Edition) by Chris Doyle.

❏ $14.95   CRUISING GUIDE TO TRINIDAD AND TOBAGO (2nd Edition) by
Chris Doyle.

❏ $26.95   CRUISING GUIDE TO VENEZUELA & BONAIRE (2nd Edition) by Chris
Doyle. Provides Anchorage information GPS and full color charts.

❏ $24.95   CRUISING GUIDE TO CUBA — *With GPS Coordinates and Charts*
(2nd Edition) by Simon Charles.

❏ $24.95   GENTLEMAN'S GUIDE TO PASSAGES SOUTH — *6th Edition With GPS Coordinates* — The "Thornless Path to Windward," by Bruce Van Sant.

❏ $15.95   CRUISING GUIDE TO THE SEA OF CORTEZ (From Mulege to La Paz)

❏ $19.95   CRUISING GUIDE TO THE FLORIDA KEYS by Capt. Frank Papy.

❏ $ 9.95   1999 CRUISING GUIDE TO ABACO BAHAMAS by Steve Dodge. (8$\frac{1}{2}$" x 11")
Containing charts from Walker's Cay south to Little Harbour. Includes GPS coordinates.

❏ $12.00   CRUISING MANUAL TO THE KINGDOM OF TONGA IN THE VAVA'U
GROUP (Chart included) The Moorings.

❏ $13.50   AT ANY COST: LOVE, LIFE & DEATH AT SEA (Hardcover)
By Peter Tangvald; thrilling autobiography of a cruising sailor whose primary home for
50 years was a 49' handcrafted wooden sailboat.

❏ $12.50   SOAP OPERAS OF THE SKY by Jeannie Kuich. A whimisical look at the soap
opera-like tales surrounding the tropical constellations.

❏ $10.00   HOME IS WHERE THE BOAT IS by Emy Thomas. A glimpse into the
cruising way of life.

❏ $14.95   THE NATURE OF THE ISLANDS: PLANTS & ANIMALS OF THE
EASTERN CARIBBEAN by Chris Doyle and Virginia Barlow.

❏ $12.95   CARIBBEAN by Margaret Zellers with breathtaking photos by Bob Krist; —
perfect tropical souvenir or gift.

❏ $29.95   YACHTSMAN'S GUIDE TO JAMAICA by John Lethbridge. Only complete guide
to cruising Jamaica including 50 ports, harbours and anchorages of this island.

❏ $12.95   THE GUIDES TO DIVING AND SNORKELING IN THE BRITISH VIRGIN
ISLANDS or USVI. (Two separate books — $12.95 Each)

❏ $14.95   THE LEEWARDS, PUERTO RICO, VIRGIN ISLANDS, CHESAPEAKE
BAY, INTRACOASTAL WATERWAY, RESTAURANT GUIDES & RECIPE
BOOKS (Five separate books — $14.95 Each.)

❏ $35.00   SOUTHERN SHORES (2nd Edition, 9" x 12", 256 pp) by Roger Bansemer. Florida
artist, Bansemer has captured on canvas the rich texture of the south from the shoreline to
the native wildlife along Florida's coast, north to Savannah & Charleston with a stop in
the Virgin Islands.

To dial →38# 1 AC #

- ❏ $14.95 SHIP TO SHORE I (A collection of 680 recipes & cooking tips from Caribbean charter yacht chefs) compiled by Capt. Jan Robinson.
- ❏ $14.95 SLIM TO SHORE (more recipes from Capt. Jan Robinson).
- ❏ $14.95 SEA TO SHORE (280 seafood recipes and cooking hints.)
- ❏ $14.95 SWEET TO SHORE (Robinson's ultimate dessert collection).
- ❏ $10.95 SIP TO SHORE (Robinson's cocktails and hors d'oeuvres collection).
- ❏ $ 7.95 MAVERICK SEA FARE: A CARIBBEAN COOK BOOK by Dee Carstarphen (Simple shipboard recipes you can prepare at home).
- ❏ $12.00 **CALENDAR:** THE BRITISH VIRGIN ISLANDS. Photography by Dougal Thornton (New year available in October of preceding year).
- ❏ $29.95 **VIDEO** (VHS), or (PAL Add $10)**:** SAILING THE WINDWARD ISLANDS by Chris Doyle & Jeff Fisher.
- ❏ $19.95 **VIDEO** (VHS): ISLAND PORTRAITS: ST. VINCENT & THE GRENADINES by Chris Doyle & Jeff Fisher.
- ❏ $19.95 **VIDEO** (VHS): CRUISING TRINIDAD & TOBAGO by Chris Doyle.
- ❏ $29.95 **VIDEO** (VHS), or (PAL Add $10)**:** CRUISING THE NORTHERN LEEWARDS by Chris Doyle.

WATERPROOF CHARTS

- ❏ $18.95 U.S. & BRITISH VIRGIN ISLANDS
- ❏ $18.95 BRITISH VIRGIN ISLANDS
- ❏ $18.95 UPPER FLORIDA KEYS
- ❏ $18.95 LOWER FLORIDA KEYS
- ❏ $ 8.50 CLEAR, WATERPROOF, REUSABLE PLASTIC STORAGE TUBE

─────── *CALL FOR A COMPLETE CATALOG* ───────

ORDER FORM VISA MasterCard DISCOVER *(For orders only, call 1-800-330-9542 or 727-733-5322).*

To order, check the appropriate box(es), fill out coupon and send check or money order to: Cruising Guide Publications, P.O. Box 1017, Dunedin, FL 34697-1017. Florida residents add 7% sales tax. See schedule for shipping charges. All books are shipped via UPS within 10 days of receipt of order.

SHIPPING & HANDLING:		
	U.S./Terr.	Canada
Other		
Up to $15.00	$ 3.50	$ 5.50	$ 7.00
15.01-30.00	4.95	6.95	9.90
30.01-40.00	6.75	8.75	13.50
40.01-50.00	7.75	9.75	15.50
50.01-75.00	8.75	10.75	17.50
Over 75.00	9.75	11.75	19.50
Additional Address Add $3.25		

$ _____ Total Merchandise

$ _____ Sales Tax 7%
(Florida residents only)

$ _____ Shipping & Handling

$ _____ Total Enclosed

Name _____

Address _____

City _____ State _____ Zip _____

Daytime telephone (_____) _____

(Prices subject to change without notice)

Boat # → 284-496-9957